SINGLE STOCK FUTURES

Founded 1807, John Wiley & Sons is the oldest independent publishing company in the United States. With offices in North America, Europe, Australia, and Asia, Wiley is globally committed to developing and marketing print and electronic products and services for our customers' professional and personal knowledge and understanding.

The Wiley Trading series features books by traders who have survived the market's ever changing temperament and have prospered—some by reinventing systems, others by getting back to the basics. Whether a novice trader, professional or somewhere in between, these books will provide the advice and strategies needed to prosper today and well into the future.

For a list of available titles, please visit our Web site at www.WileyFinance.com.

SINGLE STOCK FUTURES

An Investor's Guide

Kennedy Mitchell

John Wiley & Sons, Inc.

Published by John Wiley & Sons, Inc., Hoboken, New Jersey
Published simultaneously in Canada

For general information on our other products and services, or technical support, please contact our Customer Care Department within the United States
at 800-762-2974, outside the United States at 317-572-3993 or fax 317-572-
4002.

Wiley also publishes its books in a variety of electronic formats. Some con-
tent that appears in print may not be available in electronic books.

For more information about Wiley products, visit our web site at
www.wiley.com.

Library of Congress Cataloging-in-Publication Data

Mitchell, Kennedy E.
    Single stock futures : an investor's guide / Kennedy E. Mitchell.
       p.   cm.—(Wiley trading)
    Includes bibliographical references and index.
    ISBN 0-471-26762-7 (alk. paper)
    1. Single stock futures. 2. Speculation. 3. Futures I. Title II. Series.
  HG6041 .M58 2003
  332.63'228—dc21   2002190746

Printed in the United States of America.

10 9 8 7 6 5 4 3 2 1

To Elizabeth, who has unfailingly provided me with her love and support.

CONTENTS

ACKNOWLEDGMENTS

Thank you to John Kabala, for always reminding me to "finish the book."

INTRODUCTION

For years, the United States financial markets have been migrating toward a more derivative based environment. Many famous fund managers have taken early retirement, victims of the new economy in which the "buy and hold" strategies of latter years have produced sub-standard gains, if not losses. Equities have moved into the realm of a currency that has abandoned the gold standard, the exchange of shares now is a means of creating wealth, not procuring equity in a venture based on its own merits. The derivatives markets now arguably drive the underlying transactions in equities, and advanced strategies have taken center stage in which financial statements are much less important than measuring Delta, Theta, and Alpha. To not understand the derivatives in today's markets is a dangerous proposition, and learning about the application of derivatives like single stock futures will become required reading for the next generation of Wall Street and beyond.

With the repeal of the Shad-Johnson Accord, security futures are now trading in the United States, and have the potential to greatly color the existing landscape. Great losses that have occurred in the past can be limited through their hedging capabilities using risk transference, and the individual investor can now apply advanced trading strategies once reserved for only the most well-heeled investor. The key to success is knowledge, and this book is aimed at delivering a basic knowledge of the single stock futures market for all investors, individual to professional and all points in-between.

Chapter 1

AN OVERVIEW OF SINGLE STOCK FUTURES

This book illustrates how investors, both individual and professional, can utilize single stock futures to add new dimensions to an investment portfolio. Whether used for speculating, hedging, or more advanced strategies like pairs trading or buy-writes, investors can add single stock futures to their array of financial tools for added diversification and flexibility. Single security futures allow an investor the opportunity to establish speculative positions with reduced margin requirements versus traditional equity purchases, and greater flexibility in hedging a single security or portfolio of securities using this new instrument. The ability to use single stock futures in place of underlying equity also adds further versatility by allowing strategies that can be pursued by the individual investor whose portfolio is limited in size. Until their introduction, many advanced trading strategies that have had proven results in the professional investment community were beyond the reach of individual investors for a culmination of factors. Many of these obstacles are now eliminated due to the creativity possible with single security futures. The successful application of single stock futures requires arming yourself with as many resources as possible before approaching this new and exciting product, and the chapters ahead will discuss the product in detail and trading strategies for the application of single security futures.

It is important to understand the genesis of single stock futures and how they have come to the forefront of innovative new financial products in the United States. The Commodities Modernization Act of 2000 was the driving force behind lifting regulations that had previously forbidden the trading of single stock futures and narrow-based indices in the United States. As part of the Commodities Modernization Act of 2000, an earlier provision called the Shad-Johnson Accord that had prevented the trading of single stock futures and narrow-based indices was repealed. This provided the official green light for moving forward with single stock futures and narrow-based index trading in the United States. In 1974, Congress had aimed to include a greater number of financial instruments under the heading of "Commodity," leading to a disagreement between the Securities and Exchange Commission (SEC) and the Commodities Futures Trading Commission (CFTC). Essentially the lack of agreement between these two governing bodies brought about the idea of the Shad-Johnson Accord in the early 1980s, and this accord strictly prevented trading of single security and narrow-based indices in the United States. The original idea behind this was that it would allow the SEC and CFTC more time to work out any differences that they may have had in order to allow such trading to proceed in the future. Then, in December 2000, the Commodities Futures Modernization Act lifted the prohibition on trading of single stock futures and narrow-based indices. The timetable for the lifting of these regulations was as follows:

- August 21, 2001: The Commodities Modernization Act permits banks, trust companies, and individual investors with more than $5 million dollars in assets to trade single security and narrow-based indices on a principal to principal basis.
- December 21, 2001: Retail trading of security futures and narrow-based indices is allowed.
- August 21, 2003: Options on single security futures are allowed to begin trading.

While these dates are a guideline, the actual inception date of trading was delayed due to the remaining regulatory and technical issues that the governing agencies, brokerage firms, and industry personnel had to work out. This can only be expected when dealing with a new derivative product that has the potential to transform the landscape of securities trading in the United States in a substantial fashion. Because the applications of single security futures are broad and diverse, it is expected that a wide range of investors will benefit from their use. For this reason, regulators of the product have taken every precaution to ensure an orderly market that prevents unnecessary risk to both professional and individual investors.

Even though single stock futures may be a relatively new phenomenon in the United States, these instruments have been traded in various overseas markets while regulatory agencies in the United States continued to ponder the inclusion of security futures in domestic markets. The other exchanges and countries that have been using security futures include: Hong Kong, Stockholm, Sydney (Australia), and as of 2001 the LIFFE (London International Financial Futures and Options Exchange). The launch of what are called Universal Stock Futures (USF) on the LIFFE generated great interest in the United States, as they included trading on United States companies such as Cisco, Intel, Microsoft, Citigroup, and ATT among others. Some criticism has taken place regarding the trading volume of these contracts in other countries, however this has been blamed in part on the lack of issues that are available for trading, and the promotion of the products has been somewhat muted in these markets. Furthermore, United States citizens are prohibited under the former Shad-Johnson Accord from trading single security futures in other markets, including the LIFFE. Now that the Accord has been repealed, it will be a natural evolution to see more foreign derivative markets opening their doors to U.S.-based investors, barring any regulations indigenous to the foreign markets that may prevent such activity. At present, many foreign markets that are trading single security futures offer a "cash settlement" of positions, as is the case with the LIFFE exchange in the United Kingdom. Some argue that the nature of a physically settled security futures contract, like the ones available in the United States, is more conducive to the public interest and therefore will be more popular than their cash-settled counterparts. (More on cash versus physical settlement is covered in the next chapter.)

The volume of single stock security trades doubled between 1999 and 2000 in the markets that already allow such trading, clearly a sign that the environment for security futures continues to develop in a rapid manner. Here in the United States, there is the expectation that security futures will evolve to become the most important derivative introduced since the equity option, given the likelihood of strong interest in security futures from individual and professional investors. Furthermore, the hedging capabilities that can be realized through the use of single security futures allow members of the professional community a perfect manner in which to reduce their risk. These risks have become more concentrated with the introduction and promotion of stock option plans and outright equity offered to company employees for incentive and payroll reasons. While common portfolio approaches recommend limiting high concentrations of ownership in one stock, the use of single stock futures allows such maneuvers by protecting these types of holdings from loss if used correctly.

With the repeal of the ban on single stock futures trading, investors are able to add a dynamic component to their existing portfolio strategies. Investing, speculating, hedging, and market making can be facilitated with the use of single stock futures, while both professional and individual investors benefit from the diversity these instruments introduce to the investment arena.

Exactly what are single stock futures? They are futures contracts, within the financial futures universe, that have shares of listed public companies as their underlying asset. In other words, like other futures contracts, a single stock futures contract allows a buyer and seller to transact a standardized equity transaction for a future date. The caveat is that the price for the future transaction is decided upon. The buyer of a stock futures contract believes that the current price is attractive relative to the anticipated future price, while the seller of the contract views the price as overvalued relative to their projection for the future. Chapter 12 deals with the application of both fundamental and technical analysis to single stock futures trading, providing methods investors can use to compliment their existing strategies for hedging and speculating.

The purchase or sale of a futures contract represents an obligation to accept or deliver, at a price determined when the contract is executed, an underlying asset or commodity. These contracts allow a buyer and seller to agree on a current price for the future transaction. The original development of such contracts was primarily for agricultural markets, as producers and consumers within different sectors wanted to "lock-in" specific prices for their crops and goods. The origin of such derivatives can be traced back to Japanese rice trading during the 1640s.

Over time, futures markets have been developed to include countless financial instruments. These "agreements" allow investors to trade a wider variety of instruments without actually having to purchase the underlying asset that they represent. This has been very useful for both hedgers and speculators alike. For investors that are new to the futures markets, Appendix 1 contains an informational overview of how a futures contract works.

Similar to other financial futures, single stock futures have standardized features that allow the trading of the contracts with standardization of the underlying instrument. For example, the underlying number of shares that a single stock futures (SSF) contract represents is fixed at 100 shares. As with an option contract, the size is standardized at 100 shares and will not fluctuate. Other standardization includes contract delivery month, the underlying component (in this case the company's shares that make up the futures contract), and the minimum fluctuation that can occur in the course of trading the instrument. The concept of standardization within the futures markets is a key component that allows the trading of such contracts in a fashion that allows each party involved in a transaction to rely on the standardized features of a specific contract. Without such standardization, the trading of security futures would be much more complicated as every transaction would have different terms and conditions. By only allowing a predetermined set of variables in a security futures contract, regulators and exchanges leave only the price of the contract to be determined by both buyer and seller.

Narrow-based indices can also now trade in the United States as a result of the Commodities Modernization Act of 2000. These are indices that are composed of very few individual underlying stocks. Most sector indices that trade today are comprised of anywhere from 10 to 500 underlying equities. The new narrow-based indices will be comprised of as few as four underlying equities. In the past, such an index was prohibited from trading as it was envisioned as a structure too prone to manipulation by large purchases or sales of the stocks that construct the index.

With the new indices that will be available, more fine-tuned approaches to hedging equity baskets with well-defined equity indices will be possible. More traditional, broad-based indices are often faulted for not allowing an efficient hedge due to inconsistent movement with more narrowly-based equity portfolios.

Additionally, speculators that expect sharp movements in certain market sectors are often disappointed to find that more broad-based indices have diversified qualities that promote more subtle variations. Conversely, narrow-based indices include very few representative equities, and may therefore reflect more substantial deviations in their price movements. Recognizing these qualities, the application of a narrower-based index like those being introduced today may be more useful for speculators and hedgers in the financial community. For a sample list of narrow-based indices, see Appendix 2.

Single stock futures introduce substantial flexibility for a wide array of investors, both individual and professional. From speculating to hedging and all points between, these revolutionary instruments provide a cost-effective trading method for participants in the equity, futures, and options markets. There are several advantages to using single stock futures in place of physical equities or equity options, all of which will be covered in this text.

Speculators versus Hedgers

In all futures markets, a key distinction is made between the activities of a hedger versus those of a speculator. These roles differ in relation to their trading approach and goals, as well as margin requirements in some markets.

The label of *speculator* can bring about visions of a wild investor with money to burn, placing copious trades with a disregard for losses that may occur. However, in the futures universe, a speculator is anyone who is not a hedger, and it's that simple. Any user of futures other than a hedger is a speculator, because due to the limited life span of a futures contract, it is given that their goal is short-term gains. If you plan to trade single stock futures for profit, replacing the use of an underlying equity, you are a speculator. This is true even if you approach your use of single security futures as investing, applying the same care and methodology as you would transacting underlying common stock of a company. The only difference is that you are using single stock futures instead of actual equity shares, and you are still referred to as a speculator.

A speculator in the futures market is seeking returns, and aims to enter a trade with the idea that a profit will be made based on the identified strategy. The main goal of using futures is to generate gains in the portfolio of the speculator, through either short-term strategies or longer term investment plans that you decide can be executed through the use of security futures. A typical transaction for a speculator would be a purchase, short sale, or spread transaction that will generate sufficient profits to outweigh the risks of losing capital. This differs from the hedger, who approaches the futures markets solely as a function of looking to protect the assets that they already own through the use of future agreements. For a hedger, profit or loss is secondary to ensuring that the hedge they have established will function properly, and merely serve to offset any losses that may occur with an asset.

A *hedger* is a user of futures for the purpose of offsetting perceived loss potential in the underlying instrument. In other words, hedgers use futures contracts as insurance policies like many people use options, to protect their underlying asset in the event of adverse movement that may result in losses.

In many futures markets, particularly agricultural contracts, verified hedgers also have the benefit of a lower margin requirement for trading futures contracts. This is because their exposure is considered to have a guarantee of sorts, since they deal every day with the underlying asset that they are hedging, and are perceived to have an inventory of the product to back up their futures position. For example, suppose a corn farmer believes that corn has reached the highest price of the season, and will head lower from current prices until harvest. The farmer sells corn futures, locking-in his sale price for the post harvest delivery. This is an absolute hedge, because the farmer is going to deliver his corn that he has entered the future agreement to deliver. Unlike a speculator, he will not aim to buy back the corn futures when they trade lower a month from now. When the futures contracts he sold expire and delivery is due, the farmer will deliver the corn he owns as promised.

The use of single stock futures is also applied in two distinct manners, hedging and speculating. The key to reducing margin requirements is holding the equity that you are hedging in the same account in which you are trading a security futures contract . In Chapter 9 of this book, detailed information is provided on the official exchange guidelines for margin requirements. These may differ from your personal requirements, as brokers are allowed to increase margin requirements based on their specific guidelines. However, the exchange minimum listings in Chapter 9 should give you a solid understanding of basic margin rates.

Chapter 2

KEY DIFFERENCES BETWEEN EQUITIES AND SINGLE STOCK FUTURES

There are several key differences between single stock futures and underlying equities, which begin with the fact that one is ownership in a company (equity) and the other is *an agreement to purchase equity at some future date, at an agreed-upon price.* This chapter highlights some of the key differences, as well as similarities, of single stock futures and the equities that they represent. Understanding these differences is an important step in using single security futures in either a hedging or speculative capacity, so you can fully understand both their versatility and limitations.

When you decide to purchase shares of a company that trade on one of the major stock exchanges, you are really buying equity in that particular company. With single stock futures, you actually are just forming an agreement between yourself and another party to transact shares *at some future date.* It is important to understand that you do not in fact have a position in shares of the underlying company's stock, but you do have an agreement that you will transact these shares at a future date at a determined price. The details of the transaction are standardized, with each contract representing 100 shares of the underlying company's stock, the delivery date (or transaction date for your purchase or sale of the existing stock), and the price at which these shares will be transacted. The idea is that minus some adjustment for stock dividends and interest rate costs, the price of these futures should track the price of the underlying stock they represent. This may not always be true however, since futures can often reflect movement based on expectations and shifts in supply and demand. However, assuming all things are equal, the price of a single stock futures contract should be calculated using a fair value model that takes into account the cost of interest rates and dividends from the trade date to expiry date.

In the purest sense, single stock futures should move point for point with the underlying stock they represent, minus adjustments for dividends and interest. In option trading language, you would expect single stock futures to always have a Delta of 1.00, so that the movement of an underlying equity is mirrored by the stock futures contract. However, in some instances a single stock futures contract experiences an imbalance in supply and demand, or shifting expectations may cause the contract to temporarily sway from equilibrium with the underlying stock. For the fair value of a single stock futures contract, the formula in Figure 2.1 applies.

For example, suppose the share price of ABC Telecom was $62.00. It is the second week of January, and you take a look at the March ABC Telecom stock futures. They could be trading at $61.90, which would reflect a 0.10 cent discount under the current price at which you could purchase the ABC Telecom shares on the stock exchange. Why? Because, given that ABC Telecom pays a 0.15 cent dividend in February, and the current interest rate suggests the cost of financing every 100 shares of ABC Telecom between now and March delivery is 0.05 cents, a discount equaling the 0.10 cents is subtracted from the underlying price of ABC Telecom to determine the futures price (for March). The details of pricing an ABC Telecom futures contract for March delivery can be easily calculated using our fair value pricing model and replacing the components with our details. (See Figure 2.2.)

Holders of single stock futures are not entitled to dividends, as you can see in Figure 2.2. However, holders of single stock futures are responsible for financing the 100 shares per contract

Futures Fair Value =

(Underlying Equity Price + Interest) – Dividends

Figure 2.1   Futures fair value.

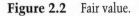

Fair Value =

($62.00 + 0.05) – 0.15 = $61.90

Figure 2.2   Fair value.

at only a 20 percent margin requirement, as indicated by the interest cost component also included in our formula. If you looked at longer dated delivery dates, such as June or September, you would see greater premium or discounts that reflect the cost of interest and dividends depending on what they may be during that period. In fact, the difference may not even be scaled as traders may see a Federal Reserve interest rate hike later in the year, which increases the interest rate expense even further.

These factors can influence the prices of single stock futures versus their underlying stock. Expectations regarding earnings, pending news, and other factors may also cause the futures to trade at either a premium or discount to the current underlying market for the actual shares. Additional comparisons can be made using Table 2.1 for reference.

TABLE 2.1   Equities and Single Security Futures Comparison

	Equities	Single Security Futures
Margin	Current Reg. T margin is 50 percent of a positions value, or less for a "pattern day trader."	Exchange minimum of 20% of total position value. May be less for certain spreads.
Voting Rights	Yes	No
Minimum Trade Size	One share	One contract, equaling 100 shares
Minimum Tick Value		
Trading Hours	9:30 A.M. EST–4:00 P.M. EST plus after-hours in some markets.	9:20 A.M. EST–4:02 P.M. EST after-hours trade may develop at some point.
Fungible	Yes	No
Delivery	Physical at settlement day	Physical at delivery date
Settlement	Based on "T+3," which means trade date plus three days.	Based on "T+3," however from contract expiration forward.
Up-Tick Rules (for short sales)	Yes	No

(continues)

TABLE 2.1   *(Continued)*

	Equities	Single Security Futures
Price Movement Limits	N/A	N/A Contracts will only be halted when the underlying shares of the security are halted.
Last Trading Day	N/A—continuous	The third Friday of the particular delivery month.
Position Limits	N/A. Although reporting is required of some large positions.	Any size of 1000 contracts or more, maybe lower in near term delivery months.

Margin

With physical equities, the current margin requirement is known as Reg. T margin, referring to the Securities and Exchanges Commission Regulation T, which sets the minimum margin requirement at 50 percent for publicly traded shares. This is higher than the requirement for single stock futures, which is currently set at 20 percent *of the value of the contract.* It is important to realize that this is the Exchange Minimum margin requirement. In other words, any brokerage firm can set its own margin requirement in excess of the exchange minimum, which is 20 percent. While some securities will adhere to a 20 percent margin requirement, others that have a greater daily standard deviation will experience higher margin requirements, as posted by your respective brokerage firm. As with Reg. T margin in securities trading, this practice has already been seen in traditional equity trading. For some Internet, biotech, and other volatile equities, margin requirements have frequently been raised above the exchange minimum for equities, which is 50 percent. As a standard, the examples contained in this guide apply exchange minimum margins throughout.

A contract's value is determined by taking the number of shares multiplied times the current price. All single stock futures currently have an underlying base of 100 shares, as seen in Table 2.1, so 100 shares multiplied times the contract price equals the total value of the contract. This amount is then mul-

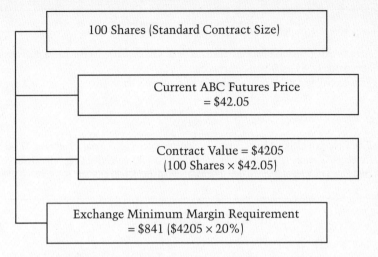

Figure 2.3   Exchange minimum margin requirement.

tiplied times 20 percent to determine the total margin requirement for the exchange minimum.

As you can see in Figure 2.3, the margin calculation for single stock futures is straightforward. By taking the standard contract size, 100 shares, and multiplying this times the current futures contract price, you determine the total value of the contract. Then, multiply this figure by 20 percent to determine the minimum exchange margin required for your purchase or sale of the contract. Again, it is important to realize that the exchange minimum requirement may be lower than what is required by your brokerage firm, as many firms add a risk premium to these minimum required margins.

Margin balances can change after the initial purchase or sale of a single stock futures contract and in most cases they probably will. For this reason, it is not advised to trade these instruments using the bare minimum margin in your account. Even small fluctuations can result in a decline below what is known as "minimum exchange maintenance margin," which in the case of single stock futures is also 20 percent (or the level determined by your brokerage firm). Any time your account equity declines below this 20 percent level, you will be required to deposit additional funds into your account.

For example, if the events in Figure 2.4 were to occur, you would then have two choices. You could either immediately

---

Day 1

An investor purchases ten contracts of Cisco futures for June delivery
at a price of $12.10 per contracts.
The exchange minimum margin of $2420 is deposited.

Day 2

The price of CSCO June futures declines to $11.90 per contract. The
investor's trading account is debited $200.00 to reflect the decline,
and the trading account is now deficient by $160.00.

Figure 2.4   Margin fluctuation.

deposit to your account the margin deficiency, which is $160.00,
or you could sell enough contracts to lower your margin requirement. Although your account incurred a loss of ($200.00),
your overall margin requirement is lower because the value of
your position has also declined. Therefore, the net result is a
margin deficiency of ($160.00). If you take no action, your broker
will promptly take the latter on your behalf to reduce your
exposure and cure your margin deficiency. This example clearly
illustrates why you should always plan on having ample additional margin in your account, particularly given the volatile
markets of recent times.

Marked to Market

An important concept in all margin calculations is the fact that
single stock futures are "marked to market." This process is
standard in all futures trading, and understanding the concept is
complimentary to maintaining a good working relationship with
your brokerage firm.

At the end of each trading day, your account will be debited
or credited after the closing price of the contracts in which you
have a position is compared against your cost basis. This is standard futures accounting used for all contracts. For calculating
the resulting debit or credit, the formula in Figure 2.5 is applied
to the positions held in your account each day.

Current Futures Price – Purchase Price

or

Short Sale Price – Current Price

= Credit or Debit to Account Balance

Figure 2.5   Calculating credit or debit to account balance.

As this formula illustrates, any change in your position value will be reflected immediately. Although this formula is said to be applied at each day's close, intraday movement that affects the value of your account in an adverse manner may trigger a notification of margin due prior to the closing. The change and update to your account equity is almost instantaneous, so you must consider maintaining sufficient balances to cover the movement of contracts on a short-term basis. It may be cumbersome to wire transfer funds into your stock futures account every time a small movement occurs, and in some cases you may be unable to deliver the margin in a manner that is agreeable with your broker, causing them to liquidate your entire position without notice. It is also a function of clearing brokers, or the firms responsible for clearing the orders of your actual brokerage firm, that in some cases may raise the margin required for specific contracts. It is in their best interest to alleviate frequent margin calls so that they remain in good standing with regard to regulations governing margin requirements. See Chapter 9 for more detailed information on margin considerations.

Trading Unit and Minimum Fluctuation

Equities and single stock futures differ greatly with regard to the minimum unit and fluctuation. With equities, the minimum unit is a single share, whereas single security futures have a minimum trading size of one contract, which is representative of 100 shares. Further, a fluctuation of 0.01 cent with an equity is the equivalent of $1.00 using a single stock futures contract. The size of every contract is standardized at 100 shares, with a minimum fluctuation of 0.01 cent, which multiplied times the contract size of 100 shares equals $1.00. This leverage can be both beneficial as well as harmful, depending on whether markets are moving in your favor or adversely. The standardization of single stock futures to represent 100 shares of the underlying equity is a necessary component in the construction of single stock futures as it provides a trade size that is accessible by a wide range of investors. The fixed share size of the contract also allows facilitated trade by allowing the market to only decide at what price a transaction will take place. However, since the contracts are fixed at 100 shares of the underlying equity that they represent, the movements associated with the contract will be representative of the contract size times the underlying contract price. This leverage component is an inherent quality in futures trading and must be understood to avoid ending up on the wrong side of a double-edged sword.

Uptick Rules and Short Sales

The rules governing short sales, or the sale of a single stock futures contract that you previously did not own, are markedly different than those that apply to trading of equities. With equities, a rule commonly referred to as the "Uptick Rule" only allows a short seller to sell into an "uptick" in an equity during certain volatile market periods. In other words, in a rapidly declining market, an investor (no matter if professional or individual) must wait for a tick higher in a stock before selling short. So, in the complete absence of buying activity, a short-seller would be unable to establish a new bearish position betting that the stock would decline even further. Although this rule was established with good intent, it is more of a nuisance than anything else, seeing as there would only be a complete absence of buyers in only the most exceptional cases. For example, even those betting on a lower share price, given a rapidly falling stock price will at some point "cover their short" and buy back shares, thus creating the uptick required for a new short sale. In panic situations, it is possible that this rule mutes the short sale effect on a stock, but it hardly cancels the overall movement.

With single stock futures, there is no uptick requirement to sell short a contract. This means that in even the most rapidly declining markets, the futures depend on the efficiency of the market itself to dictate the supply and demand. As previously stated, it would be difficult to imagine everyone was a seller, and if they were it would most likely be for a good reason. If not, then a potentially lucky buyer would bring the supply/demand relationship back into parity and the price would stabilize. The lack of any regulation governing uptick rules with single stock futures allows a more efficient market, which will afford the buyers and sellers of such contracts the opportunity to establish market equilibrium on their own terms. Whether this will create greater or less market volatility over time has yet to be determined. An interesting comparison is a currency that has a trading band and then is later allowed to freely float in the interbank market. While short-term volatility may increase when the band is removed, the medium to longer-term volatility will generally decrease as buyers and sellers face a greater degree of uncertainty and are less aggressive in their activities. A definite advantage exists using single security futures in place of underlying equities in volatile markets nonetheless, given that there are fewer limitations on the short sale of contracts versus the underlying stock.

Another major advantage for short-sellers using single stock futures is the availability of stock futures contracts. When short-selling occurs in an equity, the shares must be "borrowed" through your broker in order for you to sell them short. This occurs more often in equities that are heavily shorted, leading to a shortage of stock to borrow, and thus the investor is left with a message that their broker cannot locate stock for them to sell short. This was a common phenomenon during final days of the Internet equity bubble, and continues to be a problem for some irrationally exuberant equity issues. In fact, it is suggested that many equities rise meteorically as a direct result of no stock being available to loan for short-selling. As a result, the underlying equity continues to rise in zero gravity as there is a complete absence of speculative short-sellers who would potentially introduce an equilibrium to the price of the shares. Using single stock futures, there is a buyer for every seller and vice versa, so you can always sell a contract that you do not own initially, and most importantly it is not required that any stock be borrowed for the short sale. Security futures contracts can be traded as a long purchase or short sale, regardless of your prior position if any.

The Issue of Fungibility

The trading of single stock futures represents an agreement to transact the shares of an underlying equity at a future date. However, an investor can cancel his or her obligation by transacting the opposite side of their initial trade. In other words, a buy can be offset by a sale, and a sale offset by a purchase. The action of an offsetting future agreement is similar to closing a position in the actual equity market.

An offsetting transaction poses a caveat with the use of single stock futures. In Table 2.1 notice that equities are fungible whereas single stock futures are not. This means that when you purchase equity, you can then sell the same shares at any exchange where the stock is listed. In this day and age, the largest capitalized equities often trade simultaneously at different exchanges. For example, shares of IBM trade at the Pacific, Chicago, NASDAQ©, NYSE, Boston, and other regional exchanges. If you purchase shares at the open in New York, it is very possible you may later sell those same shares at the Pacific Exchange in San Francisco. In equity trading, the best bid price and best offer price are available for your transaction, regardless of where the first side of your trade was executed. The ability for these markets to be linked together allows the best bids and offers to be representative of a wide set of market-makers that are stationed in various posts around the country. Together, they compete for orders that are placed by investors who are looking at a composite of all of their bids and offers, a system that allows execution at the best current price available in the market.

In many cases, if you execute a trade to buy shares at the market open on one exchange and sell the shares shortly thereafter, it typically will be the case that you traded on two different exchanges. To the investor, this typically should not matter, and rarely does, as he or she is concerned with the best bid or offer in the marketplace, wherever it may reside. This fungibility allows seamless execution for the best bid and offer in the market, which is only noticed by investors when they glance at their trade confirmations and see that the trade was executed at the PSE (Pacific Exchange) or NYSE (New York Stock Exchange) or other regional market.

In contrast, single stock futures are not fungible between exchanges. The exchanges involved in trading the new product, including OneChicago LLC, NQLX (NASDAQ-LIFFE), and ISLAND Futures list single stock futures contracts independently of each other. This concept is critical in understanding how to trade single security futures. While it is envisioned that other exchanges may join the trading of security futures later in their development that may allow a fungible product, the principal will be the same as any fungibility agreement will likely exist only between a few exchanges. Any new exchange that joins the single security futures marketplace would probably only be able to structure an agreement with one other exchange for fungibility, thus it would not make the market completely funglible, although it would increase the depth of the two exchanges in question.

What this means for an investor is that the best bid and best offer for a particular security futures contract may reside at two different exchanges. An investor can transact an opening and closing side of a trade on two different single stock futures exchanges; however, this requires the contracts to be held until they mature at expiration. This process has been eased by reduced margin requirements for such activities (see Margin, Chapter 9). Nonetheless, if an investor wishes to have zero financial responsibility for the open trade and have it completely closed out in a more immediate fashion, he or she may have to exit the trade *at the best bid or offer at the same exchange where the trade was opened.*

For example, if you are looking to purchase a contract of XYZ Corp. stock futures, you see the best offer in the market is $32.25 per contract. A few days later, the stock has risen to $34.00. However, the best bid for you to sell into is actually at $33.70, because you are limited to selling at the exchange where you purchased the contract originally, seeing as you want the contract closed completely. Figure 2.6 lists sample hypothetical prices for discussion.

You can see that each exchange where XYZ Corp. single stock futures trade has a different bid and ask price. Now, assume that you purchase a contract at OneChicago for the current offer price of $33.50. A few minutes later, you decide that it was a bad decision and want to exit the contract. Although you would, in

	Bid	Offer
OneChicago	$33.00	$33.50
NQLX	$33.15	$33.65
ISLAND	$33.25	$33.75
AMEX	$33.30	$33.80
NYSE (stock)	$33.30	$33.40

Figure 2.6   Hypothetical prices.

a fungible market, be able to sell at ISLAND for $33.25 and completely close the position, you cannot. Due to the lack of fungibility, you can only exit the position at OneChicago for the bid price of $33.00. However, you can sell at ISLAND if you are willing to hold both sets of contracts to expiration at a reduced margin requirement. This feature of single stock futures may change in the future, but for now the lack of fungibility may prove to increase liquidity in the near term.

Another alternative to selling at the price of $33.00 would be to sell at the current market bid price for the physical shares of XYZ Corp., which is $33.30. A sale of 100 shares, the equivalent size of your futures contract, will effectively close your market exposure. There are other considerations to this approach, however. First, you must hold the contract and the shares until delivery date. This may seem cumbersome, particularly if you are using limited funds or if the delivery date is far in the future. Another consideration are fees that your broker may charge for delivering on a futures contract, which like delivery with an options contract can be high in relation to your actual savings in the transaction. These topics are covered in more detail in Chapter 6.

Although many market participants are critical of security futures not being a fungible product, an interesting point can be made that this will serve to further liquidity in the long run rather than hurt it. For many years after the introduction of listed equity options, trading was confined to the Chicago Board Options Exchange (CBOE). There were no issues with liquidity, and in fact the introduction of trading on different listed equity options exchanges arguably changed many positive factors surrounding listed equity option trading. It is believed that having a non-fungible product, such as single stock futures, liquidity can

actually develop at a greater pace even though a group of exchanges are trading the product independently of each other.
While liquidity may be greater at one exchange than another, the
entirety of liquidity will increase with the passing of time as the
aggregate business of each individual exchange develops. This
will allow markets to establish greater depth as time moves forward, and given the steps that each exchange is taking to ensure
liquid and smooth operations, it is unlikely that the non-
fungible nature of single security futures will pose any hindrance
to their popularity or efficiency.

Delivery

When shares of an equity are purchased or sold, they settle on a
"T+3," or trade date plus three days basis, meaning that three
days from the date of the trade is the required date for the funds
to be debited and the shares to be received for a particular transaction. This settlement procedure remains in effect with single
security futures; however, settlement occurs three days following expiration of the futures contract. Meanwhile, the settlement of an actual futures contract purchase or short sale occurs
the following business day.

With single stock futures, delivery takes on a new meaning
as this is the date on which two things occur: (1) All trading
ceases on that particular futures contract; and (2) Any outstanding obligations must be settled in accordance with the contract
specifications. If you are long a single stock futures contract at
expiration, you will be receiving the underlying 100 shares per
contract and must deposit the full contract value into your trading account. This is the amount that you are paying the individual that is making delivery of the shares to your account. If you
were short a single stock futures contract going into the delivery
date, you must have the shares of the underlying equity in your
account and you will receive the previously agreed upon price
multiplied times 100 shares per contract in your account. In
either case, if you fail to deliver funds (for a purchase or long
position) or fail to have sufficient shares of the equity in your account (for a sale or short position) then you are considered in default of your obligation for delivery. In speculative applications it

is rare to see a contract held through to delivery date, however in hedging applications it may be more common. This is discussed further in the respective chapters ahead.

It is important to realize that many brokers charge a fee for delivery services. This must be considered into the overall return on your transaction when holding a contract through to delivery, and also the impact it may have on your financial resources until the transaction settles.

Contract Expiration and Delivery Dates

Unlike underlying equities and more similar to an options contract, single stock futures have an expiration date and also a delivery date. Most often the date referred to is the delivery date, and this is the month that is always referenced in conjunction with the single stock futures contract you are trading. For example, if you are purchasing ten contracts of Intel futures for June delivery, this is how your order is classified and your broker then knows what trade to place on your behalf. The last trading day of a single security futures contract is the third Friday in the delivery month, in our example June. If you held a long contract as of the third Friday of the month, which expired in that month, you would be notified for delivery. Most likely your broker would notify you that in three business days you need funds to cover the purchase of 100 shares of the stock that your long contract represents. Like equities, single stock futures settlement reflects the T+3 method, or trade date plus three business days. However, with single stock futures it should be called E+3, or expiration plus three, since the expiration process is rather passive and delivery takes place three business days following that expiry. By applying this method of uniform settlement, it is possible for an investor who must deliver the shares unexpectedly to purchase the shares as of the expiration day, and settlement follows three business days later, coinciding with the final delivery or settlement date of the futures contracts for that particular month. This allows a rebalancing of equities by major institutional investors and market-makers so that their new transactions, if any, will settle on the same day that the contract delivery is to take place.

Single stock futures trade for delivery at the end of each quarter, plus two serial months. This ensures that there are always three consecutive months forward from the current date in which you can trade the contracts. Each contract is identified by a specific code string, depending on which exchange you are using to place your orders. Because the product is non-fungible between exchanges, the unique identification codes for contracts that are otherwise identical assists with identifying which exchange you are doing business with. Table 2.2 shows the contract calendar from OneChicago LLC.

Constructing a Security Futures Contract Symbol

Single security futures are quoted on all major quote vendor services, but understanding the construction of security futures symbols or tickers is critical. The construction of a security futures ticker symbol is indigenous to each exchange. Because the product is not fungible, each exchange that trades single security futures can have its own variation on how to construct a symbol for a specific contract, even if it is the same underlying equity and the same delivery month! For this reason, constructing contract codes is covered in Chapter 3 under each respective security futures exchange. While this is a general guideline to constructing

TABLE 2.2   Contract Calendar from OneChicago, LLC

Delivery	Jan	Feb	Mar	Apr	May	Jun	Jul	Aug	Sep	Oct	Nov	Dec
Current												
January	S	S	Q			Q						
February		S	Q	S		Q						
March			Q	S	S	Q						
April				S	S	Q			Q			
May					S	Q	S		Q			
June						Q	S	S	Q			
July							S	S	Q			
August								S	Q	S		Q
September									Q	S	S	Q
October										S	S	Q
November											S	Q
December												Q

Q = Quarterly Contract   S = Serial Month

symbols for security futures, your executing broker can provide additional information in regard to constructing correct symbols for separate single security futures exchanges.

Contract Limits and Movement

Single stock futures do not have movement limits like some other financial futures contracts do. Some broad-based index futures and other commodity futures have predetermined daily limits that prevent contracts from moving in one direction more than a certain deviation from the prior day's settlement price. These limits are in place to assist the investment community by preventing "runaway" markets or panic situations. As with the uptick rule associated with equities, many question the viability of such limits because it is often thought that markets are best left to their own devices to establish equilibrium. However in the bigger picture, limits may serve to cool volatility levels in the short run.

If you think about it, underlying equities do not have limits. Many times an investor has witnessed a company with accounting irregularities open substantially below the prior day's closing price, only to continue its descent even further. This is similar to the movement of single security futures, as they have no predetermined limits associated with daily price swings. The only cessation of single stock futures trading occurs when there is a corresponding halt in trading of the underlying stock that the contract represents. News events such as earnings releases, other news dissemination, or regulatory actions would be examples of why an equity was halted and the corresponding security futures contract halted in conjunction. Any halt of a security futures contract is handled in conjunction with the specialist that is associated with the underlying equity on the stock exchange in which that company is listed.

Single security futures do have size limitations placed on trading, which dictates that any trade or accumulation of contracts over 1000 in size is reportable, meaning the transaction that involves 100,000 common shares of underlying stock or greater. Typically this involves filing paperwork with various regulatory agencies describing your activities in a particular equity. Given the large size of such a transaction for an individual investor (each .01-cent move in an underlying equity would equal a $1,000 change in equity in such a futures position) it may be unlikely that this requirement is a problem for many security futures investors.

Understanding the Leverage

An important concept to address when comparing single stock futures to underlying equities that they represent is the leverage component. Futures contracts have leverage associated with their structure, while underlying shares of equity have no inherent leverage associated with them; essentially what you buy is what you get. You can apply modest leverage to the trading of shares by utilizing Reg. T margin which is commonly available, thereby financing 50 percent of your position and only posting half of the value of your purchase. This practice is common among many investors, given the low interest rate environment of present. However, a 50 percent margin requirement is well below the leverage available through the use of single security futures.

With single stock futures, the standardized contract sized is 100 shares. What this means is that every transaction involves a minimum of 100 shares of the underlying stock that the contract represents. Further, rather than having a margin requirement similar to Reg. T, single stock futures have a margin percentage that is set as a percent of the total value of the transaction. This is similar to the application of margin in securities trading, as the 50 percent margin you must apply is for the entire value of your transaction. The percentage margin required for the total value of your single stock futures transaction is 20 percent. Believe it or not, this is high when compared with the margin requirement for other financial futures, but the leverage quality is the same. With only 20 percent of your position "paid for," you are floating some 80 percent of the position on borrowed funds, which can create outsized gains or just as easily outsized losses depending on the direction of the equity contract that you are trading. While all investors plan to be profitable in their trading activities, it is an important function to understand how leverage can magnify losses just as quickly as gains. An appropriate approach to the use of single stock futures, keeping this in mind, is to base your transactions on an aggregate contract value that is not far from where you would transact the similar trades using underlying equity. The versatility provided by single stock futures brings other useful advantages to their application than just trying to control more equity than you are capable of covering the losses for if your future price projections turn out to be incorrect.

Standardized contract sizes have the same influence on the leverage principal as margin requirement. Because the minimum price fluctuation is 0.01 cent per security futures contract, multiplied times the number of shares in each contract (100) this equates to a $1.00 move for every 0.01 cent move in the underlying equity. If the move is in your anticipated direction this is a benefit, however if it is against your position the leverage can just as easily be a problem. Unlike equity options whose movement may not always mirror that of the underlying equity, in theory security futures should closely track the price of underlying shares. Therefore, the leverage is more pronounced than it would be in your average equity option transaction. A complete comparison between options and futures is found in Chapter 10.

Regulatory Considerations

Both the Commodity Futures Trading Commission (CFTC) and the Securities and Exchange Commission (SEC) have regulatory control over single stock futures. Since the product is a hybrid of the equity and futures world, this joint regulatory environment makes good sense for the equitable administration of this new product.

These agencies make certain that brokers dealing in security futures are properly licensed and have passed the appropriate proficiency training required for placing trades on a customer's behalf. Furthermore, they make certain that regulatory guidelines and procedures are followed according to the mandates that they hand down to the participants in the single security futures markets. Their authority extends to the farthest reaches of product involvement, from a security brokerage firm to a website that may offer advice on how to trade single stock futures.

Chapter 3

THE EXCHANGES FOR SINGLE STOCK FUTURES

Single stock futures trade at four main exchanges in the United States. Trading takes place through electronic means (with the exception of the American Stock Exchange [AMEX]), without the use of a trading floor or trading pit as you might envision, with market-makers scrambling around in brightly colored jackets. Instead, the market for single stock futures at three exchanges is a modern day electronic venue, connected through modern day technology. Meanwhile, at the other end of the spectrum, the AMEX offers single security futures trading alongside its option trading pits, transacted by floor traders through the more traditional open-outcry method.

While some investors have been critical of electronic markets over the years, they have proved to be an efficient and cost effective manner in which to trade a wide variety of financial products. In fact, the migration to further electronic exchanges in the future means that, as with the modern day Internet-based brokerage firms, fees associated with trading should only continue to decline. This is in the best interest of all the participants in the financial markets, particularly for those who trade enough size to be impacted by the costs associated with trading.

The development of an exchange for single security futures was pursued quickly following the passing of the Commodities Modernization Act of 2000, with the NASDAQ-LIFFE project gaining initial approval by regulatory agencies, followed by OneChicago, ISLAND, and AMEX. All four of the initial security futures exchanges have teams with extensive backgrounds and knowledge of futures trading, however in their quest to become the predominant exchange for the product, fungibility was ruled out as an option.

The four exchanges involved in securities futures trading have certain variances within their market-making methodology and approach to single stock futures. A description of each of the four exchanges follows.

OneChicago LLC

The OneChicago LLC group is based in Chicago, Illinois, and also has offices in New York City. The exchange was formed and financed as a joint venture between the Chicago Mercantile Exchange (CME), the Chicago Board Options Exchange (CBOE), and the Chicago Board of Trade (CBOT). These three well-known exchanges back the operations of OneChicago group logistically and financially, although the exchange itself is an independent organization. The three major exchanges backing the OneChicago group have a strong interest in seeing the venture succeed, and to its advantage OneChicago has the backing and marketing power of the other three exchanges at its side. The sheer volume of both traders and trades that are associated with the other exchanges in Chicago should lend great success to the OneChicago group moving forward, particularly with respect to hedging activities by the option market-makers at the CBOE. Single stock futures provide an excellent manner in which these market-makers can eliminate certain risks of selling option premium to the investing public by hedging their Delta exposure with the use of single stock futures, more of which is covered in this chapter.

OneChicago has organized trading at its exchange using a system called the LMM, or Lead Market Maker system. This involves a select group of designated LMMs that were selected individually by the exchange. While the beginning number of LMMs was limited, other trading groups can apply to become LMMs for review by the exchange. The original group selected by the exchange includes 24 LMMs, including: AOTUSA LLC, Bear Stearns, Botta Capital Management, Carlin Specialists, CTC LLC, Deutsche Bank, DRW Holdings, Eiger Capital Management, Equitec Proprietary Markets, Jump Trading, Knight Financial Products, Mercury Trading LP, Rock Island Index Trading, Ronin Capital, SLK-Hull Derivatives LLC, SMW Trading Company, Susquehanna Investment Group, TD Securities-LETCO DPM, TD Securities-Stafford Group, Timber Hill LLC, Tradelink LLC, Transmarket Group LLC, Wagner Scott Bear, and Wolverine Trading LP. Each of these firms has a proven expertise in providing liquid, two-way markets for various financial futures and options markets. A few of the initial firms selected for designation as LMMs are also large option market-makers, which goes hand in hand with the trading and market-making activities in the single stock futures market.

For example, the diagram in Figure 3.1 illustrates how selling an option to an investor by one of these firms can then turn into a single stock futures order, which can then turn into an order in the stock of the underlying instrument of that same futures contract. This is a circular process that should improve the liquidity of the markets in the long term.

The OneChicago group is headed by William Rainer, who was the Chairman of the Commodities and Futures Trading Commission (CFTC) from August 1999 through early 2001. He also held positions with the United States Enrichment Corporation, Greenwich Capital Markets, and Kidder, Peabody and Company, Inc.

The OneChicago exchange is a private, for-profit company that generates income by collecting exchange fees on every

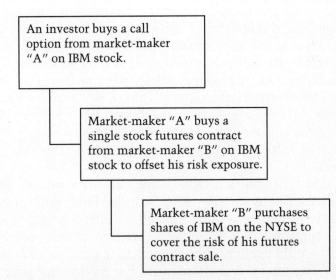

Figure 3.1   How sale of an option can become an order in the stock of the underlying instrument (of that same futures contract).

transaction that takes place via their electronic marketplace. Theoretically, this allows a steady income stream for the exchange as long as the expenses associated with running the operation are diffused, and the necessary trading volumes occur at the exchange to generate these fees. Because OneChicago decided to base their operations on an electronic network, the fees associated with operations should be very competitive. The overall migration in the financial industry from staffed exchanges to electronic marketplace has succeeded in substantially lowering transactional costs across the board.

At the onset of trading for single stock futures, the OneChicago exchange plans on offering a minimum of 80 available SSF contracts and 15 narrow-based indices (both the SSF contracts and narrow-based indices listed at OneChicago can be found in Appendix 4). It plans to add additional listings once trading evolves in this new marketplace. Initially the exchange minimum margin requirements are 20 percent, and there will be trading in the first two quarterly delivery months plus two serial months for each of the listed SSF contracts. The contracts will be settled by physical delivery at expiration.

Trading security futures at the OneChicago exchange requires a solid understanding of identifying individual security futures contracts. The resulting prices quoted will be those available for the exchange whose ticker symbol you are using. In other words, a ticker symbol for a Microsoft June delivery futures contract at OneChicago will not indicate what the current quotes are for the identical contract that may be trading on another exchange. As mentioned earlier, since products are indigenous to their respective exchange, there is no quote montage that many investors have become familiar with by investing with fungible equities. While this may seem confusing at first, constructing a futures symbol becomes more automated with repetition.

The construction of a OneChicago security futures symbol should be looked at as a two-step process. First, you must take the underlying equity symbol that the futures contract you wish to trade represents. For example, a security futures contract for Microsoft would begin with that particular stock's ticker, which is MSFT. The next step is to identify the month and year of delivery for the contract that you wish to trade. This is done using standard futures delivery codes, as outlined in Figure 3.2.

January	F
February	G
March	H
April	J
May	K
June	M
July	N
August	Q
September	U
October	V
November	X
December	Z

Figure 3.2 Monthly delivery codes for futures contracts.

The monthly contract delivery codes are fixed and will not change. As with option contract codes, each month is designated by a particular letter of the alphabet, and the year is indicated by the last digit, for example 2002 would equal 2. Additional information regarding symbol construction can be located at the OneChicago website, or through your executing broker.

By trading single security futures using the LMM system, OneChicago provides a system whereby each designated LMM has a specific number of contracts to quote (market depth) for a specific set of contracts (names) at a specific maximum spread (bid-ask differential). Some LMMs may be willing to quote two-sided markets for 50 contracts on each side for a minimum spread of 0.05 cents, while some other LMMs may request to quote a 0.15 cent spread good for 500 contracts on each side of the market. This all depends on the individual market-maker firm, and the commitment it wants to make for the exchange. In return, the firms receive benefits such as reduced exchange fees and guaranteed participation on contracts traded at the exchange.

I had the opportunity to discuss the OneChicago LLC exchange with Mr. Peter Borish, Senior Managing Director of the organization. Mr. Borish is a well-established member of the asset management community, having founded Computer Trading Corporation (CTC) in 1995 and serving as Chairman of the company. He was Director of Research at Tudor Investment Corporation from 1986 to 1994, after having left his position at the

Federal Reserve Bank of New York where he worked from 1982 to 1985.

Our discussion began by covering the general structure of One-Chicago and the products that they intend to offer. Even though OneChicago was recognized by the CFTC after the NQLX, the number of security futures contracts they plan to offer for trading from day one well exceed those listed at the NQLX. Mr. Borish also believes that the exchange has a competitive advantage in offering narrow-based indices, since these products offer both individual and professional investors the opportunity to speculate or hedge risk associated with portfolio exposure across different sectors. Mr. Borish pointed out that the markets move in a more sector rotational manner, and therefore the use of sector specific index futures that are not as correlated to the overall market like some larger index contracts can be very useful for investors.

I raised the question of popularity for the products here in the United States, given that the LIFFE version of single security futures, the so-called Universal Stock Futures, have not managed to garner a great deal of volume since their introduction. He replied that the United States launch should not be compared with the LIFFE listing of United States-based companies, given that certain restrictions apply to the listings on the LIFFE. Furthermore, Mr. Borish believes that the United States is a more derivatives-focused environment than other countries, a fact that will allow greater success in the United States for security futures products. In the United States he pointed out, the volumes of option trading far surpassed that in other countries, another indicator that the United States launch of the product will be a success.

I asked what the greatest appeal would be for using single security futures, and Mr. Borish indicated that many different investors would use the product for different reasons, however new people would be joining the market for security futures as they found qualities that applied to their individual needs and approach. The key, he said, is making certain that users of the product are educated so that the application of security futures can take place in an informed manner. In this manner, they can be used to their full potential.

I moved on to questions regarding market volatility and the general impact that was expected on the securities markets from the introduction of single stock futures. Mr. Borish indicated it was his belief that longer term volatility may even decline due to the introduction of security futures. He likened the current equity environment to a table with only three legs, being the underlying equities, equity options, and listed index derivatives. With the introduction of single security futures, the fourth leg of the table will be in place that will add stability and likely lower volatility over the long run. This makes sense, since the ability for market-makers, professional investors, and individuals to access more markets for risk control and hedging will likely improve the overall liquidity profile of the financial markets.

When I questioned the practicality of fungibility, or lack thereof when it comes to single security futures markets, Mr. Borish made the argument that fungibility would actually fracture liquidity in the long run, and his case was quite convincing. Although on the surface it would seem that having a fungible product is more appropriate for near term liquidity, in the long run it actually hurts the exchanges specializing in the particular product. A perfect example was the initial introduction of listed equity options, which Mr. Borish pointed out were not fungible for many years after their introduction. The volumes actually dropped off after the products became fungible, with more exchanges competing for the same trades. By having exchanges remain autonomous in the early days, single security futures should actually see increased liquidity in the long run as each exchange develops its own unique liquidity. I tend to agree that this approach will lead to greater competition that in turn will promote further liquidity moving forward. Furthermore, the principal of having to buy and sell a product on the same exchange is not as daunting as it may seem, given that OneChicago has put together a system to provide liquidity from day one.

Picking up on the liquidity topic, we moved on to discuss the use of OneChicago's LMM, or Lead Market Maker system. This system allows the exchange to have professional traders making continuous two-way markets for specific security futures in which they are assigned. The LMM system, Mr. Borish said, allows the exchange to retain control over the product trading at their exchange. This system allows more flexibility for the exchange than offering a limit book like other exchanges since there is a recognized element of liquidity available from day one of trading in each security futures product. The LMMs are guaranteed a certain participation in order flow in exchange for providing continuous two-sided quotes in the names they are assigned. The LMMs, he said, are also considered to provide valuable input with regard to new security futures listings moving forward. I agreed with Mr. Borish that the use of LMMs who also have extensive option market-making experience was useful, given that they can use security futures for offsetting risk with their other activities in the options trading universe.

I then discussed the users of security futures, and what techniques they may use to introduce diversity through the use of security futures in their overall approach. I suggested that there may be concerns about individual investors using security futures and incurring heavy losses through their trading activities. Mr. Borish replied that education was a key concept behind the new product, and that everyone becoming involved with the product should educate themselves before diving in head first. Furthermore, he added that it was not the exchanges expectation that investors would be using security futures with the absolute minimum margin required. The use of these products with such an approach would be ill-advised. Rather, investors should plan on having reserves to meet any margin call or deficiency, and not view security futures strictly from a "how much can I leverage up myself" point of view. Mr. Borish also pointed out that any way you look at your investing, when you buy an asset you are buying volatility, therefore individual investment decisions should be made with care by thoroughly completing research before any investments are made.

Regarding trading methods and strategies, Mr. Borish indicated that single security futures provided many opportunities for investors. He indicated that single security futures are much more capital efficient for investors to use versus other derivative products or underlying shares. From speculating by active traders to hedging by individual investors and all points between, Mr. Borish indicated that it was his belief security futures would be used for a wide array of applications. Coming from a successful background in financial management, Mr. Borish pointed out more advanced strategies such as volatility-based trading, pairs trading, and relative value approaches would be greatly facilitated by these new products. He added that large institutions that were index-based funds could also use single security futures to fine-tune their approach, and omit one or a handful of equities that they did not want to include in their equity trading baskets. Likewise, a corporate entity that was participating in a stock buyback plan could utilize single stock futures for this purpose. The fact that security futures have a physical settlement at delivery further allowed such activity with ease by larger companies.

Of special interest, we discussed the new narrow-based indices that are listed at OneChicago, and how they provide a unique opportunity for professionals and individual investors as well. These products, indices based on as few as five underlying equities in a particular sector, are ideal he said for hedging industry specific risk in portfolios. While other exchanges may offer security futures, the OneChicago group would appear to be in the lead with respect to the listing of narrow-based indices. Because the market is prone to moving in a sector rotational manner, Mr. Borish indicated that the use of indices such as those listed at OneChicago makes sense in today's market.

The NASDAQ-LIFFE

The NASDAQ-LIFFE (NQLX) exchange is also an electronic exchange developed solely for the trading of single stock futures and narrow-based indices. This exchange is an offshoot of the well-known NASDAQ© exchange that trades a great number of publicly listed shares of major companies. The NQLX was the first exchange to be approved by the Commodities and Futures Trading Commission (CFTC) to trade single stock futures following the repeal of the Shad-Johnson Accord.

The NQLX has the LIFFE (London International Financial Futures and Options Exchange) exchange, based in London, as a business partner in their organization. This allows the NQLX great insight into the workings of single stock futures trade, since the London-based LIFFE has been trading security futures for several years and has had Universal Stock Futures (USFs) listed on major U.S.-based companies since early 2001. These companies may be able to offer the NQLX project insight into what will work and what will not work with regard to trading single security futures in the United States.

There are two separate listings that will occur on the NQLX with regard to single stock futures. The first, single stock futures, will primarily be comprised of U.S.-based companies that are well capitalized and listed on one of the major U.S. stock exchanges. It is envisioned that moving forward the LIFFE may eventually offer the USF products for trade by U.S.-based investors after appropriate regulatory approvals are obtained. This will open foreign derivative markets to mainstream U.S.-based derivative traders, which will improve liquidity for all those involved in these markets.

The NQLX is headed by Mr. Thomas Ascher, who worked with Interactive Brokers Group and is a long-term member and former Director of the Chicago Board Options Exchange (CBOE). An interview with Thomas Ascher is located at the end of this chapter, in which he discusses the NQLX and single stock futures trading in his own words.

The NQLX bases its trading technology on a platform called LIFFE CONNECT, which was a system designed by the LIFFE and is currently in use at the LIFFE security futures exchange. It can be envisioned as the "trading host" or "hub," where all buy and sell orders are matched. Additionally, the system indicates the depth of the market, or the number of bids and offers and at what prices they are listed. The diagram in Figure 3.3 shows the relationship between the LIFFE CONNECT platform and orders placed on the exchange.

As the figure indicates, investors and professionals place their orders that are routed to the LIFFE CONNECT trading platform via their own specific software used for placing orders. The LIFFE CONNECT hub then matches the buy and sell orders, practically instantaneously, transmitting the fills back to the

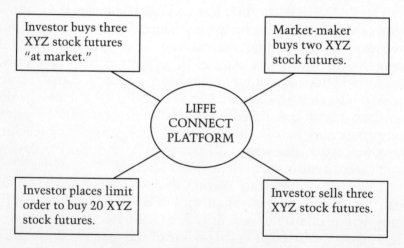

Figure 3.3   LIFFE CONNECT system.

brokers who will then disseminate the information to their clients. While the process may seem to involve a few steps, the turn around time from the placement of an order from Investor A and B to receiving a fill is only seconds. In some cases, institutional and professional investors can qualify to connect directly to the LIFFE CONNECT hub rather than going through their brokerage firm, expediting the process even further. The LIFFE CONNECT platform uses a technology commonly referred to as CLOB, or Central Limit Order Book. This means that the system matches orders according to price and time priority, and it is similar to the more traditional NASDAQ© equity platform. By using such a method, the NQLX is taking a different approach than OneChicago, as it relies on market participants to provide the major liquidity in trading. While some market-makers are present, they number fewer than their LMM counterparts on the OneChicago exchange. However, for providing continuous two-sided markets, the NQLX market-makers are given perks, perhaps a share in revenue, which is the system at the LIFFE markets, NQLX's business partner.

The NQLX, like OneChicago, is also a fully electronic exchange. Leveraging its experience from the NASDAQ© equity market trading model, the NQLX should be successful in keeping fees to a minimum given that the overhead costs are less than those encountered by a more traditional exchange. The NASDAQ© market is recognized as a leader in electronic trading, transforming the once small NASDAQ© marketplace into what is now the listing venue of choice for many companies.

At the NQLX exchange, constructing a security futures symbol is again specific to the exchange, given the nature of security futures. Because the NQLX interfaces directly with the LIFFE CONNECT platform, certain considerations were made in connection with designing the symbols for trading security futures. The NQLX utilizes a straightforward method of constructing contract symbols. For example, in the case of Intel, whose underlying equity symbol is INTC, the symbol would be truncated to INT. Then, the delivery month is added, as is a two-digit number for the year of delivery. The difference with the NQLX is that the delivery month is a three-letter reference, and not simply a single letter code. For example, September is SEP, October is OCT, and so on. Figure 3.4 illustrates the monthly delivery codes and delivery years.

January	**F**
February	**G**
March	**H**
April	**J**
May	**K**
June	**M**
July	**N**
August	**Q**
September	**U**
October	**V**
November	**X**
December	**Z**

Add last two digits of the delivery year
(Example: January, 2002 would be Jan02)

Figure 3.4   Monthly delivery codes for futures contracts.

Using Figure 3.4, you can see that the Intel security futures for September, 2002 delivery would be labeled as: INTSEP02. The NQLX omits both the corporate action indicator and a letter to identify their exchange, however a corporate action identifier will be added in the event that an action is present. However, the default symbol omits this number. If there was a reverse split or other corporate action, the symbol changes again to a two-letter equity identifier, such as IN2SEP02. In this case, you can see that INT was replaced with IN2, while the delivery month and expiry year code remains unchanged.

For more information on constructing symbols for NQLX traded futures, visit their website or contact your executing broker. Table 3.1 lists contract specifications for single security futures trading at the NQLX.

An Interview with Tom Ascher, CEO of NASDAQ-LIFFE

Mr. Thomas Ascher, the Chief Executive Officer of the NASDAQ-LIFFE (NQLX) markets was kind enough to grant an interview to be published in this guide. His background is discussed along with a narrative of our conversation regarding single security futures products and what is expected moving forward with the introduction of these derivatives.

Thomas Ascher worked with the firm Interactive Brokers LLC, as the Executive Vice President before joining the NQLX.

His duties with Interactive Brokers LLC included overseeing their entire sales and marketing efforts, and relationships with other exchanges and market participants. The firm has become a very successful entity, offering low-cost execution services in a wide variety of products to both professional and individual investors. The parent company of Timber Hill LLC, Interactive Brokers LLC was able to leverage experience and access in the futures and options markets and pass along added value to clients who utilize their services. While with the Interactive Brokers LLC group, Mr. Ascher was able to structure a strategic joint venture between the Boston Stock Exchange, Bourse de Montreal, and his own firm to create a new U.S. equity options exchange.

Mr. Ascher is a long-term member of the Chicago Board Options Exchange (CBOE), joining in 1986, and served as a director from 1994 to 1999. In 1997, Mr. Ascher was named Vice Chairman of the Board of Directors and Chairman of the Executive Committee at the CBOE. Additionally, Mr. Ascher has served on the Options Clearing Corporation (OCC) nominating committee from 2001 to present, and was also a trustee on the Cincinnati Stock Exchange from 1997 to 2001. He also participates as a member and committee chairman of the Economic Club of Chicago.

Mr. Ascher and I began our discussion of the NQLX and single security futures by reviewing that the NASDAQ-LIFFE joint venture was the first exchange to be recognized by the CFTC and other regulatory agencies as an authorized exchange for single security futures. The efforts of NQLX to structure their exchange while competing exchanges were still building their management teams allowed the group to put together a solid game plan and move on to the systems testing stage before any other exchange. Even though they were prepared, the delays posed by some regulatory agencies (my conjecture) may have impacted any benefits created by being the first exchange on the block.

I asked Mr. Ascher if there were any official projections of expected volume for the NQLX, but he declined any formal estimate given the fact that he stated volume would increase methodically, as different market participants joined in the trading of security futures as time moved on. Mr. Ascher believes that at the inception of trading for security futures a defined group of participants will be readily willing to trade the new products, such as hedge funds, active day traders, and other professionals such as market-makers. However, he sees a greater scope to the use of security futures by investors who are looking to replace equities with the use of security futures for hedging applications that may be used by a wider group of individuals. The point he stressed was to expect the volumes from these different market segments to develop over time, given that the key to bringing investors to use security futures is education. Through educating investors, which is already done as he pointed out on the NQLX website, the exchange hopes to bring knowledgeable investors to the products that trade there.

Mr. Ascher and I discussed the potential users of single security futures in more detail, and he indicated that it was expected many segments of market participants would join in the use of security futures.

More specifically, he indicated that it was natural that option market-makers would probably look to security futures for hedging and trading purposes, and that the new products facilitate these activities that occur in large volumes. For example, a floor trader selling an option to another investor may look to use single security futures to hedge or offset some of their risk. Mr. Ascher's background and longstanding interaction with other professionals at the CBOE allows him the intricate knowledge of how market-makers operate. I then posed the obvious question, did he think that over time security futures would undermine equity option volume, and actually be a competing product? To this, he emphatically stated that security futures would compliment equity options rather than compete against them, as many strategies can encompass the use of both of these derivative products. Furthermore, he went on to add that he believes security futures would increase the liquidity of derivative markets in general moving forward, given that market professionals would have another source of risk offset.

Mr. Ascher stated that security futures cannot be all things to all people, and by this he was responding to my questions about suitability. He indicated that the security futures contract may have different qualities that appeal to different types of product users, and therefore the market is rather unlimited. The one key is to make certain that enough sources are available for different types of investors to learn what they need to know about these products before becoming involved.

Moving forward, we discussed the market-making system that is implemented for trading through the NQLX. This system, known as the CLOB or Central Limit Order Book is the most equitable according to Mr. Ascher, and affords true price discovery since it is not based on an exclusive arrangement with certain market-makers for certain security futures contracts. The NQLX, he explained, guarantees a certain piece of orders to individual market-making firms that agree to make continuous two-sided markets in security futures contracts throughout the trading day. People familiar with the traditional NASDAQ© equity platform should be at home with the LIFFE CONNECT technology, and Mr. Ascher pointed out that in professional circles the LIFFE CONNECT platform is (arguably) considered the best global execution platform.

Because the software was connected through technology created by the LIFFE exchange, I then raised the issue of USF trading there, the Universal Stock Futures introduced in 2001. I indicated that the volumes, since introduced in January 2001, had been relatively low in U.S.-based equity futures. Mr. Ascher stated that he believed volumes were low due to the ban of U.S. asset managers and investors from participating in trading of USFs from day one. Furthermore, the entire infrastructure he indicated was different than the U.S. markets, where he is confident that volumes would be adequate in security futures to create a new, liquid marketplace. I then inquired what he believed the overall impact would be on volatility, an issue that has been raised since talk began of single stock futures. His reply was that he would expect a decrease in the overall equity market volatilities as time moved forward following the initial launch of single security futures.

TABLE 3.1   Contract Specifications for Single Security Futures Trading at the NQLX

Nominal Contract Size	One hundred shares of the common stock or American Depository Receipts (ADRs) of selected companies whose shares are listed on U.S. securities exchanges (i.e., NYSE) or trade over-the-counter (i.e., NASDAQ©).
Quotation	U.S. dollars per share
Minimum Tick Increment	$0.01 per share = $1 per contract
Delivery Months	The first five quarterly delivery months in a March, June, September, and December cycle as well as the nearest two serial months (i.e. January and February in December). This will ensure that the first three calendar months will always be available for trading.

(continues)

TABLE 3.1   *(Continued)*

Symbols	Three character alpha-numeric product code.
Trading Hours	09:30–16:02 EST
Last Trading Day	The third Friday of the delivery month.
Settlement Day and Time	10:00 EST on the next business day following the last trading day.
Settlement Price Calculation	The Settlement System will calculate the Daily Settlement Price based on reported prices in the two-minute period prior to the time specified for contract settlement. The first 90 seconds of the settlement period will be used to monitor spread levels. The Settlement Price will be determined during the final 30 seconds of the settlement period, according to the following criteria:

a. A single traded price during the last 30 seconds will be the Settlement Price.

b. If more than one trade occurs during the last 30 seconds of the Settlement Range, the trade weighted average of the prices, rounded to the nearest tick, will be the Settlement Price.

c. If no trade occurs during the last 30 seconds of the Settlement Range, the price midway between the active bids and offers at the time the settlement price is calculated, rounded to the nearest tick, will be the Settlement Price.

d. In the circumstances in which there is no traded price nor updated bid/ask spread during the last 30 seconds of trading, the settlement price of that contract month shall be the settlement price of the first quarterly delivery month plus or minus the latest observed calendar spread differential between the first quarterly delivery month and the contract month in question. In the event that the relevant spread price differential is not readily observable, in order to identify appropriate settlement prices, Exchange Market Services may take into account the following criteria as applicable (1) spread price differentials between other contract months of the same contract; and (2) price levels and/or spread price differentials in a related market.

EDSP Calculation (Exchange Delivery Settlement Price)	The official closing price of the underlying stock on the NASDAQ© or NYSE, as of the latest possible period before NQLX system closing time (17:00 EST).
Delivery Size	Physical delivery of 100 shares (plus or minus the impact of corporate events per standard Options Clearing Corporation (OCC) rules and practices) made through National Securities Clearing Corporation (NSCC)/Depository Trust Corporation (DTC).
Delivery Process and Date	Delivery will be carried out via the NSCC three-day delivery process.
	Three business days following the last trading day for the futures (T+3), holders of net short positions deliver

the underlying securities to holders of net long positions and payments of the settlement amounts are made. Generally, the underlying stock certificates are stored with the DTC in which book entries are used to move securities between accounts. The net financial obligations for settlement are made, via wire transfers with designated banks, in single payments from the NSCC to firms with net credit positions and to the NSCC from firms with net debit positions. These transactions are cleared through the NSCC before 13:00 EST on the settlement date.

Price Limits There are no daily price limits on Single Stock Futures. When the underlying shares cease to trade in the cash market, the Single Stock Futures based on the underlying will also cease trading in a manner coordinated with the applicable securities exchange.

Reportable Position Limits One thousand contracts, equivalent to 100,000 shares of the underlying common stock/ADR. NQLX may introduce different reportable position limits for futures positions held within one month of the last trading date.

ISLAND Electronic Communication Network

The ISLAND ECN is also providing an electronic marketplace for trading single security futures. The new venture, ISLAND Futures, is a progression from the traditional equity ECN that ISLAND began as.

The platform is an Electronic Communication Network (ECN). These platforms became very popular for equity trading during the 1990s, and continue to be a low-cost alternative to trade securities versus more traditional exchanges. The ISLAND ECN effectively provides a cyber-exchange, that is entirely electronic and provides a meeting place for buyers and sellers. It is a low-cost and effective manner in which trades can be placed, matched, and executed in a rapid fashion.

ISLAND received approval to trade single stock futures, and while they may be the first ECN to foray into the single stock futures market, other ECNs are certain to follow if the product is successful enough to warrant several competing listings for the contracts. These companies have the ability to pass along lower costs for trading security futures given their well-established electronic infrastructure. Many of the benefits of using an ECN for trading equities also apply to their use for trading security futures contracts.

Because ISLAND is able to match buyers and sellers without an extraordinary amount of effort, it often passes along savings to investors who place trades through their interface. If this trend continues, then ISLAND may be a very effective platform to utilize for the trading of single stock futures moving forward.

The American Stock Exchange

The American Stock Exchange (AMEX) also decided to offer trading of single security futures products. The AMEX is different than the other three exchanges however, because here single security futures are traded via open outcry, in contrast to the other three exchanges that are trading single stock futures.

The AMEX allows trading of security futures side by side with listed equity option trading that has taken place at the exchange for several years. By doing this, the exchange hopes to lower the costs associated with developing an entirely different exchange for the trading of the product. This should allow costs associated with trading security futures to remain low, while they are able to participate in a more traditional manner.

The AMEX is familiar with the successful trading of derivative products, as seen in their introduction of exchange traded funds (ETFs). By leveraging their experience with other derivative products, the AMEX may be able to be very successful with its listing of single security futures.

Market-makers on the AMEX floor are able to provide continuous, two-way quotes for single security futures, and in exchange they are provided participation rights similar to the structure at the OneChicago exchange, although the similarities end there between the two. Over time, it will be interesting to see security futures exchanges evolve, and the crowds choose the most effective exchange for these products.

Chapter 4

SPECULATING WITH SINGLE STOCK FUTURES

The Purchase

There are several steps involved in speculation with security futures, specifically: Identifying what timeframe you expect the underlying equity to move during, analyzing the scope of the move you expect in the underlying stock, and planning an entry and exit strategy with regard to the target investment. Additionally, it is important to determine what size position will be most beneficial to your market views, and how this translates into the standardized contract size for stock futures. If you are planning on a speculative purchase of single security futures, knowledge of these concepts is key to placing a successful trade in your target equity. (See Figure 4.1.)

Trading single stock futures to recognize price gains in an underlying equity is much like placing a trade for an individual stock, with the wrinkles of a futures contract. These include having a standardized transaction size (100 shares), a reduced margin requirement (20% minimum), and an expiration date for the contract. The nature of a security futures contract to expire is more similar to an equity option, however the comparison between these two instruments will be covered in a later chapter.

In order to calculate the profit or loss in a futures purchase that is bought and sold before the contract expires, an investor can utilize the same method of calculation used for equity investing, which is current price minus cost basis. However, when

1. Identify time duration for expected equity move.

2. Identify expected scope of equity move.

3. Plan exit strategy.

4. Plan entry strategy.

5. Determine trade size (number of contracts).

6. Execute strategy.

Figure 4.1   Trading checklist.

trading a security futures contract, the result must be multiplied times 100 shares per contract and then again by the number of contracts purchased. For example, if an investor buys two Walt Disney futures that expire in May, at a price of $42.10, and later sells two contracts at a price of $42.25, the resulting profit calculation is as follows:

Current Price or Sales Price = $42.25

Cost Basis = $42.10

The resulting gain, 0.15 cents, is multiplied times the standard contract size of 100 shares to ascertain the gain per contract of $15.00. Then, this result is multiplied times the number of contracts traded, two, to determine that the gain before commissions on this transaction is $30.00. Using this calculation method, an investor can determine what the projected gain or loss may be on a specific security futures transaction.

Suppose you expect a move in shares of ABC Financial Corp. to begin in the next few days. After your research and analysis, you expect these shares to rise by $4.00 per share, from the current price of $60.00. The "front month" contract for the ABC Financial Corp. futures is March, as the current date is January 30. Because you expect the move in this stock to occur over the next few days, you feel confident that the March contract will suit your trading needs, as the contract will not expire for some time after the move higher you are looking for has exhausted itself. Timing is extremely important in the use of single security futures, however several benefits exist over the use of equity options when time is a consideration.

With an equity option, typically an investor is purchasing an option that has a Delta of less than 1.00 (more of this is covered in Chapter 10). *Delta* is the measurement of how much a derivative moves in relation to a move in the underlying asset that it represents. Deltas range from 0.00 to 1.00, and they correspond to movement in the underlying asset according to their assigned Delta. For example, a Delta of 0.50 means that a derivative will fluctuate only half of the amount of its underlying asset, while a Delta of 0.00 indicates no correlation, while a Delta of 1.00 equals a mirrored move with the underlying instrument. Option prices with low Delta that have a higher cost typically are reflecting a "time premium" as part of their cost. This premium will decay as the time to expiration of the option grows nearer. A quick method of determining an options Delta (which only works with very liquid option markets) is to divide the amount of change in the option contract by the net change in the value of the stock's price. Suppose you own a call option that has increased in price by 0.25 cents on the day. The corresponding equity has increased by 0.60 cents, which would mean your quick Delta calculation is 0.416, or 0.42. This means that for every full point increase in your equity, you can expect your option contract to increase by 0.42 cents. This Delta calculation is only for on-the-fly calculations, but will serve as our example here. Because the Delta of your option contract is 0.42, it means that almost half of your option premium is time value that may decay. This is not the case with a single stock futures contract.

Single security futures have a theoretical Delta that is 1.00 or very close to 1.00, meaning that the movement should mirror, less an adjustment for interest expense and dividends, the underlying equity of the contract. This means that the time horizon, while important, is not as critical as when using equity options.

The next step is to identify what size position you believe is appropriate. Given that you would normally purchase 1000 shares of ABC Financial Corp. stock on the open market in this case, you decide that the appropriate action is to buy 10 contracts of ABC Financial Corp. stock futures. This is where the leverage component enters your trade. Because every single stock futures contract is composed of 100 shares of the underlying equity that it represents, the cumulative size of your position is determined by taking 100 shares multiplied times the number of contracts that you are planning to trade.

Moving forward, it is noted that the current price of ABC Financial Corp. futures are trading at $59.90, while the underlying shares of ABC are trading at $60.00. Why is the current price lower than the underlying shares (by 0.10 cents)? Because, in mid-March the ABC Financial Corp. will be paying a dividend of 0.15 cents and the additional 0.05 cents reflects the cost-of-carry, or in this case the interest cost of financing the purchase of 100 shares of ABC Financial Corp. stock between now and March expiration. These costs are passed along to the buyer of the contract by the seller, because the owner of a security futures contract has no rights to the dividends that are paid while they hold the contract. However, the long holder of the contract must front the cost of the interest expense to finance the shares of ABC that make up the contract.

Any dividends received during the period the contract is outstanding are subtracted from the current futures price, because the holder of the futures contract is not entitled to receive the dividends paid during this period. Any interest rate costs are added to the price of the futures contract, because the buyer of the futures contract is charged back the financing expense of the position they are carrying on margin.

Using our formula for the fair value of a single stock futures contract, we plug the details into our pricing model in Figure 4.2.

The model accurately confirms that the current price of ABC Financial Corp. futures should be $59.90, confirming the market price. Deciding that this is more than fair, you go ahead and place your transaction by contacting your broker or entering the trade yourself through an online system.

$$(\$60.00 + 0.05) - (0.15) = \$59.90$$

$$\text{Interest Expense} = +\,0.05$$

$$\text{Dividend Discount} = (0.15)$$

Figure 4.2   ABC futures fair value.

Even after the added cost of interest expense, your purchase costs you a total in required margin deposits of $11,980—this is your good-faith deposit for the purchase of this future agreement with the seller. The identical transaction to control the same number of shares in underlying ABC Financial Corp. stock would equal the full face value of the transaction, or $59,900. While this may be reduced by standard 50 percent Reg. T margin, you would still be required to post some $29,950 in margin compared with the $11,980 required with the use of the SSF contracts.

Remember, leverage is a two-way street. While the trading of SSFs for speculation may seem like a free lunch given the low margin requirements, an adverse move in the shares (i.e., a move sharply lower rather than the $4 .00 increase you were expecting) would create calls for more margin in your account. Meanwhile, the reduced cost of carrying the position will also influence your return on investment.

Using the same example, if your trade in ABC Financial Corp. was to pan out exactly as you expected it would, the actual return on capital is higher than if you had purchased the shares outright.

For example, your capital in use for the purchase of 1,000 ABC shares at $60.00 is $60,000. If the stock appreciates the $4.00 you expect in three days, your return on this trade is a gain of 6.7 percent. Applying standard Reg. T margin, you could improve the rate of return to 13.3 percent, basing the purchase on an outlay of $30,000. Meanwhile, a climb of $4 with your margin of $11,980 using SSFs translates to a gain of 33.4 percent. This is merely a function of the actual capital required to finance the purchase of the position. Because the margin amount you posted for the purchase of ABC stock futures can climb if the contract declines from your purchase price, the rate of return can also turn out to be much lower once the trade is exited.

Single stock futures trade in a bid and offer environment just like the equities that they represent, and your transactions can either be placed on a limit basis or using market orders, just as in trading equities. For example, if ABC Financial Corp. futures were trading $59.90 bid and $60.00 offered, you could place your bid to buy ten contracts at $59.95, your calculated fair value for the contract. On the other hand, if you expected a quick move higher in the shares and did not have the time to risk the market running away, you could "buy ten at market," or at $60.00 in this case. The futures market allows the same set of diverse order types as equity markets, as seen in Figure 4.3.

Deciding what type of order to place when trading single security futures depends on your individual trading style and approach. If there is swift two-way trading in a particular contract and you are not very price sensitive, you may choose to use market orders. On the other hand, if you are trading a large number of contracts in every order it may be worthwhile to place bids or offers where you believe the contract is fairly priced and see if your order is executed. It is always worthwhile to remember that for the most part, floor trading personnel such as market-makers and some locals are only trading single security futures for the purpose of capturing the bid-ask spread, the difference between the bid price and the sale price of a contract. It is likely that as soon as a market-maker receives a contract at his bid (and is

---

Market Order: An order to buy or sell at market indicates that you will pay the current offer or bid price for a trade.

Limit Order: This is an order to buy or sell at a specific price level that you indicate when placing your order. It cannot be executed above or below your limit price.

Stop Loss: This is a protective order to liquidate your position if the market reaches a specific level indicated. Once this level is reached, your stop loss becomes a market order to sell or buy.

OCO Order: This means *one cancels the other*. If you want to exit your trade for a profit at a higher level, or a stop loss at a lower level, you can use an OCO order instead of leaving two separate buy and sell tickets. This way, when one side of your OCO order is executed, the other side is automatically cancelled.

MOC Order: This means *market-on-close*, and indicates that you would like your order executed with the closing price range for the day.

MIT Order: A *market-if-touched* order means that your transaction will be done at market after a specific level is touched. It is used in place of a limit order to buy or sell.

Figure 4.3   Future market order types.

then long) they will immediately place the same contact for sale at the offer price (so they can become flat or neutral again) merely capturing the difference, however small, between these two prices. The repetitive nature of this action is what generates steady cash flow for the market-maker, and this income can be substantial as long as the volume of single security futures generates consistent business for their participation. For this reason, it may be frustrating in some cases to place bids and offers in the market, as your orders may take a back seat to the activities being conducted by the floor trading staff, who will most likely adjust their orders to the extent that they have first priority over yours (by raising or lowering their bid or offer, respectively). This may create a situation in which it makes more sense for you to utilize the market order system, particularly in contract markets in which the activity is brisk, and you will be assured of not paying a very large premium or discount from the last traded price.

Another use of single security futures is illustrated using the shares of Microsoft. In this example, an investor would like to speculate that Microsoft will be announcing terrific earnings due to a new operating system it has developed. Looking at the MSFT futures for December delivery, the investor sees that the contract is trading at $42.10 bid and the offer is $42.90, while the underlying MSFT shares are last traded at $42.50.

This is confusing, because it appears that whether the investor shorts the contract or decides to buy, they will be paying a discount or premium over the current market price. In effect, the market-makers are placing a straddle on the underlying MSFT share price, to protect themselves to an extent if the price of MSFT swings wildly after the earnings announcement, which it historically has proven to do. Is this allowed? Yes, because single security futures, while typically tracking the valuation model provided earlier for deriving fair value, can always trade according to market conditions or supply and demand. There is no rule that a stock future must trade in alignment with the underlying equity that it represents.

Understanding that the market-makers are nervous about the pending earnings announcement, the investor decides that the premium is not too high, so a purchase is made of 15 contracts of the MSFT stock futures for December delivery. The investor pays a price of $42.90, and is now long the contract. Figure 4.4 indicates the details of the transaction.

Investor buys 15 contracts of MSFT December futures.

Contract Price: $42.90

Aggregate Contract Value: $64,350 ($42.90 × 100 × 15)

Minimum Margin Requirement = $12,870 ($64,350 × 20%)

Figure 4.4   Transaction details.

The speculator that purchased MSFT futures in our example is a short-term trader, and his theory is that MSFT shares will see a quick jog higher following the earnings release and then they will be sold off by the traders like himself, most likely resulting in a decline in the shares for the day even though they announce fantastic earnings. The speculator believes that in any case the price of Microsoft at current levels would make a valued addition to his portfolio, in the event of a decline he will just let the contract expire and he will take delivery of the 1500 MSFT shares since he thinks $42.90 is a fair longer-term price. Therefore, with a contingency plan in place, he executes his short-term strategy by placing an offer in the market to sell his MSFT/Dec futures directly after he received confirmation that the purchase was completed at $42.90. A limit order is placed to sell 15 MSFT/Dec futures at a price of $44.10.

In deciding where to place his sell order, the investor used the quick formula in Figure 4.5 to decide what profits he believed justified the trade.

Long Position:

(Target Price – Entry Price) × (Number of Contracts) × 100

Short Position:

(Entry Price – Target Price) × (Number of Contracts) × 100

Figure 4.5   Quick formula.

Applying the calculation in Figure 4.5, the speculator figures that a profit of $1800 would be a great profit for the short duration of the trade, so he decides to proceed. The information in Figure 4.6 was put into the calculation above to derive the $1800 figure.

Soon after the trade is entered, shares of MSFT are temporarily halted for the earnings announcement. As the speculator expected, the company announces solid earnings and projections for future growth. The next morning he sees that the MSFT/Dec futures traded at $44.20, 0.10 cents above his limit order to sell. This means that he must have been filled on his order to sell 15 contracts at $44.10, and he has gained $1800 less commission costs on this transaction. Had the trade gone in the opposite direction, the investor was not worried, having plenty of available margin in his trading account for margin calls and looking to take delivery in such a case, believing any decline would be short-lived.

Single stock futures offer the speculator greater versatility and margin savings when compared to traditional equities. More advanced strategies like portfolio buy-writes, arbitrage, and matched pairs trading are covered in Chapter 7 and are applicable to use by experienced speculators who wish to exploit the full potential of single stock futures. Until the new product was introduced, more advanced strategies were difficult to implement by smaller capitalized individuals.

Trading single stock futures for speculative price movements can be more appealing to some investors than trading options based on the same equities. The calculations of Delta for equity options and the pricing of equity options based on volatility estimates can be confusing to many traders, both individual and professional alike. Given the freedom of market-makers in the option markets to assign personal volatility estimates to individual option series, the math can become quite murky when

$$(\$44.10 - \$42.90) \times 100 \times 15 \text{ Contracts} = \$1800$$

Figure 4.6 Quick formula applied.

you purchase an option and it later fails to reflect the full movement of its underlying stock. With single stock futures, this hazard is muted given that SSFs have a Delta of 1.00, meaning that they should move point for point with the underlying equities that they represent. However, this is not always the case. As with some stock options that have a Delta of 1.00 and fail to reflect underlying stock price movement at some stage, other factors such as supply and demand and future expectations may also affect the price of an SSF contract. Financial market workings can always be dissected to the most basic foundation on which they are founded, supply versus demand, and more importantly the forces that act on supply and demand to cause them to be in flux. A pending earnings report, insider information, or any other random factor may cause the lack of movement or likewise seemingly unexplainable movement in a SSF before the underlying equity has moved at all. The expectation is that the arbitrageurs will maintain the efficiency of the marketplace by exploiting these short-term differences and closing any gap that may exist between a single stock future and the underlying shares that the contract represents. This dynamic is discussed in more detail in Chapter 8.

Because single security futures are based on a contract size of 100 shares, an investor can benefit from purchasing these contracts versus the underlying equity particularly if they tend to trade in larger size. For example, and investor who is buying 10,000 shares of IBM may decide that it is easier to purchase 100 contracts of the IBM equity futures, because the transaction costs will be lower and the trade will be completed at one price. Often, even in more widely traded equities, an investor will find that larger orders to buy or sell a security are executed at several different prices depending on underlying market liquidity. As a result, single security futures may offer the flexibility to execute an order in its entirety at one price, and more quickly than utilizing conventional securities.

When executing a purchase of a security futures contract, it is critical to remember that losses in the position can exceed the amount of margin deposited in your account. Therefore, it is critical to have a solid entry *and exit* plan when entering into a security futures transaction. This way, you will be well prepared in the event that your transaction did not go as planned.

Takeover Speculation

Another speculative purchase application for single security futures can be to establish a speculative position during the acquisition or merger of a publicly listed company. For example, suppose a company called XZY Industries made an offer to purchase the shares of a close competitor, ARC Company. The shares immediately increase in value following this announcement to a price of $35.00, well below the $42.00 offer for the purchase by XZY Industries. This dynamic is seen often when companies have to vote, approve, or otherwise discuss a takeover option. The risk premium of $7.00 remains on the table, so the single security futures investor can now take action.

A purchase of ARC Company futures, at the current price of $35.00, would potentially allow another $7.00 increase once the takeover was approved. However, any breakdown in talks would lead to a rapid decline in shares of ARC Company and its corresponding single security futures. With this in mind, the true versatility of security futures is applied as investors buy ARC Company futures for $35.00, and simultaneously purchase the ARC Company $32.50 put contracts for downside insurance. In this manner, the investor has limited any risk associated with this speculative trade to $2.50 per share, for a possible payoff of $7.00 per share. Figure 4.7 illustrates the dynamics of hedging a speculative security futures purchase with a listed equity option.

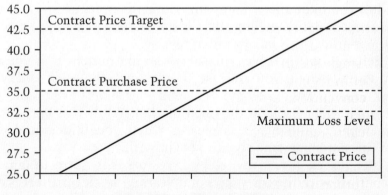

Figure 4.7 The hedged SSF.

The combination of listed equity options with security futures is a manner in which investors can unlock the true potential of these products. In the early stages of security futures development, many market commentators indicated that single stock futures were detrimental to the listed equity options markets. As it turns out, just the opposite is true. These instruments offer complimentary qualities, and when used in conjunction with one another, they can unlock new methods of creating wealth with reduced risk.

Another potential use of security futures in a takeover or merger situation is possible if both companies involved in the transaction have listed security futures contracts. This would allow an investor to establish a long position in the takeover candidate and a short position in the aggressor, therefore establishing a spread that may produce gains. Suppose that Microsoft was to buy IBM. If both of these companies had listed stock futures at that time, an investor could establish a short position in Microsoft, and a corresponding long position in shares of IBM, thereby capturing any upside movement in shares of IBM and corresponding decline in Microsoft. This type of spread is discussed in more detail in the following chapters, as are other similar strategies.

Selling Short with Single Stock Futures

The introduction of singe stock futures facilitates the process of selling short for those companies that have futures listed on their shares. While selling short is understood by a large sement of the market, let's have a quick review.

Selling short involves the sale of an instrument that you do not actually own, you are just "borrowing" the asset and will later return it after you have "covered your short" by purchasing the instrument back on the open market. While this may seem somewhat confusing, it is clearer when you understand the workings of borrowing stock to begin with.

Most stock that is owned by investors is in "Street Name." In contrast with the early days of investing, stock certificates are rarely now sent to investors who purchase equity in their accounts. This change occurred over many years, for reasons including cost control, the delay in receiving security certificates, and the safekeeping of security certificates. Additionally, any day-trading or short-term investing was ruled out in the days of stock certificates, given that an investor would have to await his original proof of purchase before selling the shares and delivering the certificates back to the broker.

Therefore, brokerage firms began holding equities that were purchased by investors, and a brokerage firm can now tell exactly what its overall exposure is based on the netting of buys and sales in any particular equity. The facility that made this possible is called the Depository Trust Company (DTC), which is the main clearing firm for equity transactions in the United States. By providing net statements on broker positions, the DTC is able to facilitate the borrowing of equity for short sales because they can instantly "see" what broker has excess holdings of a particular equity that can be loaned out to a short-seller.

When an investor decides to sell short a particular stock, a series of steps is set in motion before the sale can take place. If you wanted to sell JNR Food Company short, you will call your respective broker and request the trade. They will try to locate the stock for you to borrow for this sale. In most cases, this should not be a problem, but historically an attempt to borrow a stock for short sale has sometimes been very difficult. For example, during the dot-com meltdown, many traders and investors were disappointed to find that they could not locate stocks to borrow to sell short, as all of the available equity was either sold already or loaned, or a combination of these factors. This market condition also contributes to inflated market values for particular securities. In some cases, equities that can never be located for short sale or are in low supply for loans tend to be trading well beyond their projected market values. This situation results in overvalued price given that the speculative element that would otherwise keep prices closer to equilibrium are removed from the market, since stock cannot be borrowed for a short sale. In this manner, speculators are prevented from exerting their bearish influence on such equity issues.

Once your broker locates the stock for you to sell short, the sale can take place as soon as there is an uptick in the underlying equity that you wish to short. This is markedly different from single security futures, in which an uptick is not required for a short sale. Even in a rapidly declining security futures contract, an investor continues to have the right to sell short the contract, without waiting for an uptick in the underlying security.

After the sale is complete in a security, any decline in the stock you have sold below your sale price is to your benefit until the day you purchase back the stock to offset your initial selling transaction. Nonetheless, many investors do not realize that even if you are short a stock that was borrowed and it is declining in your favor, the stock that was borrowed for your short sale may be called at any time by the owner. In other words, you may be enjoying a profitable trade and then discover that you are forced to close the position out before you would like. Although this is somewhat rare, it can occur and is a further complication of short selling with the use of equities.

Even after the stock is located for an investor to sell short, in a rapidly declining or extremely volatile market in which trading curbs are in effect, an investor must wait for an uptick in the stock before his short sale can occur. Given that other short sale orders are waiting in cue ahead of the prospective investor, quite a lot of movement to the downside can occur before the actual sale is completed. Many investors have been faced with the disappointment of watching a rapid decline in a stock in which they have a pending short sale waiting for execution. This painful experience is the reality of being correct in your analysis, yet not enjoying the fruits of your labor. Single stock futures used in the place of underlying equities can facilitate a short sale by alleviating some if not all of the nuisances of using underlying stock.

Stock futures, by their nature of being a derivative and agreement for a future transaction, can be purchased or sold as an opening transaction. The principal that a buyer exists for every seller and vice versa in the futures market allows the ability to sell a futures contract as an opening transaction. If you believe that a particular stock's price will decline from current prices, you can sell a single stock futures contract to an individual who believes the opposite, that the stock will rise from current levels. This system also nullifies the need to borrow stock from an owner, as the contract can be sold as an opening transaction as a regular course of business. Additionally, there is nothing to borrow because you are entering into an agreement for a future transaction; you are not exchanging any physical property or equity as the case may be in short-selling an underlying stock.

The one issue that an investor who shorts a contract must remember is the delivery date of the contract that they sold short. As long as the position is closed or offset as of the last trading day in that particular contract before delivery, there is no obligation on behalf of the short-seller to deliver the stock that they sold via the futures contract. If the position is profitable and an investor wished to remain short the stock, it can be rolled forward to the next delivery date for the difference in price between the front (current) month and the next delivery date contract price. This will be covered in more detail in Chapter 6. Figure 4.8 illustrates the dynamics of a short sale using an SSF contract.

Identifying the equity you would like to sell, the scope of expected decline, and an exit strategy are all important when initiating a short sale transaction. Security futures are agreements for a future transaction, so the current ownership of an equity is not required for the ability to sell short the futures contract. The steps involved in borrowing a stock, as detailed earlier, are not necessary when an investor decides to sell short a stock futures contract. Because one is selling the agreement for a future trade, it is a reflection that they plan to sell the equity at the current price at a predetermined future date.

For example, a speculator believes that Internet stocks are trading at a price that is inflated to the fair market value for that equity, based on the application of price-to-earnings ratios and the overall outlook of the business model for free Internet companies. Using this approach, they identify a stock called Sham Technologies. In order to decide which delivery month to sell

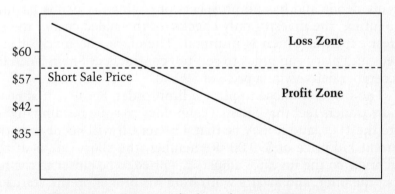

Figure 4.8   Dynamics of a short sale using an SSF contract.

short, the investor carefully considers the time frame that is projected for the expected decline in this company's share price. Deciding that it should occur in the next two months, and it is currently July, the investor believes that the most appropriate contract to short is the September delivery date, which will allow almost three full months for the decline to be realized.

Looking at the price for Sham Technology September delivery, the price indicates a bid of $90.00 and offer of $91.10. This is a wide spread, but given that the implied volatility of Sham Technology is 190 percent, the investor sees this as a fair market. While volatility should not affect the price of security futures, according to the fair market value model, deviations from this theory do occur. One is very clear in the case of Sham Technology, which has a volatility that is well beyond current market volatility. For this reason, the market-makers in Sham and likewise the equity specialist have been making a wider than usual spread, or bid-ask premium in these shares. The reasons for such activity are to allow protection to the market-makers, particularly in fast markets. With Sham Technology, the market is continually fast, so market-makers have compensated by widening the bid-ask spread to protect themselves from losing money on their activities. They have no interest in being long or short Sham Technology, and merely want to capture the difference between the bid and offer price. Furthermore, the fact that the contract is farther-dated (September is three months from the current date) also creates less liquidity in the price. However, the investor has little time to worry about rolling the contract, and feels that he would like to short the contract according to his time projection for the decline. Because Sham Technology pays no dividends and has no prospects of paying dividends far into the future, the investor only checks for the added cost of the interest expense, which is minimal. Therefore, the investor proceeds and places an order to sell ten contracts of Sham Tech for December delivery at a price of $90.50.

The investor chose to place a limit order, because it appears many traders feel that Sham Technology may be heading higher into the 100s, and it may be that a better fill will occur than the current bid price of $90.00. Remember, the short sale is at the bid price, so the investor adjusts his price to be closer to the bid than the offer, and awaits word from his broker on the status of the trade. Using limit orders in less liquid or rapidly moving markets, like the one in our example, is a good way to eliminate surprising fill levels on orders. Conversely, market orders may be more appropriate with more liquid, smaller spread contracts. Most professional investors will always choose to utilize limit orders in the futures market, as their entry and exit levels are an important part of the overall investment strategy. Figure 4.9 indicates the profit or loss potential of the short sale with Sham Technology.

While any appreciation in price in shares of Sham above $90.50 will incur losses to the investor, price declines below this level will generate capital gains. The target of the trade is $75.00, which is well below the current market value and may take several months to develop. The investor is betting that this will occur before the contract officially expires in September, since they have no interest in making delivery of the shares and merely wish to offset the position with a purchase to recognize the short term profits.

Utilizing single security futures for the purpose of speculating is beneficial for the ease of execution, the ability to sell a larger volume of shares without leaving a footprint, and the versatility that is gained from lower margin requirements for trading in these instruments. Of these benefits, one that is largely recognized by the institutional investment community is the ability to trade in single security futures without leaving a market footprint. This commonly refers to any disturbance that is

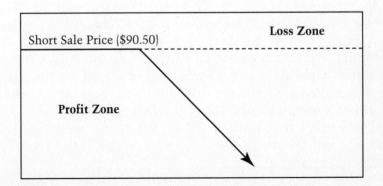

Figure 4.9   Profit or loss potential of the short sale with Sham Technology.

caused or any movement in the shares of an equity that is caused by the direct activities of a single investment or hedge fund.

For example, if XYZ fund believes that after thorough analysis the price of ZEBRA food company will rise, they may desire to establish a very large position in the underlying shares. The only problem that XYZ faces is that when they begin buying and equity in small pieces, word gets out that they are buying and given their success as of late that usually means many others join in on the purchase. As a result, shares that they are targeting a large position in generally move above what they call their bogey level, or level at which they want their average price for all transactions so that they have a decent entry point average. For this reason, XYZ may be interested in using single security futures, because they may be able to purchase a larger number of shares in a single transaction rather than breaking up their purchase order into many smaller pieces. This is possible because of the standardized contract size of security futures, 100 shares, that allows leverage in the number of shares that are controlled with a single transaction. Additionally, XYZ fund is in the business of generating short-term gains for their clients, and therefore, they do not care that they will not actually own the underlying shares and not recognize the dividends or voting rights. They are confident that their investors will be happy if they generate gains through the use of single security futures.

Going back to our example of a takeover earlier in the chapter, shorting security futures can also take place in conjunction with listed option transactions to maximize the potential of security futures.

In our previous example, XZY Industries was making an offer to buy out holders of shares in ARC Company. The shares moved up to $35.00, below the takeover price of $42.00. A speculator decided that because XZY Industries and ARC Company are in the same field and generally have a lock on the market consumers, the government will likely ban their takeover and it should be announced near term. For this reason, it makes sense to short the security futures of ARC Company, meanwhile purchasing a call option on ARC to cover the risk if the takeover is completed against all odds.

In this manner, the speculator will benefit from a decline in contract value in ARC, while also having the piece of mind that a move higher will be offset by the call option purchased for every security futures contract sold.

The use of listed equity options can be complimentary to using security futures when shorting a stock. The outright benefits of shorting single security futures over underlying equities are numerous, and should be considered when looking for short-term gains from the sale of a security.

Shorting Against the Box Explained

A very popular strategy that has been used by professional investors for some time and is now becoming used more among individual investors is the method called *shorting against the box*. This refers to the strategy of shorting an equity while maintaining a long core position in the same underlying equity.

While this may seem like a counterproductive method of investing, it can actually improve your investment results dramatically, and is particularly effective if you are a more active investor. Essentially, the theory behind shorting against the box is that, while you believe a particular equity in which you have a large stake will do well *over the long term*, in the near term you expect a decline due to various reasons that you have identified. What this means is that the best approach to investing in this equity is to maintain your long holding and sell short shares in a new transaction that will generate short-term cash flows if the decline you expect actually occurs. Of course, as with the risk of selling short in general, you will recognize a loss if the shares continue to rise instead of decline as you expect.

Utilizing single security futures for shorting against the box is a natural. Even if the underlying shares that you own are the physical common shares of an equity, the security futures can be used for the short portion of your investment plan. By shorting the futures, you can speculate on near term price declines while managing your overall long exposure in the physical equity of the underlying. Typically, an investor would short only a portion of the entire long position that is held in the underlying security. (See Figure 4.10.)

The best part of this strategy is the flexibility that it allows the investor in the event that the underlying shares do not decline. For example, in Figure 4.10, if the shares of Motorola

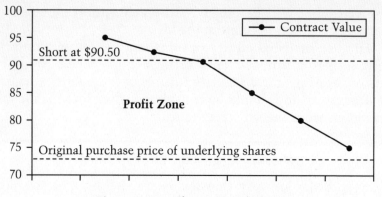

Figure 4.10   Short against the box.

stock (MOT) were to increase rather than decline in value, and you were short against the box 5 MOT contracts against your underlying 5000 shares (1/10th of your underlying holdings), and the price of MOT rose instead of declined, you could opt to hold your short contracts to delivery. In other words, even though you believed at the time shorting against the box was an appropriate strategy, you were incorrect, however there is no need to panic because you actually hold the underlying MOT shares in your equity account. Therefore, if you hold the contracts to delivery, you can just offset the trade against 500 of your underlying MOT shares and you will not recognize any loss. This assumes that your purchase price of the MOT shares was below the level where you shorted against the box. In this manner, you can decrease your risk of recognizing losses from the strategy, although you must understand that you will eliminate 500 of your 5000 share position if you manage your loss in this fashion. If your cost basis is substantially lower in the shares of MOT, you may not care that you were forced to sell 500 shares of your 5000 share position, given that the price you received was well in excess of your cost basis anyway. Further, you may believe that the issue of selling the 500 shares was a valid risk/reward judgment call.

This method of speculative short-selling with some security, since you already have a position in the underlying security, can be rewarding and an effective means of using single stock futures for shorter term gains.

Liquidity Considerations

The dynamics of most futures markets dictate that typically the most liquid months (i.e., the highest volume months) are the nearest term delivery dates. Depending on which futures contracts you are trading, liquidity will typically taper off as the delivery months become farther from the current date. This is due in part to the short term nature of the instrument, and the uncertainty that may apply to months far out in the future. Additionally, unless you are actively pursuing strategies that require trading farther-dated months, the activity will usually levitate toward what is called the "front month."

Liquidity cannot be estimated due to many factors, however great care was given to the selection of single security futures that would be chosen for trading by the respective exchanges. These considerations included but were not limited to liquidity, market capitalization, and name recognition. The ability to smoothly introduce new security futures will likely be based on the same criteria, as the product builds off of existing liquidity in securities that trade on major stock exchanges. As a rule, investors will likely find it easier to transact deals using single stock futures in the more liquid, front contract months.

Chapter 5

HEDGING WITH SINGLE STOCK FUTURES

Single stock futures can be used to offset risk associated with the underlying shares of a company's stock held in your portfolio. In fact, in highly volatile and fast-moving markets, single stock futures will likely be the instrument of choice for hedging risk to your assets.

For many years, savvy investors have relied on options to hedge their market risk for equities held in a portfolio. While this system has worked well, many facets of the process have disappointed and disinterested investors from protecting the equities that they own. This is evident in countless examples of individual investors losing substantial savings through their passive approach with 401K and other qualified retirement plans, that often have concentrated holdings of one or a few individual equities. With the use of proper hedging vehicles, such losses can be avoided. The fact that they are not readily understood in the options market lends to the potential popularity of single stock futures for this application.

When employing the use of single stock futures as a hedging device, you must understand that in theory the futures contracts pricing formula will hold and the stock futures should move in tandem with the underlying equity they represent minus adjustments for interest and dividends. Although this is the assumption, there may be cases in which the actuality deviates from this model. This should be the exception rather than the rule and prices should always return from any distorted valuation with the passing of time, allowing the convergence to occur again.

When utilizing single stock futures for hedging purposes, the steps involved are: Identifying what price protection you seek, determining what number of shares you will need to hedge and what number of security futures contracts this translates into, and the time frame that applies to your hedge. Figure 5.1 illustrates how a single stock futures contract price trades in tandem with the decline of the equity that it represents.

In Figure 5.1, the decay in price in both an underlying equity and the futures contract that represents its price should be in tandem minus any minor adjustments for dividends and interest.

Identification of the protection you are looking for is the first step in developing a plan to accurately and efficiently hedge your equity exposure. For example, if you own 50,000 shares of your company's stock in your retirement account, and the current price is $42.00 per share, how much downside risk are you looking to protect your shares from if you believe the shares are going to decline? What time frame do you want protection for? And what number of shares do you want to protect from decline? The answers to these questions must be addressed before a hedging strategy can be devised that will allow you the maximum benefit for protecting your interest and finances.

Generally speaking, many investors and holders of their own company's equity require strategies such as these for protecting their retirement savings. Many employees of companies believe that it is poor judgment to liquidate the holdings in their com-

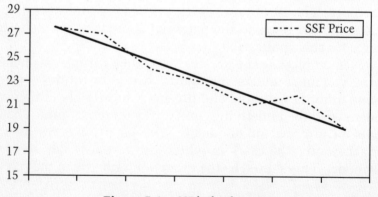

Figure 5.1   SSF hedge dynamic.

pany shares, as this reflects a lack of belief in the core mission of the corporation. While this is a generally flawed approach to begin with given that diversification is key to any sound investment strategy, the next best thing is a hedging strategy that will protect loyal company employees in the event that their shares face a short term or sustained decline from lofty levels.

Assume that the company employee would like to be protected from a decline in shares from the current price of $42.00. While the employee only paid $2.00 per share in the company's incentive plan, the gains created from the share appreciation are now considered profit, so a hedge that would mirror a sale of all 50,000 shares is what the employee is looking for. This will also prevent the position from being officially closed out, as the hedge will leave the underlying shares in place. The employee is looking to hedge exposure from the current date of December to February of next year. Therefore, the following steps are taken: The employee's broker is notified to sell 500 contracts of the company's stock futures. The employee is notified that the margin required for the sale of these contracts of 500 multiplied times the contract value, or $420,000. For this margin amount, the employee is 100 percent hedged if the equity declines below $42.00, dollar for dollar. Profits will accrue in the account holding the security futures, while the retirement account will reflect the loss of equity from any decline in shares. On the other hand, a continued increase in share value will be reflected in the retirement account and the account equity in the futures position will decline, potentially creating margin calls for the employee.

Once this strategy is executed, the employee will not recognize any gain in the shares above the hedge price of $42.00, however any decline below $42.00 will be matched dollar for dollar with the hedge against the retirement account. This type of hedging is best if it is for a short-term duration. Given the likelihood of margin calls for the futures side of the position, it may be difficult to maintain the position unless a great deal of margin collateral is placed with a broker to begin with. Therefore, the fact that the employee is holding a substantial amount of their company equity in an account will not lower the margin requirement, or serve to fulfill the margin requirement, in any way. This is due in part to the fact that the securities are held in a different account than the securities futures.

One major consideration in utilizing single security futures for the purpose of hedging equity owned in a qualified plan for tax purposes is that the hedge activity must take place in a different account, since single security futures are not considered allowable instruments for a qualified plan account. Therefore, even though the losses from share price decline are being accrued in one account, the profits from the hedge are being accrued in another account. This may also translate into different tax treatment for the gains that are created through the hedge in a traditional versus retirement account.

The following is another example of a typical hedge using single stock futures: An executive of a large manufacturing company owns 100,000 shares of stock acquired through his stock option program for employees. His benefits coordinator stated that he is able to sell any part of these shares, or all of them, if he thinks it is appropriate. Yet, he feels that this would be traitorous to the company spirit, and his wife agrees that even though they would love to sell the shares as they see the price, currently at $60.00 as high historically, they must hold the position because the company may frown on the sale.

Determined to protect himself, the employee decides to sell enough single stock futures so that his exposure is only half of what he owns in the company, or 50,000 shares. The next day he calls his discount broker and sells 500 contracts of his company's single stock futures contracts at $60.00. While the margin required for this position is $150,000 ($3,000,000 worth of stock times a 5 percent margin requirement), the executive does not need to worry about losing the margin in his account, as it is covered by the shares he owns outright in his account. Because the employee is hedging his stock that is owned outright and held in a regular brokerage account, the brokerage firm that he deals with applies only a 5% margin requirement for his short sale of the security futures (see Chapter 9 for more details). From that day forward, even though the company executive owns 100,000 shares of the underlying stock, he will only recognize capital gains and losses on 50,000 shares of his company's stock, as the other half or 50,000 shares has been hedged through the use of single stock futures. When the contract expires, he can always place the hedge on again using a forward roll or a new trade altogether in a farther dated contract. Meanwhile, the executive continues receiving dividends and voting rights on the common shares that he owns in his account. Although the movement of the shares has been hedged to some extent, the ownership continues to exist. In this case, a reduced margin requirement of only 5 percent was required because the securities and security futures are held in the same account.

Now suppose a few months later the executive sees that the price of his company shares has declined to $45.00. While the company has suffered short-term, he believes the price is ready to move higher again in the long-term. Therefore, the executive places an order to buy 500 contracts of his company's single stock futures, realizing a profit of $1500.00 per contract, or $750,000. However, this profit is offset by the identical loss he realized of $750,000 from the $15.00 decline in the price of 50,000 company common shares held in his account. He effectively protected himself from a $15.00 drop in half of the company stock, and saved $750,000 in losses. The hedge is illustrated in Figure 5.2.

While this example seems perfect, consider what would have happened if the executive had placed a hedge on at $60.00 and the stock soon thereafter climbed to $80.00. The value of half the stock held would still only be $60.00, and $20.00 in upside potential will have been lost!

This may or may not be an issue with the executive. Given that most hedgers only place such a transaction when they are comfortable with the profit they have already locked in, it will

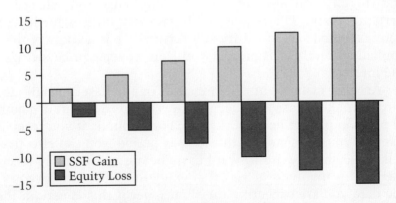

Figure 5.2 Hedging equity loss.

most likely not be an issue unless greed takes hold, which it often does. The key to using single stock futures for hedging is to remember that the decision to hedge should not be taken lightly; so that once the trade is placed it is not regretted. Investors that hedge, whether individual or professional, should not be concerned with the profit or loss in each individual leg of a hedge. Rather, the entire position should be viewed from the perspective of performing as a complete unit, offsetting risks that are associated with holding the underlying equity or asset.

Let's take another look at possible uses of an SSF for hedging underlying positions in an equity. Say that year-end is approaching, and you have a stock in your portfolio that has performed extremely well. Although you are a long-term investor, you believe that it may be prudent to lighten up your equity exposure before the New Year, yet the tax consequences of selling your stock will be extreme. The best solution in your mind would be to sell the entire amount of stock, yet the tax liability this would create is just too much for the current year.

Using single stock futures, you could effectively sell this stock without realizing any consequences of actually selling the shares, specifically the tax liability. By selling contracts of an SSF in the same stock, you can lock-in the price that you will receive for the shares at a future date, even if you decide not to hold the position to expiration. Once the New Year rolls around, you can purchase back the SSF contract in the equity, and then sell your shares. However, you will have been insulated from any decline in the shares between the date you sold the SSF contract and the day you unwind both the SSF hedge and sell the underlying stock. The use of single security futures for hedging your expected sale of equity at a future date is a strategy that if applied correctly will protect you from adverse price swings in the interim.

Another instance in which the sale or purchase of single stock futures makes sense is to hedge shares received as part of a bonus or pension plan at your workplace. For example, if you receive a fixed number of shares with each pay period, you can effectively sell these shares on a forward basis before you actually receive them. This involves the risk that you will still be employed as of the date you are expecting the shares, yet if this is certain then the sale of an underlying security futures contract in the shares of your company is an effective manner in which to lock-in a guaranteed price for your incentive shares. Remember however, you must actually deliver the shares as part of your obligation once they are received. By doing this, you ensure that the shares will be available and you will not be in default of delivery once the expiration date of the SSF contract arrives. Once again, the proper margin must also be on deposit with your broker before you can trade security futures, given that expected stock dividends would in no way be considered covering your margin obligations.

A more common use of single stock security futures for the individual investor is to hedge against adverse price movement preceding a corporate announcement such as earnings or other news. In today's marketplace, any publicly traded company that is announcing earnings is typically a candidate for high volatility, which may result in losses for the investor holding the underlying shares. Through the use of single stock futures, an investor can transfer risk to another party by hedging their exposure with security futures.

Hedging an outright position in a security is a relatively simple process. Since single stock futures are traded in a standardized contract size of 100 shares, the first step is to determine how much (if not all) of your stock exposure you would like to hedge. For example, if you would like to hedge against a price decline in shares of Qualcomm (QCOM) before its earnings announcement, and own 1000 underlying shares, a hedge in security futures would equal ten contracts.

Once the number of contracts has been determined, a sale level is determined and you proceed by placing an order to sell ten QCOM futures (at the current delivery month) at either a predetermined limit price or at market. Remember, by using a limit order you may not get your order filled, which will be problematic in the case of a hedge. Therefore, using a market order in this case may be the best manner in which to proceed. By selling the futures contracts, you now have effectively locked-in the current value of QCOM. Since your position is now completely hedged, you will not realize any price gain, however any declines will not effect your position either. You have effectively frozen your position with the added benefit of not having to sell your underlying QCOM shares, recognizing gains from your cost basis that is substantially lower.

After the earnings announcement, you can either exit your futures position by making a purchase of ten contracts, or you can choose to deliver your QCOM shares at expiration, for the price at which you sold the ten contracts before the announcement. Come delivery day, your shares will be swapped out of your account and the price at which you sold the futures contracts will be the amount you receive in your account for the shares. In the event that the announcement was bad news for the price of QCOM, and the shares declined, making delivery may be appropriate since you will effectively receive more than you can on the open market. However, this is an individual decision since longer-term equity investors, while keen to hedge against such downside moves, may wish to hold their shares indefinitely regardless of near term price fluctuations.

On the other hand, if the price of QCOM shares increases as a result of the announcement, the investor may cover the short futures contracts and realize a short-term loss from the transaction or may again make delivery instead. It is all a matter of preference and individual goals, but it is important to remember that flexibility exists for several different courses of action when using single stock futures.

Other Considerations

One of the main considerations in utilizing single security futures for any of the strategies covered in this text is the availability of contracts for the equity used in your strategy. It is difficult to replace the underlying shares of a company for which there is no securities future contract.

All of these ideas may sound great to you, but what if there is no security futures contract listed on the stock or company that you wish to transact business in? There are alternatives to this, such as trading in a listed contract that closely tracks the movement of your own company. For example, if you work at ZZ Semiconductor Company and wish to hedge your stock exposure, you may look at contracts of other companies, such as Texas Instruments or Intel. Perhaps you believe that the industry moves as a whole enough to outweigh any specific risk in trading another company's equity or security futures contract. This may pose problems if company-specific news breaks that then causes asymmetrical movement in the two prices of these shares. However, in general, the markets are moving more toward industry trends rather than individual movements.

Some strategies that involve sector analysis or speculative transactions can be used even if a listed security futures contract does not exist on your target equity. By conducting the appropriate analysis, an investor can locate equities that may have the same characteristics as those of the initially targeted equity, including the Beta, industry, and overall volatility. This may allow a substitution of sorts, in which the initial target equity for an outright purchase or short sale is replaced with an alternative equity that has a listed security futures contract. While this strategy may not be appropriate for some investors relying heavily on fundamental research or other specific factors of one company, it may be useful for more broad-based and diversified investment approaches.

Chapter 6

DELIVERY, OFFSET, AND ROLLING FORWARD

Delivery

When trading single stock futures, investors must be clear on whether they intend to take delivery or conversely offset the transaction into which they entered. Because futures contracts are an agreement to transact a specific deal at a time in the future, the only manner in which this agreement can be deemed null and void is if the investor transacts an opposite or offsetting trade. Conversely, an investor who is hedging or who actually intends to deliver or take delivery of underlying shares by way of his single stock futures activity can do so at the delivery date. Considerations that take place when planning delivery or offset include identifying markets that allow physically settled products. In other words, settlement occurs with actual common stock represented by the futures contract you are holding.

As an example, the LIFFE exchange offers only financial settle at this time, meaning that as of delivery date, a contract is settled by debiting or crediting your futures account by the gain or loss associated with the transaction. If you were to hold a LIFFE traded security futures contract to expiration and subsequent delivery, you would only be affected by cash flows rather than seeing the underlying shares delivered into or taken out of your trading account.

The U.S.-based exchanges, OneChicago, NQLX, ISLAND, and AMEX offer physically-settled single stock futures, meaning that they will expect you to take delivery of the stock you purchased futures contracts for or conversely make delivery of stock that you sold short out of your account by settlement day for the month of the contract you are trading. While financially settled contracts may be offered in the future, initial trading of security futures is centered around a physically settled product, in part to alleviate the concerns of non-fungibility.

With single stock futures, the last trading day of a contract in any given month is the third Friday of that month (those familiar with options expiry will recognize this is the same expiration schedule). An investor or hedger must decide what to do with their open contract exposure in advance of the expiration day of a security futures contract. As expiry nears in a contract, liquidity also begins to decrease, as traders focus their efforts on the next month. It is important to keep this in mind and take action well in advance of contract expiry, otherwise liquidity or a lack thereof may cause a financial impact when rolling or offsetting a position in your portfolio. My rule of thumb is to never have a position in a contract that is within ten business days of expiring. This ensures that I can roll forward or exit my position while there is still adequate liquidity in the marketplace. The timing may change depending on what security futures contract you are trading, but in general it is best to plan ahead.

As an investor, you are faced with three options as the expiry of a contract nears. You can: (1) either take delivery on a contract, meaning you will buy the underlying stock if you are long a futures contract, or sell the underlying stock if you are short a futures contract; (2) offset your position; or (3) roll it forward to a future delivery month.

With a delivery, it is important to remember that the purchase or sale will occur at the price determined when you first transacted the contract. Regardless of where the contract or underlying shares are at expiration date, you will be responsible for making delivery at the price agreed upon when you entered into your future agreement. This is the very nature of a futures contract.

In general, it makes sense to take delivery on a long position if you would like to convert your ownership to the underlying stock that is represented by your futures contract. If you believe that an equity has attractive long-term growth potential and you gained significant ground from the point you entered into the purchase and the current price, it may make sense to take delivery. However, you must pay the full contract amount for taking delivery of the shares. Now that the delivery date has arrived, you no longer are required to post a good faith deposit in the form of margin, but rather the entire contract amount is due based on the price at which you purchased the futures contract. This amount may be substantially higher than the margin posted to carry the position, and you must have these funds deposited in your account as of expiry or you will be in default on the transaction.

Conversely, if you were short a futures contract and wish to take delivery, you must deliver the shares into your account and they will be debited as of expiry and delivery. Your cost basis of these shares is the price at which you entered the futures contract agreement prior to expiry, which may be higher or lower than where the contract settles. In either case, you must have the shares available in your account by settlement day (delivery day) or you will be in default on your agreement. These shares must be paid for in full, as no margin can be used to finance the shares once they have left your account. In other words, even if you were to make delivery, you could not finance the shares with Reg. T margin in your account, as the shares would have to be in your cash account (fully paid for) before they are debited.

Offset

The opposite of delivery is offset. Offset occurs when your futures contract is essentially voided by an offsetting, or opposite transaction in the identical instrument. Most investors are familiar with the concept of offset because they often have equity trades offset in their accounts on a regular basis. The easiest way to think of offset is to picture selling a stock that you own, it's that simple. Even though a futures agreement is just that, an agreement and not ownership of anything, the principal is the same when it comes to offsetting a trade. The clearinghouse function makes this possible, which is covered in more detail later in this chapter.

Let's look at an example of offsetting a position.

An investor is long ten contracts of XYZ Corp. June stock futures at a price of $63.00. The current date is June 10th, and the last trade date for June futures is the third Friday of the month, June 21st. Therefore, you must offset your position before the close of business of June 21st. The morning of June 20th, you place an order with your broker to sell ten contracts of XYZ Corp. June stock futures at market. Once you have received confirmation that this order has been executed, you have no further obligation with regard to taking delivery of the stock after expiration. In other words, you have successfully offset your long position with the sale of ten contracts. Because you owned ten contracts outright, and then sold another ten contracts before expiry, your account will only be impacted by the change in market value from the purchase price to the sale price. Your previous obligations under the terms of the agreement are null and void because your offsetting trade cancelled them.

The opposite of offset is to actually take delivery of the underlying shares for which you owned a futures contract, as in the following example.

An investor is long ten contracts of XYZ Corp. June stock futures at a price of $63.00. The current date is June 20th, and the contract will expire later today. At the end of the day, the last trade price of XYZ Corp. stock is $67.00. Therefore, the official settlement price for XYZ June futures is listed at $67.00. You are informed by your broker that because you have decided to take delivery of the stock, you must have sufficient funds in your account to make good on receipt and payment of the stock you agreed to purchase earlier in the month. In other words, each contract of XYZ Corp. stock futures, as with other stock futures, represents 100 shares of the underlying stock. Because you owned ten contracts going into expiration, you are going to be taking delivery of 1000 shares of XYZ Corp. common shares. Therefore, you must have aggregate funds in your account for the purchase amount of $63,000. As you can see, the amount of funds you are required to have in the account is less than the current market value of your account, after the stock delivery, since XYZ Corp. common stock settled at a price of $67.00, giving the position a market value of $67,000. The $4000 differential reflects the profit the investor made from locking in the lower price when executing the futures trade earlier in the month.

However, this is an unrealized gain as the investor's reason for taking delivery in such a case would have been to establish a cost basis in XYZ of $63.00 per share for a long-term investment. If the strategy called for short-term gains, an offsetting transaction prior to delivery may have been more appropriate as it would have involved less cash outlay, and the results would have been identical.

In the delivery example, the net result of the transaction is that the position generated income of $4000, minus any fees associated with the delivery process. The same end result could have been achieved through an offsetting transaction, and the capital to make the delivery purchase of $63,000 would not have been required if the contract was offset. Instead, only the applicable margin that was required for the position would have been necessary to carry the trade until the offset occurred. However, if the investor's intent is to be a long term holder of XYZ Corp. stock, then taking delivery may make sense as they have locked-in an attractive purchase price and now wish to hold the actual common shares that entitle them to ownership in the company.

Another example may illustrate a situation in which taking physical delivery may be advantageous over offsetting a transaction.

An investor is long ten contracts of ABC Corp. June futures. Just before the last trading day of June 20th, ABC Corp. announces that it is the target of a hostile take-over bid by their competitor, XYZ Corp. While the price of the underlying shares rises to $75.00, the stock futures also rise an equivalent amount reflecting the movement in the underlying.

Because the investor believes that the takeover will occur in due course and they would like to preserve their long position in ABC Corp. without a dramatic change in market values, the investor opts to take physical delivery of the underlying ABC Corp. common stock. The investor has already locked-in a lower share price from the original futures contract transaction, and therefore is comfortable taking delivery in the hope for further gains.

In this example, the investor may even create greater gains on the position if, for example, XYZ states an agreed upon take-over price. Even though news has been disseminated that a takeover price has been reached, a small discount will remain in the market between the current market value of ABC shares and the takeover price, reflecting the risk premium that something could go wrong between the announcement date and the actual takeover date. Therefore, when the actual shares are paid for in the takeover process, the holder of ABC common will enjoy further benefits of having actually owned the common stock.

In some cases, it may make sense to take delivery if you are unable to exit a position at a favorable price in the market. While this should be a rare instance, many short-term market factors may create market conditions that create a situation in which it is more advantageous for you to offset your futures position by a trade in the underlying equity itself. Every contract represents 100 shares of the underlying, therefore a transaction involving 100 shares, a sale if you are long a futures contract or purchase if you are short a futures contract, would successfully offset your futures position. The consideration to this approach is that you would then have to hold the underlying shares purchased and the futures contract that were offsetting each other through to expiration. In lieu of holding them, you could also exit both positions at a later date, yet you then incur additional transactional fees. Taking a position in an underlying equity can be an effective way to offset a position in the equity futures if you are price sensitive or feel that it is a better alternative.

Rolling Forward

In most cases, speculators will look to either offset or to roll forward their long or short contracts in a single stock futures position. This involves the sale and purchase of a near month and farther out month of the same stock futures contract (in the case of a long position roll), or the purchase and then sale of a near month and farther out month of the same stock futures contract (in the case of a short position roll). Figure 6.1 illustrates the required steps to rolling a long position forward in a single stock futures contract.

When an investor wants to roll forward a long position, there are two transactions that will occur. First, the contracts that are currently owned must be sold, and then the farther dated month

1. Identify to what month you would like to roll forward.

2. Find the difference between the bid and offer of the months (if you are long) or the offer and bid (if you are short) to determine how much the roll will cost you.

3. Place an order to roll your position forward as either a spread transaction or transact each leg individually.

Figure 6.1   Rolling a long position forward in a SSF contract.

will be purchased. There is no limit to how far the roll forward can go, except as limited by the farthest month in the future that a contract is offered in that particular issue. Keep in mind that although dividends may lower the cost of the futures contract price in forward months, the interest expense will most likely off-set and in fact create a higher cost in forward months for some single stock futures. Additionally, there are no restrictions on the price of farther dated months being priced higher for stock futures, since the market-makers of the issue may believe that the growth potential of the underlying stock is sufficient to warrant a premium in the futures contract.

Now, let's have a look at a roll forward for a speculator who has a short position in single stock futures for XYZ Corp. (See Figure 6.2).

In this example, the investor has placed a limit on the roll wished to be transacted. By stating that the transaction is done at a limit of 0.05 cents debit, the most this transaction can cost is be $5.00. In other words, the price the investor is willing to pay or spread between the ask price of the September contract and the bid price of the December contract is 0.05 cents. The order may or may not get filled depending on market conditions, and the investor will most likely check the status of the order regularly until it is filled to make certain it is rolled forward before expiry.

The spread limit order used in Figure 6.2 is important when realizing that the roll of a futures contract is often referred to simply by the cost of the roll, and not considered as two separate orders by many traders and brokers. While retail institutions may always relay the order as two sides, and in fact a roll is

1. XYZ Corp. Sep. futures are trading 42.10–42.15.

2. XYZ Corp. Dec. futures are trading 42.10–42.20,

3. The investor places a spread order to roll forward a short position in the Sep. futures to Dec. This involves buying back the Sep. contract and selling the Dec. contract.

4. The limit order for this is placed at 0.05 cents debit, which will be executed since the "natural" is 0.05.

Figure 6.2   Short position in SSF for XYZ Corp.

always two trades, most experienced investors will refer to the roll as a debit or credit and then state the amount. In Figure 6.2, the roll would be described as buying the September to December roll for a net debit of 0.05 cents. As the market for single stock futures develops, the spread will likely be quoted for active roll months as a separate price under a special symbol. In other words, you would be able to pull up a quote for the *September-December XYZ Corp. futures roll*, priced at 0.00 bid and 0.05 offered. The roll is an important part of futures trading and is used in a wide variety of futures contracts, including single stock futures. If you are prone to holding speculative positions or wish to construct a medium- to long-term hedge for your portfolio, it is important to carefully review and understand the concepts of a forward roll for your position.

Generally speaking, you want to roll your position well before the official expiry date of your current contract holdings. This ensures maximum liquidity and prevents any timing issues if you are working limit orders for your roll forward. These transactions are relatively simple once you understand the basic concepts, and are useful for speculators who wish to hold positions, either long or short, over several different delivery periods.

The Clearinghouse

The clearinghouse plays a vital role in futures markets that is critical to the success of various contracts. This component of the markets can best be described as a middle-man, who makes certain all parties involved in a transaction meet their obligations, and also that every buyer is matched with a seller.

When your order to buy a single stock futures contract is transmitted to one of the electronic exchanges, it is matched with a corresponding sell order. These transactions are then considered a match by the clearinghouse, and you will be required to post your margin as will the seller of the contract on the other side of the trade.

If expiration day arrives, and you decide to sell your contract and thus alleviate any need for delivery, the clearinghouse again matches your sell with a buy order, and now your obligation with regard to the contract is null. This is because through the clearinghouse function, you are recognized as having no outstanding exposure. If it were not for the function of the clearinghouse, anyone who was long a futures contract would be required to deliver, and they would then receive delivery later from their sale of a contract. The clearinghouse matches the buy and sell, and therefore alleviates the need for extraneous deliveries. They can see the offset that has occurred between the purchase and sale, and therefore will not have deliveries occur between the two transactions.

Suppose in the same situation that you were to hold the contract and not sell as of expiry date. The clearinghouse would recognize that you had an *open* long contract as of expiration, and it would then expect you to receive shares and make delivery of the necessary funds into your brokerage account to cover the purchase of these shares. The clearinghouse is the entity that matches not only the buyers and sellers, but also the remaining contracts after expiry that will be required to make delivery by carefully tracking how many investors have open positions as of the expiration date of a particular contract. The Securities and Exchange Commission (SEC) approved a rule in June, 2001, that allowed the Options Clearing Corporation to clear security futures contracts for any national securities exchange, securities association, or contract market.

The Options Clearing Corporation (OCC) was founded in 1973 and is the largest clearing organization in the world for derivative products. The OCC is jointly owned by the American Stock Exchange (AMEX), the Chicago Board Options Exchange (CBOE), the Pacific Exchange (PSE), and the International Securities Exchange (ISE). Additionally, the OCC Board of Directors is comprised mostly of individuals who represent the individual clearing members that make up the OCC, numbered at approximately 135 different companies. Every year since 1993, the OCC has been rated "AAA" credit by Standard and Poor's. This is due in part to their exceptional risk management policies and procedures that ensure the credibility of the instruments that they clear.

Although the name may suggest that the OCC is solely a clearing organization for listed options, they now have assumed the lead role of being the central clearing organization for U.S.-traded single security futures. This migration is a natural progression for the organization, as it has become the predominant clearing group for derivatives and its name in the financial industry is synonymous with credibility and reliability. The OCC will support securities futures traded on any exchange or security futures market, including both fungible and non-fungible contracts. They also will support both cash and physically settled products, and will net the cash flows that occur between activity in options and futures that are based on the same equity. Additionally, one of the key roles that the OCC fills is to update or adjust positions in options and security futures to reflect corporate actions such as stock splits or stock dividends.

Chapter 7

TRADING STRATEGIES USING SINGLE STOCK FUTURES

Single security futures can be used for a wide range of strategies, for the more basic outright purchase or short sale, hedging, or advanced strategies like those covered in this chapter. The following material is intended to give an overview of various strategies, and I encourage additional research before using any of the systems mentioned.

The buy-write portfolio is a method of investing that involves purchasing an underlying equity, and selling call option premium against the position with the goal of achieving above-average gains from the sale of the option premium. Further, the sale of the option premium provides a cushion of sorts for downside swings in the target equity that normally would not be available with the outright purchase of an equity with no sale of an option. The main downside of this strategy is that you limit your upside potential to the strike price at which you sell the call option. This may prove to be only a small disadvantage when you examine the potential returns that this strategy can generate based on the use of SSFs in place of underlying equities.

When looking at companies to target for inclusion in a buy-write portfolio, it is important to take several factors into consideration, including the equity volatility, option availability, and other risks and benefits of each particular company's stock. Once you have identified the stock that you wish to include in the strategy, you purchase an equivalent number of shares using the company's SSF, and then sell the call option that you previously identified as most appropriate given your individual strategy.

Some investors choose at-the-money calls and others out-of-the money; this is simply a factor of your personal preference and analysis. What works best for one investor may not work at all for another. This is also true with regard to the time to expiration of the option you sell against the SSF, although the normal time horizon is a sale that is between 30 and 90 days before the expiry of the call option you are selling.

When selecting a portfolio of security futures for using this strategy, keep in mind that the main objective of the approach is to identify equities that will trade in either a sideways or higher pattern, which will maximize the returns generated by the use of this strategy. The only case in which the buy-write will generate losses or disappointing overall results is in a sharply declining market (unless selling short SSFs and selling covered put options). Even then however, you will have the cushion provided by the option premium that you sold and that decays in a declining market. Figure 7.1 illustrates the behavior of the buy-write portfolio.

In executing a buy-write portfolio that will deliver gains to the investor, the aim is to establish a portfolio that will require minimal adjustments between the date the portfolio is established and the expiration date of the option premium sold. Let's look at a detailed example of establishing a buy-write on a specific security futures contract.

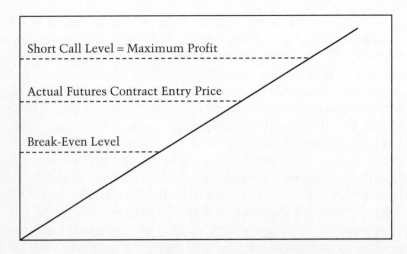

Short Call Level = Maximum Profit

Actual Futures Contract Entry Price

Break-Even Level

Figure 7.1   Behavior of the buy-write portfolio.

An investor wishes to establish a buy-write portfolio, and begins by identifying the first security future for inclusion in the strategy, which is FAST Semiconductor. The security futures for FAST are trading at $32.10, and the investor decides to purchase the contract at the current price, and then sell an equivalent number of call options against the position. For this, the investor has identified that the best option to sell is the May 35 call. It is currently mid-April, and the investor feels that the trend in FAST will be sideways to higher over the course of the next few months.

Using this information, the investor implements the strategy by purchasing ten contracts of FAST Semi futures for June delivery, at a price of $32.10. Additionally, the investor sells a total of ten FAST Semi $35.00 strike price call options for a price of $2.25. The details and cash flow of these transactions are illustrated in Figure 7.2.

The investor now has option premium incoming of $2250, and a margin requirement of $6420 for the security futures position. The position has been established, and the graph in Figure 7.3 indicates the profit and loss scenarios for the position.

As you can see in Figure 7.3, the investor will produce the maximum return if at the expiration of the call option in May,

---

1. Purchase ten contracts of June FAST Semi futures for $32.10:

   ($32.10 × 100) × 10 contracts = value of $32,100.

2. Margin requirement for stock futures is 20 percent of contract value:

   $32,100 × 20% = $6420 margin

3. Sell ten FAST Semi calls at $2.25

4. Incoming options premium of $2250 is applied toward margin.

5. Net margin requirement is $4170.

Figure 7.2   FAST semi futures.

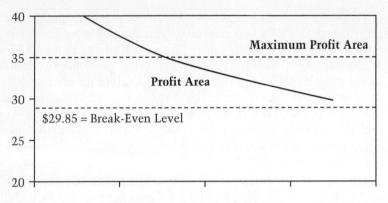

Figure 7.3   Buy-write dynamics.

FAST Semi security futures are at the call option level of $35.00 or above. The second best scenario is realized if the security futures trade sideways near or at the $32.10 level at which they were purchased, as the investor will capture the sold option premium and not lose any money on the security futures position. The break-even scenario is realized if FAST Semi futures for June delivery reach a price of $29.85. Note that in this case, the investor has been protected from $2.25 in decline in shares of FAST, which would not have been the case if the purchase was made outright. By selling the call option premium against their long security futures position, the investor was able to lower his or her cost basis and will have downside protection that is equivalent to the option premium received for the sale of the call options. The worst scenario would be if the shares of FAST declined below the break-even point of $29.85 and continued lower, in which case the investor will be losing money, even though he or she will likely capture the entire amount of option premium sold via the calls.

When using a buy-write strategy the dynamics of both options and futures must be understood completely. For example, the measurement of Delta (covered in earlier chapters) is the movement of an option relative to the underlying asset. We assume that single stock futures have a Delta of 1.00, meaning that they will move in theory point for point with the underlying asset that they represent. This assists us in deciding how to

Long ten contracts of FAST Semi with a Delta of 1.00 equals + 1000 (remember 100 shares per contract).

Short ten contracts of the FAST Semi $35.00 calls each with a Delta of 0.34 equals –340.

Cumulative Delta exposure is therefore + 660 (+1000 and –340).

Figure 7.4   Delta measurement for applying the buy-write strategy.

approach the sale of optionality against single security futures given that we have one side of the equation that will be fixed at 1.00. Using the same transaction from Figure 7.3, Figure 7.4 illustrates the use of Delta measurement for applying the buy-write strategy.

Using the facts listed in Figure 7.4, the investor is long 1000 Delta and short 340 Delta, for a total Delta position or cumulative Delta position of +660. In order to be flat, or Delta neutral, the investor could sell another 20 call options to offset his or her long Delta in the position.

Why sell only ten options to create a long Delta of +660? If your view is that the markets will rise, it makes perfect sense to only create negative Delta of 340. This is because as the market rises and underlying shares of FAST Semi rise along with the market, the Delta will also increase. Remember, Delta is a changing number for options that will reflect all movement in the shares, whether it be higher or lower. Therefore, if shares in FAST rise to the $35.00 strike price, then the short Delta from the sale of the call options will become closer to –1000, which will offset the long 1000 Delta that is created from owning the underlying security futures contracts (although in fact the price of FAST would have to increase substantially, as at $35.00 the Delta would only be about 0.50). For the trade in Figure 7.4, the following potential returns would be realized as of the option expiration in May, not inclusive of trading fees and not factoring in margin calls for the single security futures position. The return in based on the margin required for the position as of the original purchase price:

FAST Semi Futures Price	P/L	Return (%)
$35.00	$5150	+80.2
$32.10	$2250	+35.1
$29.85	$ 0	0.00

Many professional investors and funds, myself included, use a weighted sale of option premium to exploit the Delta position of an option. In other words, if the investor analyzed FAST and recognized that a move above $36.00 would be unlikely in two months, he or she could oversell the long position. This means that the investor would establish a long 10 contracts in FAST Semi futures, and then sell 20 call options against his or her position at a price of $2.25. This would create a cumulative Delta position of 320, which is the long 1000 (futures contracts) minus the short 20 calls (−680) for a cumulative long Delta of 320.

When using an oversell approach, the investor is typically more active in the financial markets and is not a passive participant, as using this approach may require purchasing additional futures contracts or buying back short call options to offset adverse movement in the underlying equity. This being said, it is more likely that a passive investor would have success using a 1-for-1 ratio of futures contracts purchased to call options sold. The returns generated from this activity can be quite substantial and offer an alternative method of approaching more volatile markets, which inherently tend to produce higher call option premiums. Furthermore, volatile market investors would be happy to receive the increased cushion associated with the call premium that they receive as a result of option sales. The key to successfully implementing the buy-write strategy using single security futures is to develop a plan and maintain your plan after execution. The downfall of the strategy is usually a trader or investor who will establish a buy-write only to tinker with the short option (i.e., buying it back to book a profit and selling another series) or will trade in and out of the security futures position. These tactics are the sign of an impatient investor who will lose money using this strategy. The single best method for generating returns with the buy-write approach is to identify your game plan, implement the strategy, and then wait for the option to expire. Of course, emergency actions may be required if the market unexpectedly declines or if you are in a compromising situation that will bring about losses in your portfolio. However, all things being equal, the positions should be maintained as when first established if there is no appropriate reason to trade. In other words, entering and exiting either leg of the strategy for the purpose of booking short-term gains is inappropriate, as it effects the core basis of the strategy that you have already implemented.

The buy-write strategy can also be used from the short side of the market. For example, if you are interested in shorting single security futures contracts on a specific equity, you can also then sell put options against your position in the short security futures contract. This allows increased return and also protection in the event that the market moves higher against your position. The premium you receive for writing the put option can also be applied toward the margin requirement for the single security futures contract.

The leverage component of single stock futures will definitely create an interesting atmosphere for the use of a buy-write strategy. Given that the option premiums written against a particular futures position can be used for margin to meet the futures requirement, the returns using a buy-write strategy with security futures versus underlying equities can be outsized. While losses may occur if the strategy is not implemented correctly, the management of Delta in this strategy combined with the margin rules provide strong incentive for the use of security futures in place of underlying equities.

Single Security Futures "Pairs Trade"

The introduction of single stock futures allows for the use of a popular strategy among hedge fund managers by all segments of investors, known as the "Pairs Trade." This involves taking positions in two or more individual securities within the same sector, however with a short and long position in the different instruments.

Pairs trading has long been a method of investing that limits systemic risk, or market risk. By establishing a pairs relationship, the investor is implementing the strategy but also enjoying the benefits of reduced correlation to the major market indices. This is an inherent benefit of the strategy, because market dynamics tend to suggest that individual issues within a particular sector will outperform or underperform in that sector. Therefore, proper identification of the issues that will be the overperformers versus those that will not do as well is beneficial to the implementation of the strategy. Other advanced strategies such as mean reversion can be applied using this basic strategy.

As an example of a pairs trade, suppose that you have identified in the semiconductor sector of the market that in your analysis the shares of Intel are attractive given that the company has reported solid earnings and institutional investors are continuing to accumulate the shares. Conversely, the shares of Texas Instruments are looking toppish, and the technical outlook in your view is rather poor. In fact, you expect a fast decline in these shares over the next few months. Therefore, you decide to establish a pairs trade, and you place an order to buy ten contracts of Intel security futures at the market price of $26.00, and sell ten contracts of Texas Instruments security futures at the market price of $34.00. Figure 7.5 indicates what action you take and your resulting position in this scenario.

Now that you have established your pairs trade, you will benefit from a decline in shares of Texas Instruments and a rise in shares of Intel. In effect, this trade is similar to a spread transac-

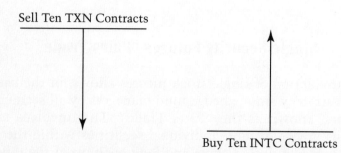

Figure 7.5   Pairs trade.

tion, however the difference is that in a spread you establish a position in different delivery months in the same security future, while with a pairs trade you trade contracts in the same delivery month with different security contracts. The benefits of this strategy include the fact that the even if your overall view is correct but the overall market declines bringing both INTC and TXN lower with it, your risk is substantially lowered thanks to the fact that you have both a long and a short position established. The largest risk to this position is that if your projections are completely incorrect in regard to the valuation of the individual contracts. For example, if INTC declines and TXN rises, your losses will be at their maximum.

Using the same example, an investor can apply the theory of reversion to the same trade. Perhaps what brought your attention to the trade was the fact that shares of INTC were down 30 percent relative to the Semiconductor Index (which was flat) over a period of the prior two months. Conversely, the shares of Texas Instruments were higher by 35 percent during this same period. As a result, you conclude that over the next few months from now, these prices should, all things being equal with the two companies, revert back to an equilibrium of sorts. In other words, shares of Texas Instruments will likely fall back toward a level of flat performance, while shares of INTC will likely rise toward the flat level of performance. If you apply this strategy, you are doing so because you believe that speculators will be shorting the shares of TXN as they overperformed, and value seekers will purchase shares of INTC as they seem to be a relative bargain in the semiconductor space. Although this example utilizes gross extremes, the premise remains the same using more detailed calculations. The important thing to remember when applying a reversion strategy is that many considerations must be made pertaining to the benchmark index, the time period being considered, the issues that are being traded relative to the index, and other factors.

Using a pairs trading strategy can benefit investors while allowing the benefits of decreased systemic risk when compared with more traditional outright purchases or sales of these contracts. However, this in most cases will also limit the potential return associated with such a strategy, particularly if the gains are realized as a result of a trending market.

The Spread Trade

Another application for trading single security futures is to use a spread trading technique. Spread trading involved the purchase or sale of multiple security futures in the same issue spread over different delivery months. This technique is popular among experienced futures traders as it allows an investor to take advantage of specific issues relating to a particular security over a predetermined time horizon. Typically, spread transactions will also require less margin than a traditional position limited to one delivery month date, since an offsetting position is held in a farther dated delivery month of the same security futures contract.

For example, suppose an investor has determined that the shares of Intel are heading lower due to a bearish technical pattern seen on the chart for this security. However, the company is in talks to be acquired by a larger company later in the year. Based on these facts, the investor decides that an appropriate position given the current date of March 12th is to sell the INTC security futures for May delivery, and buy the INTC security futures for September delivery. The trade is based on the fact that the investor feels the price of INTC will be pressured near term, yet the prospects for the company improve substantially in later dated months. Therefore, the purchase of the September delivery contract is warranted. Furthermore, the purchase of the September contract will ensure that if the company is purchased earlier than expected by their competition, then the investor will not lose an extraordinary amount of money on the speculative short for May delivery. In this example of a spread transaction, the investor is short contracts in the front month and long contracts in the back month of the spread. Within the details of this transaction, the investor is also able to adjust the number of contracts traded in each month; there is no rule that the number of contracts be equal in each month of spread. The risk of the position while both sides of the spread are still held is limited to the differential between the price at which the investor is short and the price at which they are long.

The investor's goal in this example transaction is to benefit from a widening of the spread that has been established. For example, the INTC contracts that were shorted we sold at a price of $22.10. Meanwhile, the purchase of the farther dated month of the contract was done at a price of $23.00 per contract. Therefore, the investor is paying a total of 0.90 cents for the total spread, multiplied times the contract size of 100 shares, so the total value of each spread if $90.00. The margin requirement for this position should equal the spread amount times the 20 percent margin requirement, or $18.00. The reduced margin requirement is a result of there being limited risk with regard to the position that has been established, since the investor is both short and long the same contract, albeit in different trading months. As long as each side of the spread is open (i.e., profit is not taken on one side and the contract closed) then the margin will remain at the initial level. Because the investor has paid 0.90 cents for the spread, he or she is looking for this to widen over the course of the next month or so.

What will cause a spread to widen? Anything can influence the price of the farther dated month. For example, interest rates could rise, causing the price of the September future to rise and the spread to widen. Shares of INTC may rise based on an announcement that the September earnings release will be bullish for the underlying shares. Any number of things can happen to create a widening of the spread between the May and September contracts of INTC security futures. Because of the reduced margin for establishing this trade, the investor feels confident enough to purchase 100 spreads for a cost of 0.90 cents, which equates to a position value of $9000. For this trade, the investor must place a margin deposit in his account for 20 percent of the spread value, or $1800. The profit and loss calculation made for this position on a daily marked to market basis will take the settlement value of the INTC futures for May delivery and measure them against the INTC futures for September delivery. If the spread shrinks, or declines below 0.90 cents per contract, the investor will lose money and will be required to produce further margin. However, the loss on the position is limited to 0.90 cents in total, as this is the amount that the investor paid for the spread in his or her opening transaction. If the spread widens after the purchase, the investor will recognize gains from the position for any movement above the initial 0.90 cent purchase price. Of course, as with any trading strategy that is considered, one must keep in mind that transaction costs will always effect the resulting return on a position.

Risk may be limited in spread transactions but it is not altogether gone from the equation. For example, when placing a spread transaction in farther dated contract months, lack of liquidity may become an issue. If a contract in which you establish a spread is thinly traded, then situations may arise whereby the marked to market or last reported trade price does not accurately reflect the underlying market for the security future. This will result in a request for hefty margin requirements that an investor feels are not justified given the illiquidity of the contract being to blame for the mispricing. Additionally, for liquidity reasons and others it is always advisable to use limit orders when trading spreads, so that the level you determine to be fair is where your trade can be executed and not the level which a market-maker deems appropriate.

Another consideration is that spread transactions are limited in any financial reward that they will produce relative to an outright position in a security futures contract. Although it is possible that a single stock futures spread will produce outsized gains, this is the exception rather than the rule. For example, a spread that is purchased for 0.90 cents may be fortunate to rise to $1.00, a 0.10 cent gain, if market conditions are in the favor of the spread. This may or may not be a sufficient gain to offset transaction costs that are associated with establishing the spread in the first place. Typically, although not always, spread transactions are of significant size that can either alleviate the cost of establishing the spread or cause more damage if the transaction proves to be a losing venture.

Spreads can be established for various trading objectives, including takeover or merger speculation, interest rate forecasting, or earnings speculation among other things. A perfect example of using a spread transaction for the sake of interest rate forecasting and also potentially hedging your portfolio of financial sector equities follows:

> As an investor, you own a wide variety of equities, but have a particular concentration in financial sector issues, such as banks and savings and loan stocks. This has recently become a concern, because you expect that interest rates will be rising over the course of the next three months, and you expect aggressive tightening toward the end of the year. To capitalize on the expected movement, you sell the farther dated month security futures contracts for the stocks held in your portfolio. By doing this, you have established a spread that is half formed by the equity in your portfolio and the other half

is formed by your sale of the security futures contracts. Some may argue this is a hedge, but your approach is to establish a spread because you expect near term appreciation in these equities, but selling in the outer months because as interest rates increase, financial stocks typically have fallen, their profit margins decreasing.

The number of opportunities for spread transactions are limitless, and the combined use of security futures contract in conjunction with listed equity options allows the investor to fully exploit these opportunities.

Chapter 8

ARBITRAGE PRINCIPALS

The Single Stock Futures Arbitrage

The evolution of single stock futures has allowed the development of another area of trading, which is single stock futures related arbitrage. Quite simply, these are trading desks that will attempt to profit from inefficiencies between the prices of underlying stocks and their corresponding futures contracts.

For example, a rumor of bankruptcy of a major energy trading company hits the trading desk at a major firm and it begins to aggressively sell single stock futures of Smith Energy Trading, the firm in question. For a second, the single stock futures contract drops below the price of the underlying shares of Smith Energy trading at the NYSE. A diligent arbitrage desk trader quickly purchases 100 contracts of Smith Energy stock futures, and simultaneously sells 10,000 shares of Smith Energy stock at the NYSE. The perceived benefit of this transaction is that the speculative arbitrage desk has just locked-in a profit at expiration (of the futures contract). Their profit is the difference between the price of the futures contract purchased, and the underlying shares sold, times the aggregate number of shares in the transaction, less any interest and dividend expenses. For simplicity the interest and dividend calculation is omitted from the following example.

Sold 10,000 shares of Smith Energy at $32.15.
Purchased 100 contracts of Smith Energy stock futures at $31.90.

The contract expires in 20 days, and at expiration, the expected gain is:

Sale proceeds equal $321,500 and the purchase cost was $319,000.

Therefore, the arbitrageur will expect a gross gain of $2500.

A group of traders focusing such strategies can make a decent living. On the other hand, the strategy does involve risks. Suppose that the trader had purchased the stock futures of Smith Energy first, and then was unable to sell the stock at the NYSE since the shares had been halted? The stock may then be reopened below where the trader purchased the equity futures, creating a loss on the position. Nonetheless, this type of arbitrage is considered risk-free arbitrage, because once the position is established, the risk until expiration is perceived to be nonexistent. The trader in the example using Smith Energy shares would let the single stock futures contract expire, and he or she would be able to offset this with the shares he or she had sold on the open market at the NYSE. The net result of the transaction is a wash with regard to the position risk and a profit on the transaction. The risk that does exist is considered to be execution risk, which is abundant when one side of the transaction has been placed and the other side is being transacted. This is why some arbitrageurs will work in teams or will attempt to transact both sides of an arb at once.

Another type of arbitrage occurs between option trading desks and single stock futures. When an option trader finds an option series that he or she believes is overpriced or underpriced, he or she can establish a position in that option and take an opposite position in the single stock futures contract, hoping to lock-in a risk-free profit at expiration. However, the greatest and most apparent use of single stock futures will be by floor traders who sell options to the investing public.

For some time, market-makers of exchange traded options have shied away from making large price quotes for execution in the last few minutes of trading during the day. For example, suppose an earnings report is coming out on FAST Semiconductor Company, and you want to hedge the 1,000,000 shares you own by purchasing 10,000 puts out of the money for 0.25 cents each. If you placed this order near the end of the trading day, it most likely would not be done given the historical implied volatility in FAST shares is somewhere around 225 percent. The market-makers will not want to sell you that many options, without being able to hedge their sale by actually transacting an adequate amount of stock to adjust their Delta exposure. On the other hand, if they were to sell you these options and the price of FAST increased the next day on positive earnings news, you would lose the $250,000 in protective option premium that you paid. The market-maker would have profited by that amount in just a matter of hours.

When an option sale occurs, the market-maker will adjust the Delta exposure created by a purchase or sale of underlying shares of the same company. And, if the option sale is large, this can take time, particularly if the shares of the underlying company are thinly traded. As in our example, if shares of FAST were trading at $15.20 bid and $15.25 ask, and there were only 1000 shares bid and 3000 shares offered (10 × 30), the market-maker would have to work all day to hedge the option sale (particularly to accomplish this without leaving a footprint in the marketplace, that is not moving the stock). This information suggests that the trade could not be handled under such circumstances, not until the introduction of single stock futures at least.

Using the stock futures that trade on FAST, the market-maker could hedge the option sale by purchasing 1000 contracts of FAST stock futures. The trader only wants to hedge the Delta position by purchasing 100,000 shares, so this can be accomplished with a 1000 contract purchase. In this manner, everyone wins, the investor's stock is now hedged before the earnings release, the option market-maker is comfortable with the market exposure and hedge, and the single stock futures market-maker is happy to sell the contracts as he purchased them at a lower price. The entire market place can effectively be considered more fluid and efficient with the introduction of single stock futures, given the circular nature of transactions that occur between market-makers and traders in many different financial instruments.

The market for single security futures counts on the arbitrageurs to maintain the market using the fair value method.

For example, if the price of a single security futures contract deviates from the underlying equity based on a large sell order, the arbitrage community is expected to take the action shown in Figure 8.1.

By selling the overpriced shares of XYZ company on the NYSE, and simultaneously buying the single security futures that make up those shares, the arbitrage desk in our example has managed to lock-in what is considered to be a risk-free profit. In other words, it will hold the short shares in XYZ and use them to offset the long shares of XYZ that it will take physical delivery of later when the futures contract expires and delivery takes place. The type of activity in our example is not new to the markets, and actually takes place in many different instruments. The arbitrageurs, while out to make a profit like any market participant, also serve an important function in that they play a major role in keeping prices of underlying instruments in line with their derivative counterparts, and vice versa. Although the profit margins can be very slim for this type of activity, the repetitive nature of this activity allows for the firms and individuals involved in these practices to generate strong results, if they apply it correctly.

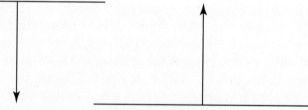

Figure 8.1   XYZ futures fair value = $26.12.

Chapter 9

MARGIN

One of the most important considerations in the trading of single stock futures is a clear understanding of the margin mechanism, how margin works, and what types of collateral can be posted.

To simplify margin, it can be reduced to being called a good faith deposit. When you transact a futures contract with another party, you are agreeing to a future transaction at a futures date at an agreed upon price. What this means is that so far, everyone has made an agreement but there are no guarantees that you will perform as expected under the rules and procedures governing the contract that you executed. In a perfect world, margin would not be required because everyone would be bound by their word, yet as we all know this is not practical, particularly when it involves monetary instruments. Therefore, the concept of margin was developed as a deposit that will ensure you comply with your end of the deal when it is time (i.e., when delivery date is reached).

Accordingly, margin is reflected as a percentage of an underlying assets value. In other words, the value of your entire transaction is multiplied by the percentage of required margin and this is the required deposit or funds that you must hold in your account. This percentage is fixed, which is further protection for not only the counterparty to your trade, but the futures exchange system as a whole. The best way to understand the concept is to remember that while the margin percentage remains fixed at 20 percent of the entire position value for outright purchases or short sales, (and lower for hedging and spreads this is an assumption, as margin can change based on market conditions, and if ruled appropriate by the governing agency and exchanges), the margin required changes based on the current value of the underlying asset. The following example indicates how margin is required for the trade of a single stock futures contract:

DAY 1

You purchased ten contracts of Intel stock futures, for March delivery, at a price of $21.00. Your initial margin requirement is 20 percent of the entire value of the position, calculated as follows:

$$\$21.00 \text{ (price of execution)} \times 100 \text{ shares}$$
$$\text{(standardized contract size)} \times 10 \text{ (number of contracts traded)}$$

Using this formula, you derive that the total value of your position is $21,000. Your margin requirement is 20 percent of this amount, the current margin level, which equals $4200. If you have at least $4200 deposited into your account, you will cover the margin requirement for this specific trade according to the minimum exchange required margins. Note that I say exchange minimum margin, as this is the 20 percent level that is understood to be the current exchange minimum for outright purchases or sales. However, your broker can raise this amount and is not required to charge you the absolute exchange minimum. They can charge you 30 percent if they like, to cover what they will indicate are certain risks associated with trading of these contracts. It is important to inquire with your executing brokerage firm and determine what level they will charge for your transactions. If they indicate that they charge exchange minimum margins then you can expect 20 percent, or whatever the exchange minimum is at that point in time.

Why would margins fluctuate? Any disaster, world event, volatility, or other factor could bring about a hike in margin requirements to a level that is determined to better protect the financial community. Many investors do not realize that the Reg. T margin, or the standard margin that you are used to using in your equity accounts that allows you to only pay for 50 percent of your stock purchase, can also be raised at any time by the governing agencies if they see it as appropriate. While such a move is unlikely given the selling pressure it could excerpt on the markets, it is always possible depending on the market environment.

DAY 2

The price of INTC futures declines to $19.00. Using our formula to calculate the margin requirement, you are now deficient in margin. Because your account has incurred losses of $2000 ($2.00 per contract × 100 shares per contract × 10 contracts), your account balance now is $2200 (your original $4200 deposit less the $2000 loss in value). Your broker will immediately request that you deposit an additional $1600 in your account, or you will face liquidation of enough contracts to cover your margin deficiency. For example, at the current price of $19.00 per contract, the margin required per contract is $380. If you fail to deliver additional margin into your account to cover the decline in account equity, your broker would have to sell 5 contracts to alleviate the need for $1600 in margin. The sale of six contracts would free-up $1600 of your margin requirement, yet these are not monies that you recoup from your initial deposit of $4200, as the funds have been lost on the trade.

The reason that you have to deliver the funds immediately following a decline in the market value of your position is because the margin is a deposit. Therefore, for continued good faith you have to replenish any amount of the deposit that is lost due to a decline in market value. Again with respect to protecting the financial system as a whole, the futures industry uses a marked to market approach. This means that the value of your position is marked to the underlying asset price at every moment. While most firms only update your mark to market at the end of each trading day, larger speculators and traders may see this activity intraday, and it is for the investors, brokerage firm, and financial system protection. If you could imagine that a great number of investors made wrong investment decisions that later moved against them, if this system was not used they could be liable for large loss at the time of contract expiration and delivery. In some cases, investors who utilize single stock futures as in the first example may not posses the entire $22,000 that the position reflects. They may be leveraging their assets and only depositing $4200 to cover the required minimum for the trading of the equivalent 1000 shares in INTC. By marking their position to market, the risk associated with their default or inability to pay for an adverse movement in the underlying stock is reduced.

Margin for Short Sales

Margin for short sales is handled in the identical fashion as for long purchases, yet an adverse adjustment in your mark-to-market occurs when the underlying instrument rises versus declines. When selling short you effectively are hoping for a decline in the value of the contract, and any gain will create a debit in your margin balance.

DAY 1

Expecting a decline in shares of OIL Corp., you sell short five December futures at a price of $45.25. Your margin requirement is as follows:

Margin Required = $(5 \times 100 \times 45.25) \times 20\%$
Margin Required = $4525

The initial margin is deposited, and then the next day you realize that the price of OIL Corp. has actually risen rather than declined as you expected. The resulting increase in the value of shares has caused the following amount to be subtracted from your margin balance:

DAY 2

OIL Corp. rises to $46.00

Margin Required = $4600.00
Account Value = $4150.00
Margin Deficiency = ($450.00)

While margin requirements can become deficient through adverse price movements, you can also see positive marked to market activity if a position is moving in the direction that you forecasted. For example, suppose in our previous example that the price of INTC gained ground to $23.00. The resulting $1.00 increase in value for each contract, multiplied times ten contracts, would equal $1000. Therefore, your new account margin balance would equal your original $4200, plus the $1000 in additional equity that was posted as a result of your gain in the position. The marked to market system is a two-way street, which allows the investor the potential of immediate gains as well as losses.

An easy formula for calculating your margin excess or deficiency depending on where the market is for your single security futures contract is shown in Figure 9.1.

The formula in Figure 9.1 allows investors to quickly and easily determine if they are in a position of holding excess margin in their accounts (and how much excess) or if they are currently in a position of being deficient in margin and will experience a margin call by their broker.

These examples underscore the need for investors to maintain sufficient margin in an account that is active in trading single security futures. While the leverage can be beneficial, it should not be viewed as a work-around to maintaining sufficient excess capital in your account for the purpose of meeting margin requirements and calls as they may occur.

The following are margin guidelines that should be used in regard to exchange minimum regulations as furnished by the Commodities Futures Trading Commission (CFTC) for single security futures. While these guidelines are useful for guidance toward your respective strategy, it is also prudent to check with your executing brokerage firm to determine what margin levels they are willing to extend to you. Often, their requirements will be higher than the minimums listed for each strategy.

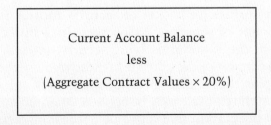

Current Account Balance

less

(Aggregate Contract Values × 20%)

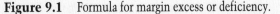

Figure 9.1 Formula for margin excess or deficiency.

Other Margin Requirements

Long security future or short security future on a stock or narrow-based security index.   Initial margin is 20 percent of the current market value of the underlying security future, and maintenance margin is also 20 percent of the current market value of the underlying security.

Long security future (or a basket of security futures representing each component of a narrow-based securities index) and long put option on the same underlying security.   Initial margin is 20 percent of the current market value of the long security futures, plus payment for the long put in full. Maintenance margin is the lower of: (1) 10 percent of the aggregate exercise price of the put plus the aggregate put out-of-the-money amount, if any; or (2) 20 percent of the current market value of the long security future.

Short security future (or basket of security futures representing each component of a narrow-based securities index) and short put option on the same underlying security (or index).   Initial margin requirement is 20 percent of the current market value of the short security future, plus the aggregate put in-the-money amount, if any. Proceeds from the put sale may be applied. Maintenance margin is 20 percent of the current market value of the short security future, plus the aggregate put in-the-money amount, if any.

Long security future and short position in the same security (or securities basket) underlying the security future.   Initial margin required is the required margin under Reg. T securities rules for the short stock or stocks. The maintenance margin is 5 percent of the current market value as defined in Reg. T of the stock or stocks underlying the security future.

Long security future (or basket of security futures representing each component of a narrow-based securities index) and short call option on the same underlying security (or index).   Initial margin is 20 percent of the current market value of the long security future, plus the aggregate call in-the-money amount, if any. Proceeds from the call sale may be applied. Maintenance margin is 20 percent of the current market value of the long security future, plus the aggregate call in-the-money amount, if any.

Long a basket of narrow-based security futures that together tracks a broad-based index and short a broad-based security index call option contract on the same index. Initial margin required is 20 percent of the current market value of the long basket of narrow-based security futures, plus the aggregate call in-the-money amount, if any. Proceeds from the call sale may be applied. Maintenance margin is 20 percent of the current market value of the long basket of narrow-based security futures, plus the aggregate call in-the-money amount, if any.

Long a basket of narrow-based security futures that together tracks a broad-based security index and short a broad-based security index put option contract on the same index. Initial margin required is 20 percent of the current market value of the short basket of narrow-based security futures, plus the aggregate in-the-money amount, if any. Proceeds from the put sale may be applied. Maintenance margin is 20 percent of the current market value of the short basket of narrow-based security futures, plus the aggregate put in-the-money amount, if any.

Long a basket of narrow-based security futures that together tracks a broad-based security index and long a broad-based security index put option contract on the same index. Initial margin equals 20 percent of the current market value of the long basket of narrow-based security futures, plus payment for the long put in full. Maintenance margin required is the lower of: (1) 105 of the aggregate exercise price of the put, plus the aggregate put out-of-the-money amount, if any; or (2) 20 percent of the current market value of the long basket of security futures .

Short a basket of narrow-based security futures that together tracks a broad-based security index and long a broad-based security index call option on the same index. Initial margin required is 20 percent of the current market value of the short basket of narrow-based security futures, plus payment for the long call in full. Maintenance margin required is the lower of: (1) 10 percent of the aggregate exercise price of the call, plus the aggregate call out-of-the-money amount, if any; or (2) 20 percent of the current market value of the short basket of security futures.

Long security future and short security future on the same underlying equity or index. Initial margin required is the greater of: (1) 5 percent of the current market value of the long security future; or (2) 5 percent of the current market value of the short security future. The maintenance margin required is the greater of: (1) 5 percent of the current market value of the long security future; or (2) 5 percent of the current market value of the short security future.

Long security future, long put option, and short call option. The long security future, long put, and short call must be on the same underlying security and the put and call must have the same exercise price (conversion). Initial margin required is 20 percent of the current market value of the long security future, plus the aggregate call in-the-money amount, if any, plus pay for the put in full. Proceeds from the call sale may be applied. The maintenance margin requires 10 percent of the aggregate exercise price, plus the aggregate call in-the-money amount, if any.

Long security future, long put option, and short call option. The long security future, long put, and short call must be on the same underlying security and the put exercise price must be below the call exercise price (collar). Initial margin required is 20 percent of the current market value of the long security future, plus the aggregate call in-the-money amount, if any, plus payment for the put contract in full. Proceeds from the call sale may be applied. Maintenance margins requires the lower of: (1) 10 percent of the aggregate exercise price of the put plus the aggregate put out-of-the-money amount, if any; or (2) 20 percent of the aggregate exercise price of the call, plus the aggregate call in-the-money amount, if any.

Short security future and long position in the same security (or securities basket) underlying the security future. Initial margin required is the initial margin required under Regulation T for the long stock or stocks. Maintenance margin is 5 percent of the current market value, as defined in Regulation T, of the long stock or stocks.

Short security future and long position in a security immediately convertible into the same security underlying the security future, without restriction, including the payment of money. Initial margin is the initial margin required under Regulation T for the long security. Maintenance margin is 10 percent of the current market value, as defined in Regulation T, of the long security.

Short security future (or basket of security futures representing each component of a narrow-based securities index) and long call option or warrant on the same underlying security (or index). Initial margin is 20 percent of the current market value of the short security future, plus pay for the call in full. The maintenance margin requires the lower of: (1) 10 percent of the aggregate exercise price of the call, plus the aggregate call out-of-the-money amount, if any; or (2) 20 percent of the current market value of the short security future.

Short security future, short put option, and long call option. The short security future, short put, and long call must be on the same underlying security and the put and call must have the same exercise price (reverse conversion). The initial margin is 20 percent of the current market value of the short security future, plus the aggregate put in-the-money amount, if any, plus pay for the call in full. Proceeds from put sale may be applied. The maintenance requirement is 10 percent of the aggregate exercise price, plus the aggregate put in-the-money amount, if any.

Long (short) a basket of security futures, each based on a narrow-based security index that together tracks the broad-based index and short (long) a broad based-index future. The initial margin required is 5 percent of the current market value of the long (short) basket of security futures. The maintenance margin is 5 percent of the current market value of the long (short) basket of security futures.

Long (short) a basket of security futures that together tracks a narrow-based index and short (long) a narrow based-index future. The initial margin is the greater of: (1) 5 percent of the current market value of the long security future(s); or (2) 5 percent of the current market value of the short security future(s). The maintenance required is the greater of: (1) 5 percent of the current market value of the long security future(s); or (2) 5 percent of the current market value of the short security future(s).

Chapter 10

SECURITY FUTURES VERSUS EQUITY OPTIONS

Option contracts on individual equities and single security futures have some similarities, yet also possess qualities that are indigenous to each instrument. Understanding these qualities is important, particularly when looking to replace your options trading activity with single security futures or combining security futures with options for more advanced strategies.

An option contract is comprised of 100 shares of underlying equity, just as a single stock future is standardized in size with 100 shares. However, as its name implies an option contract gives the holder *an option to transact the deal at a future date, at a predetermined price.* Remember with single security futures, you have *entered an agreement to the deal at a future date at a predetermined price.* This means that as a holder of an option contract, if the expiry date of the option was to arrive and you took no action, you would not be liable for default or other consequences from entering the trade. If you let your contract expire in the options market, it is your discretion to do so and not exercise your rights under the provisions of the option. Exercising an option can be compared to taking delivery of a futures contract, yet again the option is different from the commitment that is implied with the holder of a futures contract.

In previous chapters we discussed offsetting a futures position. In essence, this action cancels the agreement that you have entered when trading a futures contract. However, the failure to offset or roll-forward a futures position will result in a commitment to the transaction as of the delivery date.

Movement of option contracts in most cases will differ greatly from the movement of a single security futures contract. Option prices are measured using *the Greeks*, a reference to the terms used to describe the relationship option prices have to different influences in the marketplace. These include: An options sensitivity to interest rates (Rho), changes in volatility (Vega), the rate of time decay (Theta), the amount an option moves relative to the underlying instrument that it represents (Delta), and the rate at which the Delta changes (Gamma). These qualities are also limitations that are not recognized through the use of single security futures.

Delta, or the rate at which an option contract moves relative to the underlying instrument it represents, is a critical measurement in option trading. Without a Delta measurement, an option trader or investor would not know how much an option would move relative to the underlying asset on which it is based. In other words, if you purchase a call option on Microsoft with a strike price of $65.00 for June expiration, and the underlying stock is currently at $64.50, how much will your contract increase in value for every point in the underlying stock increase? This is where the Delta comes into play.

First, think of the option strike price as the price at which the futures contract has been executed. Come delivery date, or option expiry date in this case, your option is worth whatever the strike price is relative to the underlying equity, not the amount of premium that you paid for the right to buy the option contract. If, in this example, you purchased the option on Microsoft for $1.50, this reflects the premium, or the amount that you paid for the right to own the option contract expiring in June. As of expiration date, *you effectively have the option to buy the underlying stock at $65.00 per share*, which is the strike price of your contract. Therefore, if the underlying shares are trading below $65.00, your option will be expired worthless, as there would be no point in purchasing the stock at $65.00 if you could purchase the same equity on the open market (on the exchange in the physical shares) for a lower price. When you add the option premium you paid for the right to buy at $65.00 of $1.50 per contract, your actual cost basis would jump even higher to $66.50. This is different than a single security futures contract, which represents an obligation to purchase the shares at a future date. If you agreed to purchase a futures contract at $65.00, then you have already agreed to transact the shares at that price. It is not optional if you would like to buy Microsoft (MSFT) at the price of $65.00. The only way for an investor to eliminate the obligation to transact the shares is to engage in an offsetting or roll forward transaction. Figure 10.1 illustrates our option trade in Microsoft.

In the sample transaction in Figure 10.1, the investor who purchases this call must be expecting the price to increase above $66.50 if he is trading it for speculative reasons. Otherwise, it would not make sense to buy this contract.

Suppose that the price of MSFT increased by $1.00 the next day. The investor is surprised to see that the call contract is now valued at $2.00, which is the new premium required to purchase the contract. The contract has only increased by 0.50 cents relative to the move of $1.00 in shares of MSFT. This has occurred because the Delta, or the amount that an option moves relative to the underlying shares it represents, was 0.50. Deltas will always have a range between 0.00 and 1.00, depending on where an equity price is relative to that option at any given moment. Generally speaking, option contracts that are at the money, or have a strike price that coincides with the current price of the underlying asset, will have a Delta of 0.50. This is interpreted as meaning that the option contract will move only half as much as the underlying equity that it represents. Deltas will change as the underlying value of the asset changes, and the odds increase that the option contract will expire with intrinsic value. A Delta will

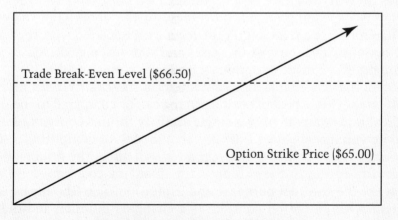

Figure 10.1 Option trade in Microsoft.

increase toward 1.00 as it becomes more likely that an option contract will have value at expiry, while option contracts that will likely not have value at expiry will have smaller Deltas, closer to zero. For the scope of our discussion, this is the best way to think of Delta, even though many other calculations such as standard deviation of equities and other details come into play when measuring an accurate Delta.

As an example of Delta increasing toward 1.00, in Figure 10.1, shares of MSFT would have to increase to approximately $70.00 from the current $64.50 before the $65.00 call option had a Delta that equaled 1.00. Therefore, until the price equaled this level the investor purchasing an option contract would not expect to receive a one-for-one return relative to the underlying asset.

This is where single security futures are different from an option contract, because a stock futures contract that is priced at fair value will always have a Delta of 1.00. In other words, a single stock future will move dollar for dollar with the underlying equity that it represents, assuming that the contract is fairly priced at the time it is purchased. This indicates that speculative applications may be facilitated through the use of single security futures relative to options, depending on the investment strategy involved. Why not then purchase an equity option contract with a Delta of 1.00 or at least close to 1.00? That is an appropriate strategy for some investors, but as you purchase an option contract that is closer to a Delta of 1.00, meaning that the odds are increased that it will expire with value, the cost of the contract also increases. Additionally, as the underlying share price fluctuates, so will the Delta, so a beginning Delta of 1.00 may decrease sharply depending on the movement of the underlying shares. Therefore it is a trade-off on the leverage associated with the use of options since the cost increases and your leverage decreases as purchases are made of options with Delta closer to 1.00.

An options *Rho* is a measurement of its sensitivity to interest rates. This aspect of option pricing can be compared to the interest rate component of a single security futures contract, with some variances. Given the fair value model for computing a security futures contract, interest rates will affect the pricing of a security future to the extent of the financing cost between the date of the contract purchase and expiration. The Rho measurement with an option contract is a changing number, and indicates the sensitivity of the option price to changing interest rates during that instrument's life cycle. The Rho is used for option valuation, however the effect that a change in interest rates inflicts on an option can vary from one contract to another. Meanwhile, a change in interest rates with regard to pricing a single security futures contract has a uniform effect, given the formula used for deriving the fair value of a single stock future at any given time.

Vega, or the change in an option's theoretical value to a change in volatility, is strictly a component of option pricing. This measurement attempts to compensate for an increase or decrease in the expected standard deviation of an option, based on changes in volatility as measured by the Vega. In the case of security futures, a Vega measurement is not required since the movement of the contract should adhere to a Delta, or movement, of one for one with the underlying equity. Consequently, shifts in volatility will not be necessary to measure changes in value of a security futures contract. The value of the underlying contract will track the physical stock underlying the futures regardless of an increase or decrease in volatility during the life of the future. An adjustment for volatility would have to be made prior to a purchase or sale by the market-maker, who theoretically may adjust prices above or below fair value to account for volatility that is associated with a particular futures contract. Once the futures contract is purchased or sold by an investor, it is not necessary to revalue the contract as the agreement will move in lock step with the price of the underlying shares.

In the area of time decay, the benefits of using single security futures over equity options are significant. Listed equity option time decay, or the sensitivity to same known as *Theta*, is one of the largest disadvantages of purchasing long option premium. Investors that purchase equity options often end up disappointed that their option expired worthless. Because the price of options that are deeply in the money, or have Deltas close to 1.00 like a security futures contract are expensive relative to options out-of-the-money, many investors opt to invest in option contracts that have a high Theta. This in turn means that the decay of option premium will be rapid, all things being equal. Time decay can result in a losing trade even if the investor properly analyzed and predicted movement in the underlying equity. In this sense, options are a wasting asset, whereas a futures contract will not reflect time decay because the contract is not based on premium but directly on the price of the underlying asset. Investors may find that the use of a futures contract for speculative applications can be more rewarding than using equity options, particularly if the use of options for that investor is limited to buying out-of-the-money puts or calls.

Another key difference between the purchase of options versus single stock futures is the issue of margin. Option contracts on equities are not marginable and must be paid for in full when purchased long in an account. This differs of course from the purchase of single security futures, which are purchased on margin that is your good faith deposit for the performance of the contract. When you purchase an option contract, you are buying that contract and not entering into a forward agreement, therefore the full value of the contract must be paid for in advance. The ability to use margin for purchasing single security futures allows more flexibility for short term speculators who have limited investment capital.

Overall, single security futures have similarities and differences, however, these tools can be used in conjunction to compliment qualities that are unique to each of the two. By implementing strategies that involve the use of both single security futures and listed equity options, new avenues for profitable speculation and accurate hedging activities can find their way into every investor's portfolio.

Examples of how these contracts can be used together are numerous. For instance, suppose that you are considering a speculative purchase of IBM stock. Instead, you decide that the leverage you can have through the use of single stock futures is appealing. Therefore, you decide to purchase five contracts of the IBM security futures for June delivery, at a price of $78.00. The margin requirement for this purchase is $7800 (5 contracts × 100 shares × $78.00 × 20%). The only problem that you can see is that the shares of IBM are quite volatile, so although you are convinced that the price of the shares will increase, you are worried about short-term volatility. You decide that to protect yourself against a sudden decline, a purchase of one put option with a strike price of $75.00 is appropriate for every futures contract you own. The price of each put option is $1.25 ($125.00, when multiplied times the option contract size of 100 shares). The graph in Figure 10.2 illustrates the profit and loss potential of this position.

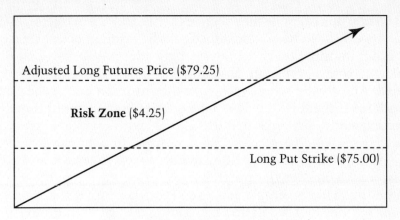

Figure 10.2   Profit and loss potential.

Through the use of a protective put option, any decline in shares of IBM below the $75.00 put strike price will not add to your losses. The position is effectively hedged at a price of $75.00, while the upside is unlimited. The complete cash outlay for this position is the cost of margin for the long futures, $7800, plus to cost of the option premium that equals $8425. The added cost of the put protection means that the break-even level of the futures purchase is $79.25, the original level of $78.00 plus the option premium of $1.25 per contract. Your losses are limited to $2125, which equals the difference between the price at which you purchased the IBM equity futures, minus the strike price of your put protection, plus the option premium. By purchasing protection, you are limiting the downside of this trade strategy while leaving any profit potential unlimited.

Even though the purchase of a put for each long futures contract means that you are raising your cost basis, it may be well worthwhile considering the potential volatility and uncertainty of equity performance. Using the same example, suppose the following situation was to occur:

An investor purchases five long IBM security futures at a price of $78.00. The following day, before the market opens, there is an announcement of accounting irregularities at the company, and the stock is indicated to open at $55.00 per share, and $55.00 per futures contract. Consequently, the value of the position has decreased by $11,500.

While this example may seem extreme, today's markets can be unforgiving in some circumstances. In the event of news releases, or other information that may strongly affect the price of an underlying equity, typically any stop-loss order would not be triggered. An investor would recognize the entire decline in the price of shares if there is a market halt or after-hours announcement. Consequently, any order that was entered with a broker to prevent such losses would not be executed in most circumstances.

As a quick note on option trading, many investors and professionals consider option trading for speculative purposes as gambling. This is simply not the case. To address the issue of using options for speculation being similar to gambling, envision a trip to Las Vegas. There, when you place your bets, the dealer at your game of choice will usually say "no more bets" or wave her hand over the table before dealing cards or before the roulette wheel slows beyond a certain stage. This is a calculated gesture, as once this is said you cannot bargain with the house and offer them a portion of your bet if they let you have the balance back for the next hand. That is, suppose I played a hand of black jack and was dealt my first card and it was a four, the dealer received her first card and it is an Ace. At this point, I should probably cancel my bet if I can get anything back from my original $50.00 placed on the table. If the house were to say, you can cancel, but we are going to only give you $30.00 back from your $50.00 bet I would probably jump at that chance, knowing my odds were lower at 21 than the dealer's. The fact is, this would shift the odds and there will never be a casino that would let me cancel my bet and refund some of my money during a hand. This is where gambling and option trading differ. If you can control the emotion and risk of option trading, you can always exit a position at the bid price or ask price in the market (depending on if you are long or short an option). It is placing a trade and "letting it ride" that is gambling, assuming you will be right at any cost and not being willing to take a loss that is smaller than your entire investment.

Chapter 11

ANALYSIS OF SINGLE SECURITY FUTURES

Single security futures can be traded using whatever type of analysis works best for you, whether you utilize technical analysis, fundamental analysis, or combination of both.

The application of fundamental analysis includes using earnings projections, company stock reports, and other details specific to each company's financial health to determine the best security which you should be invested in.

Technical research on the other hand, involves the application of charting and other technical indicators that can be used for measuring the potential of price increase or decrease in an underlying security futures contract. While fundamental analysis is used on the underlying equity itself, as a security future represents the underlying shares, technical applications can be applied to either the underlying shares or a futures contract, depending on your preference. While the charts should appear similar between a security future and the underlying asset, directly reviewing the futures charts can often be helpful as it may uncover certain key levels in the contract that cannot be discovered through the direct review of the underlying security. One necessary consideration, however, is that there be sufficient trading history in an underlying contract before its chart can be properly interpreted.

The division that runs between fundamentalists and technicians runs deep, however there has been some attempt to move in a new direction with the application of techno-fundamentalism, which is the combination of both types of analysis that works well for some investors. Fundamentalists generally believe that the release of earnings news, company fiscal conditions, and other details such as price-to-earnings (P/E) ratios and earnings per share carry the most weight when considering trading a particular security, or in this case single security futures contract.

Conversely, technicians generally discount all of the information upon which fundamentalists rely, including earnings, P/E, etc. Instead, they attempt to measure the movements of equities and observe patterns in prior movements that may repeat in the future. By discovering these patterns, it is assumed that certain reactions will occur again in the market as they did historically. There is also a deeper interpretation that technical study is the study of the psychology of the market, and a graph represents how the market as a whole reacts to a stock's price at given levels. Similar to an EKG that is interpreted by a cardiologist, skilled technicians can decipher charts to determine the health of the markets or the overall health of a particular security. The bottom line is that the best analysis method for an investor to use is the analytical method that best compliments their own style. For example, if you are a true believer in technical analysis yet you cannot seem to interpret a chart to save your life, it is just as worthless as using no analysis at all. Experimentation with different types of analysis is the single best method of determining what system works best for your individual needs and success.

Technical Analysis in Detail

Technicians generally believe that the equity markets are completely efficient, and that any news or fundamental data that may present itself, including news releases, earnings releases, analyst recommendations, and so on are already reflected in the price of a security. This means that no matter how insightful an investor's research may be, the end result is that all of this data is already reflected in the price of the security, and therefore it is relatively useless to a technician. During recent years, technical analysis has become a more popular method of analyzing investments in general, although in most cases it is used in conjunction with fundamental research. Many investors find this combined approach rewarding, since using both methods allows for a review of traditional equity information while also using technical analysis to identify important trends and support and resistance levels in particular securities and the overall market. The use of technical research is heavily depended on by shorter to medium term traders, who utilize this method of identifying key levels in certain stocks, without which critical entry and exit points may be missed. With shorter duration trading, timing is everything.

Identifying Trends

The basis of technical research is the principle of trends, which can be classified as major or minor trends within the overall scope of equity movement. A major trend typically occurs over the course of a year or more, while trends that last several days or months can be considered minor trends. Some trends can even be measured on a short time frame as intraday, and these would definitely fall into the minor trend category.

The idea behind a trend is that prices, when they begin to move, generally will continue to move in the prevailing direction. It is a derivative of Newtonian theory that an object in motion will tend to remain in motion. If prices begin moving higher, they should continue to move higher all things remaining equal. The shortcomings of always expecting a trend nonetheless are just that, all things generally will not remain equal in the equity markets. Any influence on supply or demand can shift expectations, and therefore disrupt the equilibrium between supply and demand, which in turn affects an equity's trend potential. The identification of trends is critical however, and can be seen in a basic example in Figures 11.1a and 11.1b.

Trends can exist as uptrends or downtrends, depending on the current market climate for a particular security. The measurement and identification of these trends will assist an investor in deciding if his or her approach is in agreement with the market or against the overall market opinion. This raises the question of whether an investor will have more success investing with the trend or against a trend.

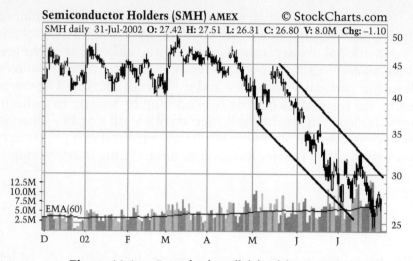

Figure 11.1a   Example of a well-defined down-trend.

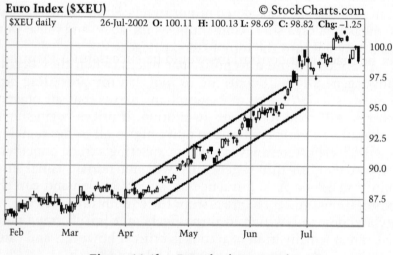

Figure 11.1b   Example of an up-trend.

There are countless phrases that refer to the age-old question of investing with trends, such as "don't fight the market" and "the trend is your friend." Within the use of technical analysis, there are two types of investors, contrarians and trend followers. As their name suggests, contrarians will generally fight a trend and try to bet against the market, while trend followers will trade with the direction of the prevailing market. Contrarians believe that the entire market cannot be correct, and therefore the minority, in this case themselves, will be correct when deciding the future price of a particular security. The interesting thing about this idea is that the underlying market, or majority of investors, is actually correct if a trend is in place and in motion. The contrarians, while believing that they will be the only correct party to an investment, are actually fighting against the actuality that the majority is enjoying profits on an investment. This invalidates some of the principal basis behind contrarian investing, and reduces such strategies to the undesirable basis that contrarian investors simply believe themselves to be smarter than the market. This cannot actually be proven because the market is indeed smarter than the investor since the prevailing trend a contrarian is fighting exists. The existence of the trend purely undermines the contrarian philosophy that the fewest number of investors make the greatest gains. In fact, the internet equity gains during the late 1990s proved that the majority of investors could actually be making the majority of gains, while the minority of contrarians incurred the most losses. An argument can be made that contrarians would be successful if identifying turning points after a trend ceases, yet this would not truly qualify as a contrarian since the trend ceasing would indicate the majority of investors were no longer aiming for movement in one direction.

Investing in the same direction of a trend, while seemingly easy, is a profitable manner in which to invest. For years I belonged to the camp that believed investing with trends was not an appropriate strategy, as it involved no substantial knowledge or specialized analysis. Years later, I tried investing within a trend for the heck of it and it turned out to be one of my most profitable trades. The basis of my investment strategy now includes identifying trends and not fighting the overall market sentiment or direction.

Another key principal to grasp when using technical analysis is the proper identification of support and resistance levels in a specific security. Using charts to identify these levels is important in establishing a potentially profitable position, given that entry and exit points can mean the difference between margin calls or no margin calls using security futures.

Resistance levels can be identified by looking for consistent levels in which selling pressure emerges in a security futures contract, whether you are using an intraday or longer-term chart. Applying the identification can assist an investor in preventing a purchase near or at a resistance level. As a general rule, any strong resistance level that prices manage to break above becomes a support level, and the validity of a resistance level can be measured by the number of times prices were rebuffed from that area. For example, a single stock futures contract that has increased in value to a price of $24.10 on six different occasions but was turned back has a strong level of selling interest located there. A break above $24.10 becomes a bullish signal for that contract as a result, and the level should then become support moving forward.

On the other hand, if prices of a security futures contract decline to a level of $15.00 on a few occasions and find buying interest there, an investor can determine by studying this price action that the contract has a solid level of support at $15.00. Meanwhile, a decline below that level should be interpreted as being bearish in the future, and the level should also become resistance moving forward.

Technical analysis is about watching the price action of a security and allowing the market for that security to paint a picture of what levels are important. By studying areas of support and resistance and adding these pieces of information to your investment approach, any investor will benefit.

Analyzing Data

When viewing charts, most technical analysis educational guides cover the types of patterns that you may see, rather than methods in which you can study and analyze the data itself. There are several manners an investor can use to plot data when charting, including bar charts, line charts, and my preferred method of candlestick charts.

Data in a bar chart is typically interpreted with the formation of a single vertical line, with a notch on the left side indicating the opening price and a notch to the right side of the bar indicating the closing price on that particular day (using a daily chart).

The height of the bar is reflected as the daily trading range, with the high and low marked by the ends of each bar. This method of charting is used frequently, and allows a simple methodology for studying daily trading ranges and the overall patterns indicated on a security chart.

A line chart is simply what its name suggests, a single line that reflects the movements of an underlying security. The line fluctuates connecting the last trade points in a security. This method of charting is most often applied when using shorter term charts, such as intraday. While it allows an overall view of activity in the underlying market, it can be misleading in thinner, less actively traded futures instruments.

The last type of chart plotting is the candlestick chart. These charts are actually an analysis within an analysis. By this I mean that each individual candlestick has an interpreted meaning. Candlesticks used for this type of charting have several different names, and combinations of candlesticks in particular arrangements have a meaning unto themselves. By using candlestick charts, an investor can attempt to forecast the medium to longer term directional movement of a security by viewing chart patterns, and can also become aware of overall market sentiment based on the analysis that each individual candlestick represents. For more information on charting with candlesticks, I recommend *Beyond Candlesticks*, by Steve Nison.

Specialized Market Patterns

Within technical analysis there exists several specialized patterns that may appear on charts, signaling certain movement that has occurred historically after the appearance of similar patterns. This approach is based on the idea that what happened following the formation of such a pattern will happen again in the future. There is validity to this idea, because the patterns depicted on a chart of a security are an illustration of investors behavior en masse. It is the psychology of the market, and generally the psychology of the market or the tendency of people to behave in certain patterns has not changed much throughout time. Having said this, the idea that certain behavior will occur in the future is a conclusion with odds in your favor, given that you study the human behavior that occurred in the prior instance. If this premise was not accurate, then it would be the same to say that the entire basis of human psychological study was based on an inaccurate foundation and had no validity. A discussion of specific chart patterns and what they are interpreted as meaning follows.

Head and Shoulders Pattern

The head and shoulders pattern (see Figure 11.2) represents three peaks in market activity, interpreted as a left shoulder, head in the middle, and right shoulder. There are specific identification qualities of each peak, which include that the left shoulder typically will have the highest corresponding volume, followed by the head, and the right shoulder will see the lowest corresponding volume. Using a volume overlay can be very helpful in determining if the pattern is valid. Typically, a resulting decline after the break through the neckline of the pattern will see a descent in prices that equals the distance between the neckline and the top of the "head" spike in the pattern. Take this distance and project it downward from the break point in the neckline. This equals the target for the fall in prices after a breach of the neckline. The

Figure 11.2   Example of a head and shoulders top pattern.

head and shoulders pattern is a widely recognized chart pattern, and if identified successfully it can lead to trading opportunities.

Triangles and Wedges

A very frequent pattern seen in security futures charts are triangles. These patterns can be one of three varieties: symmetrical, descending, or ascending. An example of each type of triangle is shown in Figures 11.3a, 11.3b, and 11.3c.

These patterns will often assist in forecasting subsequent movement in a particular security if analyzed correctly. The symmetrical triangle, as its name suggests, is an evenly formed triangle that has congruent sides. These types of triangles are normally formed during a trend, and the trend will usually continue in the prior direction after the triangle is completed. Therefore, symmetrical triangles are usually considered continuation patterns since they form during a period of consolidation and the prevailing trend then takes over. Usually, triangles will complete their formation before the apex of the triangle (formed by drawing two trend lines to form the triangle) is reached.

Ascending triangles are formations that, as illustrated in Figure 11.3c, are formed by ascending lower triangle points and a

Figure 11.3a   Example of a bearish descending triangle pattern.

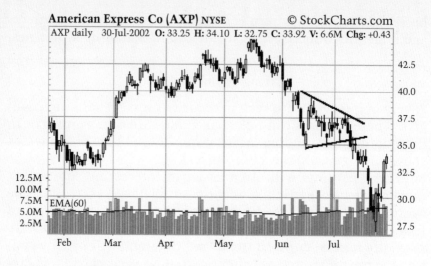

Figure 11.3b   Symmetrical (continuation) triangle.

Figure 11.3c   Sharp example of a bullish ascending triangle pattern.

fixed level of resistance that forms the triangle top. This pattern can be interpreted by the actual price action, which indicates that buyers are increasing the level in which they are comfortable making a purchase with the passing of time. However, there is also a level of resistance overhead that is turning back upside gains at a specific level. The idea is that the increasing buying pressure will ultimately be able to remove the layer of overhead resistance, resulting in a break higher. Ascending triangle patterns will usually result in a break to the upside, once the top triangle line is breached. Once the level of resistance is broken, it then becomes support for later declines.

The third commonly seen triangle formation is the descending triangle, and it is the mirror image of an ascending triangle pattern. Instead of levels in which buyers are presently increasing, a descending triangle pattern is formed by the level of selling interest declining with the passing of time. In other words, investors are becoming less price sensitive and want to exit a security regardless of the price decline. The base of this triangle is support, however, the pattern historically indicates that the selling momentum is increasing to the point at which the support can be breached. Because of this, the descending triangle pattern is indicative of a market that will usually break to the downside once the triangle formation is complete.

Another formation that is often seen in technical analysis is a *wedge*. These patterns are formed by a tight-trading range in an instrument that takes place over the course of several trading sessions. The two main types of wedges are a falling wedge and a rising wedge (see Figures 11.4a and 11.4b).

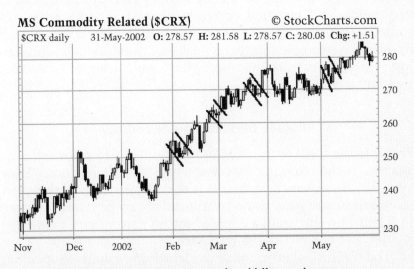

Figure 11.4a   Numerous examples of falling wedge patterns.

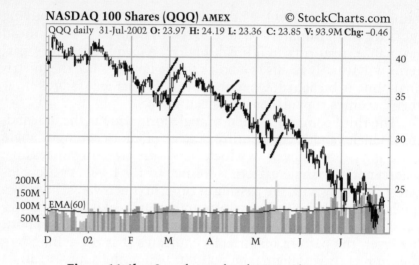

Figure 11.4b   Several examples of rising wedge patterns.

Wedges are generally considered to be continuation patterns, however, they are inverse to the direction in which the trend should continue. For example, a completed falling wedge will typically lead to a continuation higher in a security, while a completed rising wedge will commonly indicate that a security is ready for a fresh leg to the downside. These patterns can be very helpful if identified correctly, since their formations are sometimes misinterpreted as the end of a downtrend or uptrend. By properly recognizing these wedges, investors can eliminate losses stemming from the improper identification of an end to a trending move.

Double Tops and Double Bottoms

Probably the most recognized or mentioned pattern in technical analysis is the famous "double top" or "double bottom." However, the interesting note to this is that the majority of these patterns are misdiagnosed, and the results can be severe. Figures 11.5 and 11.6 illustrate a double bottom pattern and a true double top, and can be used as reference.

The traditional error made in identifying a double top or bottom is to assume that the base of the pattern will be violated.

Figure 11.5   Example of a double bottom.

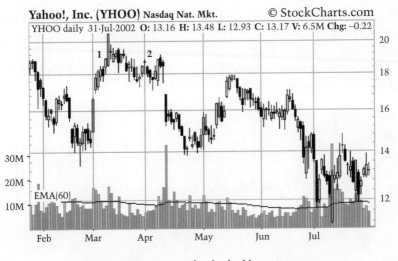

Figure 11.6   Example of a double top pattern.

Only this break indicates the true formation of either pattern, and a lack of break beyond the base will typically indicate a false reading. Keeping this in mind, it is critical to identify double tops or bottoms only after they have broken down through their base. Many investors will preemptively buy or sell when it is believed that a pattern is formed, however confirmation of the pattern is the most important consideration, particularly when dealing with either topping or bottoming formations.

As the name suggests, double tops or bottoms will generally indicate a bottom or top to a particular market. This formation generally signals that a medium to longer term change in momentum has occurred, and prices will likely reverse direction for a substantial length of time moving forward.

Even more severe in terms of expected corrective activity is the triple top pattern pictured in Figure 11.7.

These patterns, while relatively rare, often signal a more significant turning point for a security. The interpretation of this pattern is simply that support or resistance held back three consecutive attempts to break that particular level, and consequently the ensuing corrective activity is typically quite severe.

Flags

The flag is a formation that can occur in both a bullish and bearish market. This pattern is formed of two components, a flag staff and the actual flag.

Flags are generally interpreted as indicative of an impending break-out or break-down in a specific security futures contract.

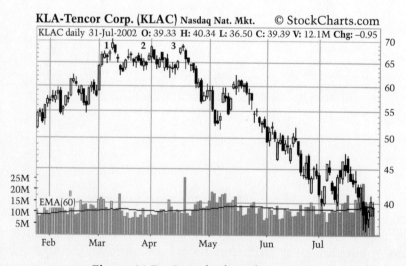

Figure 11.7   Example of a triple top pattern.

As a rule of thumb, a flag pattern will travel the distance of the flag staff after breaking out or breaking lower. This allows a guide for measuring the expected movement that will occur following a formation of a flag pattern. Essentially, a flag pattern is the formation of a sharp trend followed by the formation of a continuation wedge, mentioned earlier in this chapter. Once the continuation triangle is broken, the flag will usually trade to the measured objective. In some cases, a flag staff will be formed with a symmetrical triangle pattern at the end of the staff, and this is referred to as a pennant formation and has the same measuring techniques.

While this guide offers a brief overview of more familiar chart patterns, I would recommend that anyone who is interested in technical analysis look into a text entitled "Encyclopedia of Chart Patterns" by Thomas N. Bulkowski. It offers a complete guide to chart patterns and a unique approach to measuring the success and failure rate of each pattern, which is very useful when applying technical analysis to actual investment decisions.

Chapter 12

PROVEN TRADING STRATEGIES

One of the most important considerations when trading single security futures is how to manage your position once it is executed. While planning is a critical step in your overall transaction as well as execution, it is the management of your position that will ultimately affect the outcome of your efforts. As an example, many well-known futures funds will admit that only ten percent of their trades are actually winning, or correct, trades based on an overall ratio of their projections of future price. Any investor who hears this may then wonder how such fund managers remain in business. The answer is that they have extraordinary position management skills that allow profitability regardless of the ratio of correct price projections to incorrect. Human nature is to blame when it comes to trade management or the lack thereof in investors. The natural tendency is to hold a losing trade hoping that the market will turn around, and take quick profits with the fear that what is newly gained will be lost. The chart in Figure 12.1 illustrates the natural tendencies of managing trades for the majority of short-term or speculative investors using futures.

As in Figure 12.1, the majority of investors who use futures actually have an opposite natural tendency than that which will lead to a long and successful use of the instrument. The habit to liquidate profitable positions and "book the profit" and the disappointing quality of holding losing contracts with the hope that they will turn around tomorrow is a losing battle, whereby losses

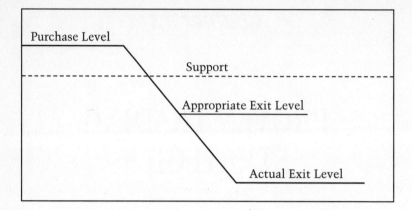

Figure 12.1   Natural tendencies of managing trades.

will, with a mathematical certainty, outweigh gains in the long run.

The opposite behavior of that in Figure 12.1 is what separates profitable traders from those that have a short relationship with the product. In other words, when speculating if you consistently liquidate losing trades based on an appropriate analysis of levels of support being breached, and continually hold your profitable positions and even add to them, you mathematically have odds of being profitable in the long term. This is where the idea of being able to succeed with only a small percentage of your trades being "correct" comes into play. As a speculator, you must accept when you are wrong and liquidate your position, while adding contracts to a position that is moving in your favor. Figure 12.2 illustrates the relationship of these two methods.

As you can see in Figure 12.2, the method of dealing with a decline from purchase price in XYZ security futures is to liquidate the position immediately after it breaches support that was identified when you placed your original trade. Conversely, Figure 12.2 indicates that on your profitable ABC security futures trade you made a significant profit by adding contracts as the price moved in your favor.

By utilizing this method, you will be profitable in the long run even if the majority of your trades are based on incorrect premises. The bottom line is that if you are able to apply this

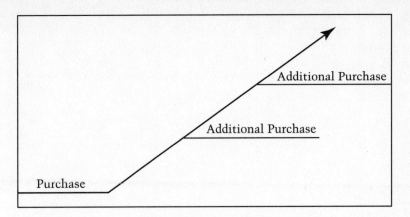

Figure 12.2 Opposite behavior.

methodology to your trading, you will consistently make more money speculating than you lose.

The necessity of trading single security futures is to have a game plan that accurately defines your entry and exit levels. Any activity in the instrument requires that you have well defined your entry and exit level, and have a contingency plan if things fail to go as planned, before you execute your first security futures transaction.

Chapter 13

SECURITY FUTURES PROFICIENCY REVIEW SECTION

The Commodity Futures Modernization Act of 2000 contained an amendment that added language to the Securities and Exchange Act of 1934. The changes require the National Futures Association (NFA) to ". . . have rules that ensure that members and natural persons associated with members meet such standards of training, experience and competence necessary to effect transactions in security futures products and are tested for their knowledge of securities and security futures products." To that end, the NFA, the NYSE, and the National Association of Securities Dealers Regulation (NASDR) have developed a proficiency test for participants in the single security futures marketplace. What this means is that any licensed broker, whether holding a Series 3 commodities license or Series 7 securities license, must complete the proficiency requirement in order to handle customers or proprietary orders for singe stock futures. Moving forward, the Series 3 and Series 7 exams will have material included that covers security futures, however individuals licensed prior to this period must take the proficiency exam. The proficiency sessions are structured much like the current continuing education programs required for both Series 3 and Series 7 registration holders. It is broken down into five modules, some of which a licensed person can opt-out of if they meet criteria. The outline for the modules is: (1) Securities Concepts, (2) Futures Concepts,

(3) Specifics of Single Security Futures, (4) Regulatory Requirements, and (5) Branch Manager/Office Director. Within these five modules, a Series 7 registered individual would be exempt from modules number one, and if not a branch manager number five. Meanwhile, a branch manager of a futures firm that is Series 3 registered would be exempt from module two only, and required to take the remaining four sections. These modules cover the major issues relating to their respective categories, and are followed by eight to ten multiple choice questions per category. These proficiency requirements are structured to be a supplement to, and not replacement for, the standard licensing exams that were taken by Series 3 and Series 7 registered persons.

This section of the book is intended to provide the necessary information required for successful completion of the security futures proficiency test. Used in conjunction with independent review of security futures products and the official documentation available through the NFA and NASDR, this study guide will assist in developing a strong understanding of the required knowledge for single security futures representatives.

Refer to the glossaries for basic futures and option market terminology and language used in the securities trading markets. These terms are useful for preparing to take the continuing education module to obtain authorization for trading single security futures. Additionally, individual investors can utilize these two complete glossary sections as a complete reference guide for terminology used when investing with single stock futures.

Appendix 1

BASIC FUTURES PRINCIPALS FOR THE BEGINNER

A futures contract is an agreement, between a buyer and seller, to transact a specific product, at an agreed upon price, on a future date. The concept is very similar to a forward contract, however futures markets have an element of standardization which is not found with most forward markets. In other words, in most forward contract markets the grade, quantity, and other details regarding a specific transaction can vary widely. Through the use of futures however, the random factors are removed and the quantity of an underlying asset, the contract expiry date, and other factors are all standardized. The only factor left to be determined is the price of the contract, which of course will fluctuate on the exchange in which a particular futures contract trades.

A buyer of a futures contract is stating that according to the terms of the deal, he or she will accept delivery of a product upon which the contract is based at the future date for that specific contract. Contracts trade in every quarterly month (March, June, September, and December) and many futures markets (including single security futures) offer two serial months in addition to the quarterly expiration months. What this means is that if the current month is March, then the March, April, May and June contracts would be available for trading. The front two quarterly months and two serial months are offered in single security futures, as an example. To determine what contracts are available at any given time for different exchanges, it is best to consult the particular exchange in which each product trades for a contract schedule.

If an investor is purchasing a futures contract, the simple premise behind the trade is that the individual views the current price for the underlying asset as low relative to where they are forecasting the future price for the same asset. Since several delivery months are trading at one time into the future, an investor can forecast the price moving forward for a particular time horizon, using the contract that best reflects the time period during which he or she expects the underlying asset to increase in value. If an investor does not feel that an asset will increase in value in the future, it would not be prudent to purchase a futures contract.

When I discuss delivery months, the term *delivery* is used for the purpose of identifying when the contract that the buyer is entering into with the seller comes due. When a contract matures (also known as expiry), delivery follows shortly thereafter. In the case of single security futures, delivery follows contract expiry by three business days. On delivery date, the buyer of a futures contract is obligated to purchase the underlying asset that is represented by the futures contract. Remember, every futures contract has standardized qualities, therefore every contract represents a certain amount of an underlying asset. On delivery date, the buyer of the contract must accept delivery of the underlying asset that is being delivered by the seller of the contract. The important thing to remember is that the full, previously agreed upon purchase price of the underlying asset is required on delivery date in order for the buyer of a futures contract to receive delivery of the underlying asset.

This is an important consideration given the inherent leverage that is introduced through the use of a futures contract. Because a buyer and seller are agreeing to transact a deal in the future, when the contract is executed the full amount of the purchase by the buyer is not required. Instead, the buyer must post what is known as a good faith deposit called *margin* in order to guarantee the performance under the contract. This deposit is based on a percentage of the total value of an underlying contract. Therefore, if a single contract represents 100 shares of an underlying asset, the full value is derived by taking the contract value multiplied times the contract size, in this case 100 shares, to determine the entire contract value. While the margin deposit may only be a small portion of this contract value (in the case of security futures 20 percent of the entire contract value is required as an absolute minimum) it is just that, a portion of the contract that is just a deposit on the full face amount of the obligation. Come delivery date, if the buyer of a futures contract wishes to take delivery of the underlying asset, he or she would have to provide the remaining 80 percent of the underlying asset value as based on the price when the contract was executed with the seller. A good comparison would be your home mortgage. If you place a down payment that reflects your willingness to perform under the contract (loan), the bank that holds your mortgage will not deliver the title to you until the remaining amount due under the contract is provided. Because futures can be purchased and sold just like an equity, however, if an investor were to sell his or her contract to another buyer before the delivery date (as if you sold your home before receiving the title) then the buyer would receive the cash difference between the purchase price paid for the contract and the subsequent sale price.

In futures markets, there are two types of delivery—physical and cash. The first, physical delivery, means that you actually receive the underlying asset on delivery date when you provide the capital required. On the other hand, cash settled futures mean just that. As of the delivery date, an investor will receive the cash difference between the contract expiry price and the price at which the contract was initially purchased. In other words, the transaction is reduced to a cash basis on all sides, thereby eliminating the need for delivery of an actual underlying asset. These types of futures contracts have become popular among various futures exchanges particularly the "financial futures complex," futures based on financial instruments such as bonds and indexes. Single security futures are physically settled in the United States, however exchanges such as the LIFFE in the United Kingdom offer cash settled instruments.

A seller of a futures contract is forecasting that prices of an underlying asset will fall relative to the current value of the instrument. Also, selling a futures contract is a more convenient manner in which short-term gains can be recognized rather than holding a contract through to the delivery date. A seller of a contract is agreeing in principal to make delivery of a product on a predetermined date in the future, for a predetermined price. Sellers typically will be those who are betting that prices in the future will decline as the current value for the same underlying asset is inflated or overpriced.

The same principals for delivery apply, only in the case of a seller, the underlying asset must be delivered to the buyer of the contract. This may pose a problem for the seller, because in the futures markets you do not need to actually own the underlying asset in order to sell a futures contract. In other words, an investor may believe that the value of Intel stock may fall between now and three months forward. Therefore, a sale is made of the Intel futures contract, however the investor who sells this contract has no ownership of the underlying asset. If the delivery date of the contract arrives, and the price of Intel shares has actually risen against previous expectations, then the investor will incur a loss. The investor would have to purchase the shares at the current price they are available, which is going to be higher than when the futures contract was sold. The loss will be the difference between the two.

In many if not most cases, futures contracts are used for short- to medium-term speculation and hedging applications, and therefore delivery is not a concern or reality for many individuals. The nature of the futures market and the principal "middle man" of all transactions is the clearinghouse. This function allows the offsetting of transactions, and matching of buys versus sales. The clearinghouse actually takes over the control of transactions after they take place, meaning that their role makes it possible to forget the identity of every buyer and seller. This recordkeeping is up to the individual brokerage firms where the trades take place. The clearinghouse guarantees the performance of every trade, and therefore it can be viewed as the real counterparty to every transaction. Due to this dynamic, a futures contract can be purchased and then sold, or sold and then purchased, and no delivery in then required. This is known as offsetting a position, and is similar to offsetting any transaction in the financial markets, such as a simple equity trade. The only difference is that in the futures markets this offsetting transaction actually eliminates your obligation with respect to any type of delivery action.

Appendix 2

NARROW-BASED INDICES

Along with the introduction of single security futures, the OneChicago LLC exchange introduced trading on a group of narrow-based indices that are sector specific. These indices are useful for both individual as well as professional investors, and can be utilized for a wide variety of speculative and hedging applications. The following is a listing of the initial narrow-based indexes offered by OneChicago.

Airlines
AMR Corp/Del (AMR)
Continental Airlines Inc. CL B (CAL)
Delta Air Lines (DAL)
Southwest Airlines (LUV)
UAL Corp (UAL)

Biotech
Amgen Inc. (AMGN)
Biogen Inc. (BGEN)
Chiron Corp (CHIR)
Genzyme Corp—Genl Division (GENZ)
Human Genome Sciences (HGSI)

Computers
Apple Computer Inc. (AAPL)
Dell Computer Corporation (DELL)
International Business Machines (IBM)
Research in Motion (RIMM)
Sun Microsystems (SUNW)

Defense
General Dynamics (GD)
Lockheed Martin (LMT)
Northrop Grumman Corp (NOC)
Raytheon Co (RTN)

Investment Banking
Goldman Sachs Group, Inc. (GS)
Lehman Brothers Holdings (LEH)
Merrill Lynch & Co., Inc. (MER)
Morgan Stanley Dean Witter & Co. (MWD)

Oil Services
Baker Hughes Inc. (BHI)
BJ Services (BJS)
Halliburton Co (HAL)
Schlumberger Ltd (SLB)
Weatherford International (WFT)

Retail
Autozone Inc. (AZO)
Best Buy Company Inc. (BBY)
Circuit City Stores (CC)
Home Depot Inc. (HD)
Wal-Mart Stores Inc. (WMT)

Semiconductor Components
Broadcom Corp-CL A (BRCM)
Intel Corporation (INTC)
Micron Technology Inc. (MU)
Texas Instruments (TXN)
Xilinx Inc (XLNX)

As you can see, these indexes are referred to as being narrow-based because the underlying equities that make up each particular index are few in number. As a result, they will track the movements of the representative sector more closely, and may allow a more effective means of hedging an equity portfolio or speculating on directional moves of a particular market sector.

For example, the exchange indicates on its website (http://www.OneChicago.com) that a particular application for hedging may be to sell the financial index to hedge against adverse movement in interest rates. Since interest rates that rise are typically bearish for financial sector based equities, it may offset a decline in shares that you hold in your portfolio in the event that a sudden move higher occurs in interest rates. Other economic announcements or events may also effect the holdings in your portfolio across different sectors, resulting in the need to hedge exposure through the use of a narrow-based index.

For some time, investors have been critical of using larger index-based products for hedging or speculating. This was due in part to the fact that such indexes are so well diversified that they fail to reflect movements that may occur in just a handful of underlying equities in a particular sector. Now that more narrow-based index products are trading, it may be easier to hedge industry specific risk for a portfolio. Additionally, today's markets are heavily section rotational, so narrow-based indices are the perfect vehicle for speculating in different sectors of the underlying equity market. Lately equities tend to move by industry rather than individually, which adds further weight to the argument for using narrow-based indices in speculative trading applications. Furthermore, spreads mentioned earlier in this text can also be applied through the use of the indexes, further reducing risk while providing opportunity for gain.

Appendix 3

TAX CONSIDERATIONS

According to general tax principals for trading securities, gains that are classified as being long-term in nature are taxed at a rate of 20 percent, while short-term gains are taxed at the investor's income tax rate. The breakdown between these two time frames is anything over 12 months is long-term while any investment with a duration of less than 12 months is considered short-term.

The Internal Revenue Service has enforced tax codes that treat any futures contract trading in what is referred to as a "60/40 split." Because futures trading is considered short-term due to the nature of the contracts to expire at a predetermined date, this treatment is considered fair to all market participants. The 60/40 split means that the first 60 percent of gains that an investor accrues from futures trading activity is taxed at a rate of 20 percent, while the remaining 40 percent of gains from futures trading activity is taxed at a rate equal to the income tax rate of that particular investor.

For example, if an investor accrues total gains from futures investing over the course of a single tax year that equal $10,000, then $6000 of this revenue would be taxed at a rate of 20 percent, equal to $1200, while the remaining amount of gain equaling $4000, would be taxed at the investor's personal tax rate (depending on total income). Additional rules apply to individual investment strategies, which may vary.

Capital gains from buying single security futures are treated as short-term gains, unless the investor holds a contract through to delivery. In this case, tax rules would apply as if the underlying asset was held for the entire duration of the trade. Therefore, if the contract was held through to delivery and delivery was taken on the underlying shares, tax considerations would be that the asset be taxed according to traditional investment holdings (as if the underlying shares had been held from day one).

Regarding the short sale of a single security futures contract, the current tax treatment involves determining if delivery of shares has occurred. In other words, until the actual delivery of shares takes place, or as the tax code states until the investor has custody of the underlying asset. This means that the gain or loss is not realized until the position is closed out or the shares are delivered, whichever comes first.

These guidelines are meant to be an overview for investors. It is critical to check with your personal tax advisor or attorney regarding tax treatment for single security futures trading as the tax codes regarding this new product are continually evolving.

Appendix 4

SECURITY FUTURES CURRENTLY AVAILABLE FOR TRADING

Underlying Security	Exchange(s) Where Traded
American Express (AXP)	OneChicago
Advanced Micro Devices (AMD)	NQLX
American International Group (AIG)	OneChicago, NQLX
Amgen Inc. (AMGN)	OneChicago, NQLX
AMR Corp/Del (AMR)	OneChicago
AOL Time Warner, Inc. (AOL)	OneChicago, NQLX
Applied Materials (AMAT)	OneChicago, NQLX
AT&T Corporation (T)	OneChicago, NQLX
Bank Of America Corp (BAC)	OneChicago, NQLX
Bank One (ONE)	OneChicago
Best Buy Company Inc. (BBY)	OneChicago
Biogen Inc. (BGEN)	OneChicago
Bristol-Myers Squibb Co (BMY)	OneChicago, NQLX
Broadcom Corp-Cl A (BRCM)	OneChicago
Brocade Communications Sys (BRCD)	OneChicago, NQLX
Cephalon Inc. (CEPH)	OneChicago
Check Point Software Tech (CHKP)	OneChicago
ChevronTexaco Corp (CVX)	OneChicago, NQLX
Cisco Systems, Inc. (CSCO)	OneChicago, NQLX

Citigroup, Inc. (C)	OneChicago, NQLX
Coca-Cola Company (KO)	OneChicago, NQLX
Dell Computer Corporation (DELL)	OneChicago, NQLX
eBay, Inc. (EBAY)	OneChicago, NQLX
EMC Corporation (EMC)	OneChicago, NQLX
Emulex Corp (EMLX)	OneChicago
Exxon Mobil Corporation (XOM)	OneChicago, NQLX
Ford Motor Company (F)	OneChicago, NQLX
General Electric Company (GE)	OneChicago, NQLX
General Motors Corp (GM)	OneChicago, NQLX
Genzyme Corp—Genl Division (GENZ)	OneChicago, NQLX
Goldman Sachs Group, Inc. (GS)	OneChicago
Halliburton Co (HAL)	OneChicago
Home Depot Inc. (HD)	OneChicago, NQLX
Honeywell International (HON)	NQLX
Idec Pharmaceuticals Corp (IDPH)	OneChicago
Intel Corporation (INTC)	OneChicago, NQLX
International Business Machines (IBM)	OneChicago, NQLX
InVision Technologies Inc. (INVN)	OneChicago
J.P. Morgan Chase & Co. (JPM)	OneChicago, NQLX
Johnson & Johnson (JNJ)	OneChicago, NQLX
Juniper Networks Inc. (JNPR)	NQLX
KLA-Tencor Corporation (KLAC)	OneChicago
Krispy Kreme Doughnuts Inc. (KKD)	OneChicago
Merck & Co., Inc. (MRK)	OneChicago, NQLX
Merrill Lynch & Co., Inc. (MER)	OneChicago, NQLX
Micron Technology Inc. (MU)	OneChicago, NQLX
Microsoft Corporation (MSFT)	OneChicago, NQLX
Morgan Stanley Dean Witter & Co. (MWD)	OneChicago, NQLX
Motorola, Inc. (MOT)	OneChicago
Newmont Mining Corp Hldg Co (NEM)	OneChicago
Nokia Corporation ADR (NOK)	OneChicago
Northrop Grumman Corp (NOC)	OneChicago
Novellus Systems Inc. (NVLS)	OneChicago

Oracle Corporation (ORCL)	OneChicago, NQLX
PepsiCo Inc. (PEP)	OneChicago, NQLX
Pfizer (PFE)	OneChicago, NQLX
Philip Morris (MO)	OneChicago
Procter & Gamble Co (PG)	OneChicago, NQLX
QLogic Corp (QLGC)	OneChicago
QUALCOMM, Inc. (QCOM)	OneChicago, NQLX
SBC Communications Inc. (SBC)	OneChicago, NQLX
Schlumberger Ltd (SLB)	OneChicago
Siebel Systems, Inc. (SEBL)	OneChicago, NQLX
Sprint Corp-PCS Group (PCS)	OneChicago
Starbucks Corp (SBUX)	OneChicago
Sun Microsytems (SUNW)	OneChicago, NQLX
Symantec Corp (SYMC)	OneChicago
Texas Instruments Incorporated (TXN)	OneChicago, NQLX
Tyco International Ltd (TYC)	OneChicago
UAL Corp (UAL)	OneChicago
VERITAS Software Corporation (VRTS)	OneChicago, NQLX
Verizon Communications Inc. (VZ)	OneChicago, NQLX
Wal-Mart Stores Inc. (WMT)	OneChicago, NQLX
Walt Disney Company (DIS)	NQLX
Xilinx Inc. (XLNX)	OneChicago

Appendix 5

USEFUL WEB SITE REFERENCE GUIDE

Web Site	Description
http://www.OneChicago.com	This is the official website of the OneChicago LLC exchange, and provides useful contract specifications and analytical tools, as well as important product announcements.
http://www.NQLX.com	This is the official website for the NASDAQ-LIFFE security futures exchange, and provides useful contract specifications and analytical tools, as well as important product announcements.
http://www.IslandFutures.com	This is the official website for the ISLAND futures group. They can also be accessed through their securities website http://www.islandfutures.com.
http://www.AMEX.com	This is the official website for the American Stock Exchange that will contain information regarding their single security futures products.

http://www.thectr.com

The Center for Futures and
Financial Education provides a
great deal of information for
beginning as well as experienced
traders interested in the financial
markets.

http://www.stockcharts.com

This website provides interactive
charting services that are very
useful in forecasting equity and
market trends.

http://www.CFTC.gov

This is the official website for the
Commodities Futures Trading
Commission. News releases and
regulatory issue regarding security
futures can be found at this
website.

http://www.SEC.gov

This is the official website of the
United States Securities and
Exchange Commission. They will
update regulatory issues regarding
single security futures.

http://www.nfa.futures.org

This is the National Futures
Exchange website, and it posts
information regarding various
regulatory and licensing
requirements for trading single
security futures products.

Glossary 1

FUTURES AND OPTIONS TERMINOLOGY*

Across the board   All the months of a particular futures contract or futures option contract, for example, if all the copper contracts open limit up, they were limit up across the board.

Actuals   The physical or cash commodity, which is different from a futures contract. *See Cash commodity/cash market.*

Arbitrage   The purchase of a commodity against the simultaneous sale of a commodity to profit from unequal prices. The two transactions may take place on different exchanges, between two different commodities, in different delivery months, or between the cash and futures markets. *See Spreading.*

Arbitration   The procedure available to customers for the settlement of disputes. Brokers and exchange members are required to participate in arbitration to settle disputes. Arbitration is available through the exchanges, the NFA, and the CFTC.

Assignment   Options are exercised through the option purchaser's broker, who notifies the clearinghouse of the option's exercise. The clearinghouse then notifies the option seller that the buyer has exercised. When futures options are exercised, the buyer of a call is assigned a long futures contract, and the seller receives the corresponding short. Conversely, the buyer of a put is assigned a short futures contract upon exercise, while the seller receives the corresponding long.

At the market   When issued, this order is to buy or sell a futures or options contract as soon as possible at the best possible price. *See Market order.*

At-the-money   An option when its strike price is equal, or approximately equal, to the current market price of the underlying futures contract.

*Glossary courtesy of The Center for Futures Education, Inc.

Bar chart   A graphic representation of price movement disclosing the high, low, close, and sometimes the opening prices for the day. A vertical line is drawn to correspond with the price range for the day, while a horizontal tick pointing to the left reveals the opening price, and a tick to the right indicates the closing price. After days of charting, patterns start to emerge, which technicians interpret for their price predictions.

Basis   The difference between the cash price and the futures price of a commodity: Cash – Futures = Basis. Also used to refer to the difference between prices at different markets or between different commodity grades.

Bear call spread   The purchase of a call with a high strike price against the sale of a call with a lower strike price. The maximum profit receivable is the net premium received (premium received – premium paid), while the maximum loss is calculated by subtracting the net premium received from the difference between the high strike price and the low strike price (high strike price – low strike price net premium received). A bear call spread should be entered when lower prices are expected. It is a type of vertical spread.

Bear market (bear/bearish)   When prices are declining, the market is said to be a *bear market*; individuals who anticipate lower prices are *bears*. Situations believed to bring with them lower prices are considered *bearish*.

Bear put spread   The purchase of a put with a high strike price against the sale of a put with a lower strike price in expectation of declining prices. The maximum profit is calculated as follows: (high strike price – low strike price) – net premium received where net premium received = premiums paid – premiums received.

Bear spread   Sale of a near month futures contract against the purchase of a deferred month futures contract in expectation of a price decline in the near month relative to the more distant month. (e.g., selling a December contract and buying the more distant March contract)

Bearish   When market prices tend to go lower, the market is said to be *bearish*. Someone who expects prices to trend lower is *bearish*.

Beta   A measure correlating stock price movement to the movement of an index. Beta is used to determine the number of contracts required to hedge with stock index futures or futures options.

Bid   The request to buy a futures contract at a specified price; the opposite of offer.

Board of trade   An exchange or association of persons participating in the business of buying or selling any commodity or receiving it for sale on consignment. Generally, an exchange in which commodity futures and/or futures options are traded. *See also Contract market and Exchange.*

Board orders   *See Market-if-touched order.*

Break   A sudden price move; prices may break up or down.

Break-even   Refers to a price at which an option's cost is equal to the proceeds acquired by exercising the option. The buyer of a call pays a premium. His break-even point is calculated by adding the premium paid to the call's strike price. For example, if you purchase a May 58 cotton call for 2.25¢/lb. when May cotton futures are at 59.48¢/lb., the break-even price is 60.25¢/lb. (58.00¢/lb. + 2.25¢/lb. = 60.25¢/lb.). For a put purchaser, the break-even point is calculated by subtracting the premium paid from the put's strike price. Note that, for puts, you do not exercise unless the futures price is below the break-even point.

Broker   An agent who executes trades (buy or sell orders) for customers. The broker receives a commission for these services. Other terms used to describe a broker include: Account Executive (AE), Associated Person (AP), Registered Commodity Representative (RCR), and NFA Associate.

Bull call spread   The purchase of a call with a low strike price against the sale of a call with a higher strike price; prices are expected to rise. The maximum potential profit is calculated as follows: (high strike price – low strike price) – net premium cost, in which net premium cost = premiums paid – premiums received. The maximum possible loss is the net premium cost.

Bull market (bull/bullish)   When prices are rising, the market is said to be a *bull market*; individuals who anticipate higher prices are considered *bulls*. Situations arising that are expected to bring higher prices are called *bullish*.

Bull put spread   The purchase of a put with a low strike price against the sale of a call with a higher strike price; prices are expected to rise. The maximum potential profit equals the net premium received. The maximum loss is calculated as follows: (high strike price – low strike price) – net premium received in which net premium received = premiums paid – premiums received.

Bull spread   The purchase of near month futures contracts against the sale of deferred month futures contracts in expectation of a price rise in the near month relative to the deferred. One type of bull spread, the limited risk spread, is placed only when the market is near full carrying charges. *See Limited risk spread.*

Bullish   A tendency for prices to move up.

Butterfly spread   Established by buying an at-the-money option, selling two out-of-the-money options, and buying an out-of-the-money option. A butterfly is entered anytime a credit can be received (i.e., the premiums received are more than those paid).

Buy stop/sell stop order   *See Stop order.*

Buyer   Anyone who enters the market to purchase a good or service. For futures, a buyer can be establishing a new position by purchasing a contract (going long), or liquidating an existing short position.

Puts and calls can also be bought, giving the buyer the right to purchase or sell an underlying futures contract at a set price within a certain period of time.

Calendar spread   The sale of an option with a nearby expiration against the purchase of an option with the same strike price, but a more distant expiration. The loss is limited to the net premium paid, while the maximum profit possible depends on the time value of the distant option when the nearby expires. The strategy takes advantage of time value differentials during periods of relatively flat prices.

Call   The period at market opening or closing during which futures contract prices are established by auction.

Call option   A contract giving the buyer the right to purchase something within a certain period of time at a specified price. The seller receives money (the premium) for the sale of this right. The contract also obligates the seller to deliver, if the buyer exercises his right to purchase.

Carrying charges   The cost of storing a physical commodity, consisting of interest on the invested funds, insurance, storage fees, and other incidental costs. Carrying costs are usually reflected in the difference between futures prices for different delivery months. When futures prices for deferred contract maturities are higher than for nearby maturities, it is a carrying charge market. A full carrying charge market reimburses the owner of the physical commodity for its storage until the delivery date.

Carryover   The portion of existing supplies remaining from a prior production period.

Cash commodity/cash market   The actual or physical commodity. The market in which the physical commodity is traded, as opposed to the futures market, in which contracts for future delivery of the physical commodity are traded. *See also Actuals.*

Cash flow   The cash receipts and payments of a business. This differs from net income after taxes in that non-cash expenses are not included in a cash flow statement. If more cash comes in than goes out, there is a positive cash flow, while more outgoing cash causes a negative cash flow.

Cash forward contract   *See Forward contract.*

Cash market   A market in which goods are purchased either immediately for cash, as in a cash and carry contract, or in which they are contracted for presently, with delivery occurring at the time of payment. All terms of the contract are negotiated between the buyer and seller.

Cash price   The cost of a good or service when purchased for cash. In commodity trading, the cash price is the cost of buying the physical commodity on the current day in the spot market, rather than buying contracts in the futures market.

Cash settlement Instead of having the actuals delivered, cash is transferred upon settlement.

Certificate of Deposit (CD) A large time deposit with a bank, having a specific maturity date and yield stated on the certificate. CDs usually are issued with $100,000 to $1,000,000 face values.

Certificated stock Stocks of a physical commodity that have been inspected by the exchange and found to be acceptable for delivery on a futures contract. They are stored at designated delivery points.

Charting When technicians analyze the futures markets, they employ graphs and charts to plot the price movements, volume, open interest, or other statistical indicators of price movement. *See also Technical analysis* and *Bar chart.*

Churning A situation in which a broker engages in excessive trading to derive a profit from commissions while ignoring his client's best interests.

Clearinghouse An agency associated with an exchange that guarantees all trades, thus assuring contract delivery and/or financial settlement. The clearinghouse becomes the buyer for every seller, and the seller for every buyer.

Clearing margin Funds deposited by a futures commission merchant with its clearing member.

Clearing member A clearinghouse member responsible for executing client trades. Clearing members also monitor the financial capability of their clients by requiring sufficient margins and position reports.

Close or closing range The range of prices found during the last two minutes of trading. The average price during the close is used as the settlement price from which the allowable trading range is set for the following day.

Commercials Firms that are actively hedging their cash grain positions in the futures markets (e.g., millers, exporters, and elevators).

Commission The fee that clearing houses charge their clients to buy and sell futures and futures options contracts. Also the fee that brokers charge their clients.

Commission house Another term used to describe brokerage firms because they earn their living by charging commissions. *See also Futures Commission Merchant.*

Commodity A good or item of trade or commerce. Goods tradable on an exchange, such as corn, gold, or hogs, as distinguished from instruments or other intangibles like T-Bills or stock indexes.

Commodity Credit Corporation (CCC) A government-owned corporation established in 1933 to support prices through purchases of excess crops, to control supply through acreage reduction programs, and to devise export programs.

Commodity Futures Trading Commission (CFTC) A federal regulatory agency established in 1974 to administer the Commodity Exchange Act. This agency monitors the futures and futures options markets through the exchanges, futures commission merchants and their agents, floor brokers, and customers who use the markets for either commercial or investment purposes.

Commodity pool   A venture in which several persons contribute funds to trade futures or futures options. A commodity pool is not to be confused with a joint account.

Commodity Pool Operator (CPO)   An individual or firm who accepts funds, securities, or property for trading commodity futures contracts, and combines customer funds into pools. The larger the account, or pool, the more staying power the CPO and his clients have. They may be able to last through a dip in prices until the position becomes profitable. CPOs must register with the CFTC and NFA, and are closely regulated.

Commodity-product spread   The simultaneous purchase (or sale) of a commodity and the sale (or purchase) of the products derived from that commodity; for example, buying soybeans and selling soybean oil and meal. This is known as a *crush spread*. Another example is the crack spread, in which the crude oil is purchased and gasoline and heating oil are sold.

Commodity Trading Advisor (CTA)   An individual or firm that directly or indirectly advises others about buying or selling futures or futures options. Analyses, reports, or newsletters concerning futures may be issued by a CTA; he may also engage in placing trades for other people's accounts. CTAs are required to be registered with the CFTC and to belong to the NFA.

Confirmation statement   After a futures or options position has been initiated, a statement must be issued to the customer by the commission house. The statement contains the number of contracts bought or sold, and the prices at which the transactions occurred, and is sometimes combined with a purchase and sale statement.

Congestion   A charting term used to describe an area of sideways price movement. Such a range is thought to provide support or resistance to price action.

Contract   A legally enforceable agreement between two or more parties for performing, or refraining from performing, some specified act (e.g., delivering 5000 bushels of corn at a specified grade, time, place, and price).

Contract market   Designated by the CFTC, a contract market is a board of trade set up to trade futures or option contracts, and generally means any exchange on which futures are traded. *See Board of trade* and *Exchange*.

Contract month   The month in which a contract comes due for delivery according to the futures contract terms.

Contrarian theory   A theory suggesting that the general consensus about trends is wrong. The contrarian takes the opposite position from the majority opinion to capitalize on overbought or oversold situations.

Controlled account   *See Discretionary accounts.*

Convergence   The coming together of futures prices and cash market prices on the last trading day of a futures contract.

Conversion   The sale of a cash position and investment of part of the proceeds in the margin for a long futures position. The remaining money is placed in an interest-bearing instrument. This practice allows the investor/dealer to receive high rates of interest, and take delivery of the commodity if needed.

Conversion factor   A figure published by the CBOT used to adjust a T-Bond hedge for the difference in maturity between the T-Bond contract specifications and the T-Bonds being hedged.

Cover   Used to indicate the repurchase of previously sold contracts as, "he covered his short position." Short covering is synonymous with liquidating a short position or evening up a short position.

Covered position   A transaction that has been offset with an opposite and equal transaction; for example, if a gold futures contract had been purchased, and later a call option for the same commodity amount and delivery date was sold, the trader's option position is "covered." He holds the futures contract deliverable on the option if it is exercised. Also used to indicate the repurchase of previously sold contracts as, he covered his short position.

Crack spread   A type of commodity-product spread involving the purchase of crude oil futures and the sale of gasoline and heating oil futures.

Cross-hedge   A situation in which a hedger's cash commodity and the commodities traded on an exchange are not always of the same type, quality, or grade. A hedger may have to select a similar commodity (one with similar price movement) for his hedge.

Crush spread   A type of commodity-product spread that involves the purchase of, for example, soybean futures and the sale of soybean oil and soybean meal futures.

Day order   An order which, if not executed during the trading session the day it is entered, automatically expires at the end of the session. All orders are assumed to be day orders unless specified otherwise.

Day-trader   Futures or options traders (often active on the trading floor) who usually initiate and offset position during a single trading session.

Dealer option   A put or call on a physical good written by a firm dealing in the underlying cash commodity. A dealer option does not originate on, nor is it subject to the rules of an exchange.

Debt instruments   (1) Generally, legal IOUs created when one person borrows money from (becomes indebted to) another person; (2) Any commercial paper, bank CDs, bills, bonds, and so on; (3) A document evidencing a loan or debt. Debt instruments such as T-Bills and T-Bonds are traded on the CME and CBOT, respectively.

Deck   All orders in a floor broker's possession that have not yet been executed.

Deep in-the-money   An option that is so far in-the-money that it is unlikely to go out-of-the-money prior to expiration. It is an arbitrary term and can be used to describe different options by different people.

Deep out-of-the-money   Used to describe an option that is unlikely to go in-the-money prior to expiration. An arbitrary term.

Default   Failure to meet a margin call or to make or take delivery. The failure to perform on a futures contract as required by exchange rules.

Deferred delivery   Futures trading in distant delivery months.

Deferred pricing   A method of pricing in which a producer sells his commodity now and buys a futures contract to benefit from an expected price increase. Although some people call this hedging, the producer is actually speculating that he can make more money by selling the cash commodity and buying a futures contract than by storing the commodity and selling it later. (If the commodity has been sold, what could he be hedging against?)

Delivery   The transportation of a physical commodity (actuals or cash) to a specified destination in fulfillment of a futures contract.

Delivery month   The month during which a futures contract expires, and delivery is made on that contract.

Delivery notice   Notification of delivery by the clearinghouse to the buyer. Such notice is initiated by the seller in the form of a Notice of Intention to Deliver.

Delivery point   The location approved by an exchange for tendering and accepting goods deliverable according to the terms of a futures contract.

Delta   The correlation factor between a futures price fluctuation and the change in premium for the option on that futures contract. Delta changes from moment to moment as the option premium changes.

Demand   The desire to purchase economic goods or services (and the financial ability to do so) at the market price constitutes demand. When many purchasers demand a good at the market price, their combined purchasing power constitutes demand. As this combined demand increases or decreases, other things remaining constant, the price of the good tends to rise or fall.

Derivative   A financial instrument whose characteristics and value are based on the characteristics and value of another financial instrument or product.

Diagonal spread   Uses options with different expiration dates and different strike prices; for example, a trader might purchase a 26 December German Mark put and sell a 28 September German Mark put when the futures price is $0.2600/DM.

Direct hedge   When the hedger has (or needs) the commodity (grade, etc.) specified for delivery in the futures contract, he is direct hedging. When he does not have the specified commodity, he is cross-hedging.

Discount   (1) Quality differences between those standards set for some futures contracts and the quality of the delivered goods. If inferior goods are tendered for delivery, they are graded below the standard, and a lesser amount is paid for them. They are sold at a discount; (2) Price differences between futures of different delivery months; (3) For short-term financial instruments, *discount* may be used to describe the way interest is paid. Short-term instruments are purchased at a price below the face value (discount). At maturity, the full face value is paid to the purchaser. The interest is imputed, rather than being paid as coupon interest during the term of the instrument; for example, if a T-Bill is purchased for $974,150.00, the price is quoted at $89.66, or a discount of 10.34 percent (100.00 – 89.66 = 10.34). At maturity, the holder receives $1,000,000.

Discount rate   The interest rate charged by the Federal Reserve to its member banks (banks that belong to the Federal Reserve System) for funds they borrow. This rate has a direct bearing on the interest rates banks charge its customers. When the discount rate is increased, the banks must raise the rates it charges to cover its increased cost of borrowing. Likewise, when the discount rate is lowered, banks are able to charge lower interest rates on its loans.

Discretionary accounts   An arrangement in which an account holder gives power of attorney to another person, usually his broker, to make decisions to buy or to sell without notifying the owner of the account. Discretionary accounts often are called managed or controlled accounts.

Downtrend   A channel of downward price movement.

Economic good   That which is scarce and useful to mankind.

Economy of scale   A lower cost per unit produced, achieved through large-scale production. The lower cost can result from better tools of production, greater discounts on purchased supplies, production of by-products, and/or equipment or labor used at production levels closer to capacity. A large cattle feeding operation may be able to benefit from economies such as lower unit feed costs, increased mechanization, and lower unit veterinary costs.

Efficiency   Because of futures contracts' standardization of terms, large numbers of traders from all walks of life may trade futures, thus allowing prices to be determined readily (it is more likely that someone will want a contract at any given price). The more readily prices are discovered, the more efficient are the markets.

Elasticity   A term used to describe the effects price, supply, and demand have on one another for a particular commodity. A commodity is said to have elastic demand when a price change affects the demand for that commodity; it has supply elasticity when a change in price causes a change in the production of the commodity. A commodity has inelastic supply or demand when they are unaffected by a change in price.

Equity   The value of a futures trading account with all open positions valued at the going market price.

Eurodollar Time Deposits   U.S. dollars on deposit outside the United States, either with a foreign bank or a subsidiary of a U.S. bank. The interest paid for these dollar deposits generally is higher than that for funds deposited in U.S. banks because the foreign banks are riskier and they will not be supported or nationalized by the U.S. government upon default. Furthermore, they may pay higher rates of interest because they are not regulated by the U.S. government.

Even up   To close out, liquidate, or cover an open position.

Exchange   An association of persons who participate in the business of buying or selling futures contracts or futures options. A forum or place where traders gather to buy or sell economic goods. *See also Board of trade* or *Contract market.*

Exchanges in the United States

Cantor Exchange (CX)
Chicago Board of Trade (CBT)
Chicago Mercantile Exchange (CME)
Kansas City Board of Trade (KCBT)
Minneapolis Grain Exchange (MGEX)
New York Board of Trade (NYBOT)
New York Mercantile Exchange (NYMEX)

International Exchanges

Bourse de Montreal (ME)
EUREX Frankfurt (EUREX)
Euronext Amsterdam/Brussels/Paris (ENP)
Hong Kong Exchange and Clearing Ltd. (HKEx)
International Petroleum Exchange of London (IPE)
London International Financial Futures Exchange (LIFFE)
Singapore Commodity Exchange Ltd. (SICOM)
Singapore Exchange Ltd. (SGX)
Sydney Futures Exchange Corporation Ltd. (SFE)
The Tokyo Commodity Exchange (TOCOM)
The Tokyo International Financial Futures Exchange (TIFFE)
Winnipeg Commodity Exchange (WCE)

Exchange rates   The price of foreign currencies. If it costs $0.42 to buy one Swiss Franc, the exchange rate is 0.4200. As one currency is inflated faster or slower than the other, the exchange rate will change, reflecting the change in relative value. The currency being inflated faster is said to be becoming weaker because more of it must be exchanged for the same amount of the other currency. As a currency becomes weaker, exports are encouraged because others can buy more with their relatively stronger currencies.

Exercise   A situation in which a call purchaser takes delivery of the underlying long futures position, or in which a put purchaser takes delivery of the underlying short futures position. Only option buyers may exercise their options; option sellers have a passive position.

Expiration   An option is a wasting asset (i.e., it has a limited life, usually nine months). At the end of its life, it either becomes worthless (if it is at-the-money or out-of-the-money), or is automatically exercised for the amount by which it is in-the-money.

Expiration date   The final date at which an option may be exercised. Many options expire on a specified date during the month prior to the delivery month for the underlying futures contract.

Ex-pit transactions   Occurring outside the futures exchange trading pits. This includes cash transactions, the delivery process, and the changing of brokerage firms while maintaining open positions. All other transactions involving futures contracts must occur in the trading pits through open outcry.

Federal Reserve Board   The functions of the board include formulating and executing monetary policy, overseeing the Federal Reserve Banks, and regulating and supervising member banks. Monetary policy is implemented through the purchase or sale of securities, and by raising or lowering the discount rate—the interest rate at which banks borrow from the Federal Reserve. A board of directors comprised of seven members that directs the federal banking system, is appointed by the President of the United States and confirmed by the Senate.

Fill or Kill order (FOK)   Also known as a quick order, is a limit order which, if not filled immediately, is canceled.

Financial futures   Include interest rate futures, currency futures, and index futures. The financial futures market currently is the fastest growing of all the futures markets.

First notice day   Notice of intention to deliver a commodity in fulfillment of an expiring futures contract can be given to the clearinghouse by a seller (and assigned by the clearinghouse to a buyer) no earlier than the first notice day. First notice days differ depending on the commodity.

Floor broker   A person who executes orders on the trading floor of an exchange on behalf of other people. They are also known as pit brokers because the trading area has steps down into a pit where the brokers stand to execute their trades.

Floor trader   Exchange members present on the exchange floor to make trades on their own behalf. They may be referred to as scalpers or locals.

Forward contract   A contract entered into by two parties who agree to the future purchase or sale of a specified commodity. This differs from a futures contract in that the participants in a forward contract are contracting directly with each other, rather than through a clearing corporation. The terms of a forward contract are negotiated between the buyer and seller, while exchanges set the terms of futures contracts.

Forward pricing   The practice of locking-in a price in the future, either by entering into a cash forward contract or a futures contract. In a cash forward contract, the parties usually intend to tender and accept the commodity, while futures contracts are generally offset, with a cash transaction occurring after offset.

Free market   A marketplace in which individuals can act in their own best interest, free from outside forces (freedom means freedom from government) restricting their choices, or regulating or subsidizing product prices. Free market also refers to the political system in which the means of production are owned by free, non-regulated individuals.

Full carry   When the difference between futures contract month prices equals the full cost of carrying (storing) the commodity from one delivery period to the next. Carrying charges include insurance, interest, and storage.

Fundamental analysis   The study of specific factors, such as weather, wars, discoveries, and changes in government policy, which influence supply and demand and, consequently, prices in the market place.

Futures Commission Merchant (FCM)   An individual or organization accepting orders to buy or sell futures contracts or futures options, and accepting payment for his services. FCMs must be registered with the CFTC and the NFA, and maintain a minimum capitalization of $300,000.

Futures contract   A standardized and binding agreement to buy or sell a predetermined quantity and quality of a specified commodity at a future date. Standardization of the contracts enhances their transferability. Futures contracts can be traded only by auction on exchanges registered with the CFTC.

Futures Industry Association (FIA)   The futures industry's national trade association.

Gambler   One who seeks profit by taking noncalculated or man-made risks. If one flips a coin to determine his course of action, he is gambling as to the outcome. If one bets on the horses, the outcome of a sports event, or some other man-made event, he is gambling. A gambler is distinguished from a speculator in that a speculator could profit from price change if he knew enough about the supply and demand factors used to determine price. He also trades economic goods, thus benefiting mankind.

Gap   A term used by technicians to describe a jump or drop in prices (i.e., prices skipped a trading range). Gaps are usually filled at a later date.

Geometric index   An index in which a 1 percent change in the price of any two stocks comprising the index impacts on it equally. The Value Line Average index is composed of 1700 stocks and is a geometric index.

Give-up   A trade executed by one broker for the client of another broker and then "given-up" to the regular broker (e.g., a floor broker with discretion must have another broker execute the trade).

Good Till Cancelled (GTC)   A qualifier for any kind of order extending its life indefinitely (i.e., until filled or canceled).

Grantor   Someone who assumes the obligation, not the right, to buy (for a put) or sell (for a call) the underlying futures contract or commodity at the strike price. *See also Writer.*

Guarantee fund   One of two funds established for the protection of customers' monies; the clearing members contribute a percentage of their gross revenues to the guarantee fund. *See also Surplus fund.*

Guided account   An account that has a planned trading strategy and is directed by either a CTA or a FCM. The customer is advised on specific trading positions, which he must approve before an order may be entered. These accounts often require a minimum initial investment, and may use only a predetermined portion of the investment at any particular time. Not to be confused with a discretionary account.

Hedge ratio   The relationship between the number of contracts required for a direct hedge and the number of contracts required to hedge in a specific situation. The concept of hedging is to match the size of a positive cash flow from a gaining futures position with the expected negative cash flow created by unfavorable cash market price movements. If the expected cash flow from a $1 million face-value T-Bill futures contract is one-half as large as the expected cash market loss on a $1 million face-value instrument being hedged (for whatever reason), then two futures contracts are needed to hedge each $1 million of face value. The hedge ratio is 2:1. Hedge ratios are used frequently when hedging with futures options, interest rate futures, and stock index futures, to aid in matching expected cash flows. Generally, the hedge ratio between the number of futures options required and the number of futures contracts is 1:1. For interest rate and stock index futures, the ratios may vary depending on the correlation between price movement of the assets being hedged and the futures contracts or options used to hedge them. Most agricultural hedge ratios are 1:1.

Hedger   One who hedges; one who attempts to transfer the risk of price change by taking an opposite and equal position in the futures or futures option market from that position held in the cash market.

Hedging   Transferring the risk of loss due to adverse price movement
through the purchase or sale of contracts in the futures markets.
The position in the futures market is a substitute for the future
purchase or sale of the physical commodity in the cash market. If
the commodity will be bought, the futures contract is purchased
(long hedge); if the commodity will be sold, the futures contract is
sold (short hedge).

High   The top price paid for a commodity or its option in a given time
period, usually a day or the life of a contract.

Index   A specialized average. Stock indexes may be calculated by establishing a base against which the current value of the stocks,
commodities, bonds, and so on, will change; for example, the S&P
500 index uses the 1941–1943 market value of the 500 stocks as a
base of 10.

Inelasticity   A statistic attempting to quantify the change in supply or
demand for a good, given a certain price change. The more inelastic demand (characteristic of necessities), the less effect a change in
price has on demand for the good. The more inelastic supply, the
less supply changes when the price does.

Inflation   The creation of money by monetary authorities. In more
popular usage, the creation of money that visibly raises the price of
goods and lowers the purchasing power of money. It may be creep-
ing, trotting, or galloping, depending on the rate of money creation
by the authorities. It may take the form of *simple inflation*, in
which case the proceeds of the new money issues accrue to the
government for deficit spending; or it may appear as *credit expansion*, in which case the authorities channel the newly created
money into the loan market. Both forms are inflation in the broader
sense.

Initial margin   When a customer establishes a position, he is required
to make a minimum initial margin deposit to assure the performance of his obligations. Futures margin is earnest money or a performance bond.

Interest   What is paid to a lender for the use of his money and includes
compensation to the lender for three factors: (1) Time value of
money (lender's rate)—the value of today's dollar is more than tomorrow's dollar. Tomorrow's dollars are discounted to reflect the
time a lender must wait to "enjoy" the money, not to mention the
uncertainties tomorrow brings. (2) Credit risk—the risk of repayment varies with the creditworthiness of the borrower. (3) Inflation—as the purchasing power of a dollar declines, more dollars
must be repaid to maintain the same purchasing power. Interest is
one of the components of carrying charges (i.e., the cost of the
money needed to finance the commodity's purchase or storage).
The market rate of interest can also be used to establish an opportunity cost for the funds that are tied up in any investment.

Interest rate futures   Futures contracts traded on long-term and short-term financial instruments: U.S. Treasury bills and bonds and Eurodollar Time Deposits. More recently, futures contracts have developed for German, Italian, and Japanese government bonds, to name a few.

Inter-market   A spread in the same commodity, but on different markets. An example of an inter-market spread would be buying a wheat contract on the Chicago Board of Trade, and simultaneously selling a wheat contract on the Kansas City Board of Trade.

In-the-money   A call is in-the-money when the underlying futures price is greater than the strike price. A put is in-the-money when the underlying futures price is less than the strike price. In-the-money options have intrinsic value.

Intra-market   A spread within a market. An example of an intra-market spread is buying a corn contract in the nearby month and selling a corn contract on the same exchange in a distant month.

Intrinsic value   The amount an option is in-the-money, calculated by taking the difference between the strike price and the market price of the underlying futures contract when the option is in-the-money. A COMEX 350 gold futures call has an intrinsic value of $10 if the underlying gold futures contract is at $360/ounce.

Introducing Broker (IB)   An individual or firm that can perform all the functions of a broker except one. An IB is not permitted to accept money, securities, or property from a customer. An IB must be registered with the CFTC, and conduct its business through an FCM on a fully disclosed basis.

Inverted market   A futures market in which near-month contracts are selling at prices that are higher than those for deferred months. An inverted market is characteristic of a short-term supply shortage. The notable exceptions are interest rate futures, which are inverted when the distant contracts are at a premium to near month contracts.

Last trading day   The last day on which a futures contract is traded.

Law of Demand   Demand exhibits a direct relationship to price. If all other factors remain constant, an increase in demand leads to an increased price, while a decrease in demand leads to a decreased price.

Law of Supply   Supply exhibits an inverse relationship to price. If all other factors hold constant, an increase in supply causes a decreased price, while a decrease in supply causes an increased price.

Letter of acknowledgment   A form received with a Disclosure Document intended for the customer's signature upon reading and understanding the Disclosure Document. The FCM is required to maintain all letters of acknowledgment on file. It may also be known as a Third Party Account Controllers form.

Leverage   The control of a larger sum of money with a smaller amount. By accepting the liability to purchase or deliver the total value of a futures contract, a smaller sum (margin) may be used as earnest money to guarantee performance. If prices move favorably, a large return on the margin can be earned from the leverage. Conversely, a loss can also be large, relative to the margin, due to the leverage.

Liability   (1) In the broad legal sense, responsibility or obligation. For example, a person is liable to pay his debts, under the law; (2) In accounting, any debt owed by an individual or organization. Current, or short-term, liabilities are those to be paid in less than one year (wages, taxes, accounts payable, etc.). Long-term, or fixed, liabilities are those that run for one year or more (mortgages, bonds, etc.); (3) In futures, traders deposit margin as earnest money, but they are liable for the entire value of the contract; (4) In futures options, purchasers of options have their liability limited to the premium they pay; option writers are subject to the liability associated with the underlying deliverable futures contract.

Limit   See Position limit, Price limit, and Variable limit.

Limit move   The increase or decrease of a price by the maximum amount allowed for any one trading session. Price limits are established by the exchanges and approved by the CFTC. They vary from contract to contract.

Limit orders   A customer sets a limit on price or time of execution of a trade, or both; for example, a buy limit order is placed below the market price. A sell limit order is placed above the market price. A sell limit is executed only at the limit price or higher (better), while the buy limit is executed at the limit price or lower (better).

Limited risk   A concept often used to describe the option buyer's position. Because the option buyer's loss can be no greater than the premium he pays for the option, his risk of loss is limited.

Limited risk spread   A bull spread in a market in which the price difference between the two contract months covers the full carrying charges. The risk is limited because the probability of the distant month price moving to a premium greater than full carrying charges is minimal.

Line-bar chart   See Bar chart.

Liquidate   Refers to closing an open futures position. For an open long, this would be selling the contract. For a short position, it would be buying the contract back (short covering, or covering his short).

Liquidity (liquid market)   A market that allows quick and efficient entry or exit at a price close to the last traded price. The ability to liquidate or establish a position quickly is due to a large number of traders willing to buy and sell.

Locals   The floor traders who trade primarily for their own accounts. Although locals are speculators, they provide the liquidity needed by hedgers to transfer the risk of price change.

Long   One who has purchased futures contracts or the cash commodity, but has not taken any action to offset his position. Also, purchasing a futures contract. A trader with a long position hopes to profit from a price increase.

Long hedge   A hedger who is short the cash (needs the cash commodity) buys a futures contract to hedge his future needs. By buying a futures contract when he is short the cash, he is entering a long hedge. A long hedge is also known as a substitute purchase or an anticipatory hedge.

Long-the-basis   A person who owns the physical commodity and hedges her position with a short futures position is said to be long-the-basis. She profits from the basis becoming more positive (stronger); for example, if a farmer sold a January soybean futures contract at $6.00 with the cash market at $5.80, the basis is –.20. If he repurchased the January contract later at $5.50 when the cash price was $5.40, the basis would then be –.10. The long-the-basis hedger profited from the 10> increase in basis.

Low   The smallest price paid during the day or over the life of the contract.

Maintenance margin   The minimum level at which the equity in a futures account must be maintained. If the equity in an account falls below this level, a margin call will be issued, and funds must be added to bring the account back to the initial margin level. The maintenance margin level generally is 75 percent of the initial margin requirement.

Managed account   *See Discretionary account*

Margin   In futures it is a performance bond or "earnest money." Margin money is deposited by both buyers and sellers of futures contracts, as well as sellers of futures options. *See Initial margin.*

Margin call   A call from the clearinghouse to a clearing member (variation margin call), or from a broker to a customer (maintenance margin call), to add funds to their margin account to cover an adverse price movement. The added margin assures the brokerage firm and the clearinghouse that the customer can purchase or deliver the entire contract, if necessary.

Marked to market   The IRS's practice of calculating gains and losses on open futures positions as of the end of the tax year. In other words, taxpayers' open futures positions are marked to the market price as of the end of the tax year and taxes are assessed as if the gains or losses had been realized.

Market-if-touched order (MIT)   This type of order is similar to stop orders in two ways   (1) They are activated when the price reaches the order level; (2) They become market orders once they are activated; however, MIT orders are used differently from stop orders. A buy MIT order is placed below the current market price, and establishes a long position or closes a short position. A sell MIT order is placed above the current market price, and establishes a short position or closes a long position.

Market order   An order to buy or sell futures or futures options contracts as soon as possible at the best available price. Time is of primary importance.

Market-share weighted index   An index in which the impact of a stock price change depends on the market-share that stock controls. For example, a stock with a large market-share, such as IBM with over 600 million shares outstanding, would have a greater impact on a market-share weighted index than a stock with a small market-share, such as Foster Wheeler, with approximately 34 million shares outstanding.

Market-value weighted index   A stock index in which each stock is weighted by market value. A change in the price of any stock will influence the index in proportion to the stock's respective market value. The weighting of each stock is determined by multiplying the number of shares outstanding by the stock's market price per share; therefore, a high-priced stock with a large number of shares outstanding has more impact than a low-priced stock with only a few shares outstanding. The S&P 500 is a value weighted index.

Maturity   The period during which a futures contract can be settled by delivery of the actuals (i.e., the period between the first notice day and the last trading day). Also, the due date for financial instruments.

Maximum price fluctuation   *See Limit move.*

Minimum price fluctuation   The smallest allowable fluctuation in a futures price or futures option premium.

Monthly statement   An account record for each month of activity in a futures and/or futures options account. Quarterly statements are required for inactive accounts.

Moving average   An average of prices for a specified number of days. If it is a three (3) day moving average, for example, the first three days' prices are averaged (1, 2, 3), followed by the next three days' average price (2, 3, 4), and so on. Moving averages are used by technicians to spot changes in trends.

Naked   When an option writer writes a call or put without owning the underlying asset.

National Futures Association (NFA)   A "registered futures association" authorized by the CFTC in 1982 that requires membership for FCMs, their agents and associates, CTAs, and CPOs. This is a self-regulatory group for the futures industry similar to the National Association of Securities Dealers, Inc. in the securities industry.

Nearby   The futures contract month with the earliest delivery period.

Net position   The difference between total open long and open short positions in any one or all combined futures contract months held by an individual.

Neutral calendar spread *See Calendar spread.*

Nominal price (or nominal quotation) The price quotation calculated for futures or options for a period during which no actual trading occurred. These quotations are usually calculated by averaging the bid and asked prices.

Normal market The deferred months' prices for futures contracts are normally higher than the nearby months' to reflect the costs of carrying a contract from now until the distant delivery date. Thus, a normal market, for non-interest rate futures contracts, exists when the distant months are at a premium to the nearby months. For interest rate futures, just the opposite is true. The yield curve dictates that a normal market for interest rate futures occurs when the nearby months are at a premium to the distant months.

Notice of Intention to Deliver During the delivery month for a futures contract, the seller initiates the delivery process by submitting a Notice of Intention to Deliver to the clearinghouse, which, in turn, notifies the oldest outstanding long of the seller's intentions. If the long does not offset his position, he will be called upon to accept delivery of the goods.

Offer To show the desire to sell a futures contract at an established price.

Offset *See Offsetting.*

Offsetting Eliminating the obligation to make or take delivery of a commodity by liquidating a purchase or covering a sale of futures. This is affected by taking an equal and opposite position: either a sale to offset a previous purchase, or a purchase to offset a previous sale in the same commodity, with the same delivery date. If an investor bought an August gold contract on the COMEX, he would offset this obligation by selling an August gold contract on the COMEX. To offset an option, the same option must be bought or sold (i.e., a call or a put with the same strike price and expiration month).

Offsetting positions (1) Taking an equal and opposite futures position to a position held in the cash market. The offsetting futures position constitutes a hedge; (2) Taking an equal and opposite futures position to another futures position, known as a spread or straddle; (3) Buying a futures contract previously sold, or selling a futures contract previously bought, to eliminate the obligation to make or take delivery of a commodity. When trading futures options, an identical option must be bought or sold to offset a position.

Omnibus account An account carried by one Futures Commission Merchant (FCM) with another. The transactions of two or more individual accounts are combined in this type of account. The identities of the individual account holders are not disclosed to the holding FCM. A brokerage firm may have an omnibus account including all its customers with its clearing firm.

One Cancels Other (OCO)   A qualifier used when multiple orders are entered and the execution of one order cancels a second or alternate order.

Open   (1) The first price of the day for a contract on a securities or futures exchange. Futures exchanges post opening ranges for daily trading. Due to the fast-moving operation of futures markets, this range of closely related prices allows market participants to fill contracts at any price within the range, rather than be restricted to one price. The daily prices that are published are approximate medians of the opening range; (2) When markets are in session, or contracts are being traded, the markets are said to be open.

Open interest   For futures, the total number of contracts not yet liquidated by offset or delivery (i.e., the number of contracts outstanding). Open interest is determined by counting the number of transactions on the market (either the total contracts bought or sold, but not both). For futures options, the number of calls or puts outstanding; each type of option has its own open interest figure.

Open outcry   Oral bids and offers made in the trading rings, or pits. Open outcry is required for trading futures and futures options contracts to assure arms-length transactions. This method also assures the buyer and seller that the best available price is obtained.

Open trade equity   The gain or loss on open positions that has not been realized.

Opening range   Upon opening of the market, the range of prices at which transactions occurred. All orders to buy and sell on the opening are filled within the opening range.

Opportunity cost   The price paid for not investing in a different investment. It is the income lost from missed opportunities. Had the money not been invested in land, earning 5 percent, it could have been invested in T-Bills, earning 10 percent. The 5 percent difference is an opportunity cost.

Option contract   A unilateral contract giving the buyer the right, but not the obligation, to buy or sell a commodity, or a futures contract, at a specified price within a certain time period. It is unilateral because only one party (the buyer) has the right to demand performance on the contract. If the buyer exercises his right, the seller (writer or grantor) must fulfill his obligation at the strike price, regardless of the current market price of the asset.

Option seller   See *Grantor* and *Writer*.

Order   (1) In business and trade, making a request to deliver, sell, receive, or purchase goods or services; (2) In the securities and futures trade, instructions to a broker on how to buy or sell. The most common orders in futures markets are market orders and limit orders (which see).

Original margin   See *Initial margin*.

Out-of-the-money   A call is out-of-the-money when the strike price is above the underlying futures price. A put is out-of-the-money when the strike price is below the underlying futures price.

Overbought   A technician's term to describe a market in which the price has risen relatively quickly—too quickly to be justified by the underlying fundamental factors.

Oversold   A technical description for a market in which prices have dropped faster than the underlying fundamental factors would suggest.

Pit   The area on the trading floor of an exchange where futures trading takes place. The area looks like a pit because it is octagonal with steps descending into the center. Traders stand on the various steps, which designate the contract month they are trading.

Pit broker   A person on the exchange floor who trades futures contracts for others in the pits. *See also Floor broker.*

Pit trader   *See Floor trader.*

Point   *See Minimum price fluctuation.*

Point and figure chart   A graphic representation of price movement using vertical rows of "x"s to indicate significant up ticks and "o"s to reflect down ticks. Such charts do not reveal minute price fluctuations, only trends once they have established themselves.

Point balance   Prepared by an FCM, a point balance is a statement indicating profit or loss on all open contracts by computing them to an official closing or settlement price.

Pool   *See Commodity pool.*

Portfolio   The group of investments held by an investor.

Position   Open contracts indicating an interest in the market, be it short or long.

Position limit   The maximum number of futures contracts permitted to be held by speculators or spreaders. The CFTC establishes some position limits, while the exchanges establish others. Hedgers are exempt from position limits.

Position trader   A trader who establishes a position (either by purchasing or selling) and holds it for an extended period of time.

Power of attorney   An agreement establishing an agent-principal relationship. The power of attorney grants the agent authority to act on the principal's behalf under certain designated circumstances. In the futures industry, a power of attorney must be in writing and is valid until revoked or terminated.

Premium   The price paid by a buyer to purchase an option. Premiums are determined by "open outcry" in the pits.

Price   A fixed value of something. Prices are usually expressed in monetary terms. In a free market, prices are set as a result of the interaction of supply and demand in a market; when demand for a product increases and supply remains constant, the price tends to decline. Conversely, when the supply increases and demand remains constant, the price tends to decline; if supply decreases and demand remains constant, prices tend to rise. Today's markets are not purely competitive; prices are affected by government controls and supports that create artificial supplies and demand, and inhibit free trade, thus making price predictions more difficult for those not privileged with inside government information.

Price discovery mechanism   The method by which the price for a particular shipment of a commodity is determined. Factors taken into account include quality, delivery point, and the size of the shipment. For example, if the price of corn is $3.50 per bushel on the CBOT, the local price of corn per bushel can be discovered by taking into consideration the distance from Chicago that corn would have to be shipped, the difference in quality between local and Chicago corn, and the amount of corn to be transported. Once these factors are considered, both the buyer and seller can arrive at a reasonable price for their area.

Price limit   The maximum price rise or decline permitted by an exchange in its commodities. The limit varies from commodity to commodity and may change depending on price volatility (variable price limits). Not all exchanges have limits; those that do set their limits relative to the prior day's settlement, for example, the CBOT may set its limit at 10> for corn. On day two, corn may trade up or down 10> from the previous day's close of $3.00 per bushel (i.e., up to $3.10 or down to $2.90 per bushel).

Price weighted index   A stock index weighted by adding the price of one share of each stock included in the index, and dividing this sum by a constant divisor. The divisor is changed when a stock split or stock dividend occurs because these affect the stock prices. The MMI is a price weighted index.

Primary markets   The principal market for the purchase and sale of physical commodities.

Purchase and sale statement   A form required to be sent to a customer when a position is closed; it must describe the trade, show profit or loss and the commission.

Purchaser   Anyone who enters the market as a buyer of a good, service, futures contract, call, or put.

Pure hedging   A technique used by a hedger who holds his futures or option position without exiting and re-entering the position until the cash commodity is sold. Pure hedging also is known as conservative or true hedging, and is used largely by inexperienced traders who are wary of price fluctuation, but are interested in achieving a target price.

Put   An option contract giving the buyer the right to sell something at a specified price within a certain period of time. A put is purchased in expectation of lower prices. If prices are expected to rise, a put may be sold. The seller receives the premium as compensation for accepting the obligation to accept delivery, if the put buyer exercises his right to sell. *See also Limited risk.*

Pyramiding   Purchasing additional contracts with the profits earned on open positions.

Quotation   Often referred to as a *quote.* The actual, bid, or asked price of futures, options, or cash commodities at a certain time.

Rally   An upward price movement. *See Recovery.*

Range   The difference between the highest and lowest prices recorded during a specified time period, usually one trading session, for a given futures contract or commodity option.

Ratio writing   A situation in which an investor writes more than one option to hedge an underlying futures contract. These options usually are written for different delivery months. Ratio writing expands the profit potential of the investor's option position. For example, an investor would be ratio writing if he is long one August gold contract and he sells (writes) two gold calls, one for February delivery, the other for August.

Recovery   Rising prices following a decline.

Registered Commodity Representative (RCR)   A person registered with the exchange(s) and the CFTC who is responsible for soliciting business, "knowing" his/her customers, collecting margins, submitting orders, and recommending and executing trades for customers. A registered commodity representative is sometimes called a *broker* or *account executive.*

Regulations (CFTC)   The guidelines, rules, and regulations adopted and enforced by the Commodity Futures Trading Commission (the CFTC is a federal regulatory agency established in 1974) in administration of the Commodity Exchange Act.

Reparations   Parties that are wronged during a futures or options transaction may be awarded compensation through the CFTC's claims procedure. This compensation is known as reparations because it "repairs" the wronged party.

Reportable positions   Positions in which the reporting level has been exceeded. *See also Reporting level.*

Reporting level   An arbitrary number of contracts held by a trader that must be reported to the CFTC and the exchange. Reporting levels apply to all traders; hedgers, speculators, and spreaders alike. Once a trader has enough contracts to exceed the reporting level, he has a "special account," and must report any changes in his positions.

Resistance   A horizontal price range in which price hovers due to selling pressure before attempting a downward move.

Retender   The right of a futures contract holder, who has received a notice of intention to deliver from the clearinghouse, to offer the notice for sale on the open market, thus offsetting his obligation to take delivery under the contract. This opportunity is only available for some commodities and only within a certain period of time.

Ring   A designated area on the exchange floor where traders and brokers stand while executing trades. Instead of rings, some exchanges use pits.

Risk disclosure document   A document outlining the risks involved in futures trading. The document includes statements to the effect that: you may lose your entire investment; you may find it impossible to liquidate a position under certain market conditions; spread positions may not be less risky than simple "long" or "short" positions; the use of leverage can lead to large losses as well as large profits; stop-loss orders may not limit your losses; managed commodity accounts are subject to substantial management and advisory charges.

There is a separate risk disclosure document for options that warns of the risks of loss in options trading. This statement includes a description of commodity options, margin requirements, commissions, profit potential, definitions of various terms, and a statement of the elements of the purchase price.

Rolling hedge   Changing a futures hedge from one contract month to another. Rolling a short hedge may be advisable when more time is needed to complete the cash transaction to avoid delivery on the futures contract. Hedge rolling may also be considered to keep the hedge in the less active, more distant months, thus reducing the likelihood of swift price movements and the resulting margin calls.

Round turn   A complete futures transaction (both entry and exit) (e.g., a sale and covering purchase, or a purchase and liquidating sale). Commissions are usually charged on a "round-turn" basis.

Scalper   A floor trader who buys and sells quickly to take advantage of small price fluctuations. Usually a scalper is ready to buy at the bid and sell at the asked price, providing liquidity to the market. The term is used because these traders attempt to "scalp" a small amount on a trade.

Security deposit   *See Margin.*

Segregated account   An account separate from brokerage firm accounts. Segregated accounts hold customer funds so that if a brokerage house becomes insolvent, the customers' funds will be readily recognizable and will not be tied up in litigation for extended periods of time.

Selective hedging   The technique of hedging in which the futures or option position may be lifted and re-entered numerous times before the cash market transaction takes place. A hedge locks-in a target price to minimize risk. Lifting the hedge lifts the risk protection (increasing the possibility of loss), but also allows the potential for gain.

Sell stop order   *See Stop order.*

Selling hedge   *See Short hedge.*

Settlement   The clearinghouse practice of adjusting all futures accounts daily according to gain or loss from price movement.

Settlement price   Established by the clearinghouse from the closing range of prices (the last 30 seconds of the day). The settlement price is used to determine the next day's allowable trading range, and to settle all accounts between clearing members for each contract month. Margin calls and invoice prices for deliveries are determined from the settlement prices. In addition to this, settlement prices are used to determine account values and determine margins for open positions.

Short   Someone who has sold actuals or futures contracts, and has not yet offset the sale; the act of selling the actuals or futures contracts, absent any offset.

Short covering   Buying by shorts to liquidate existing positions.

Short hedge   When a hedger has a long cash position (is holding an inventory or growing a crop) he enters a short hedge by selling a futures contract. A sell or short hedge is also known as a substitute sale.

Short-the-basis   When a person or firm needs to buy a commodity in the future, they can protect themselves against price increases by making a substitute purchase in the futures market. The risk now faced is the risk of a change in basis (cash price – futures price). This hedger is said to be short-the-basis because he will profit if the basis becomes more negative (weaker); for example, if a hedger buys a corn futures contract at 325> when cash corn is 312>, the basis is –.13. If this hedge is lifted with futures at 320> and cash at 300>, the basis is –.20, and the hedger has profited by the $.07 decrease in basis.

Sideways   A market with a narrow price range (i.e., little upward or downward price movement).

Special account   An account that has a reportable position in either futures or futures options. *See also Reporting level.*

Speculation   An attempt to profit from commodity price changes through the purchase and/or sale of commodity futures. In the process, the speculator assumes the risk that the hedger is transferring, and provides liquidity in the market.

Speculator   One who buys and sells stocks, land, and so on, risking his capital with the goal of earning a profit from price changes. In contrast to gamblers, speculators understand and evaluate existing market risks on the basis of data and experience, while gamblers are those who seek out man-made risks or "invest" in a roll of the dice.

Spot   The market in which commodities are available for immediate delivery. It also refers to the cash market price of a specific commodity.

Spread   (1) Positions held in two different futures contracts, taken to profit from the change in the difference between the two contracts' prices (e.g., long a January soybean contract and short a March soybean contract would be a bull spread, used to profit from a narrowing in the difference between the two prices); (2) The difference between the prices of two futures contracts. If January beans are $6.15 and March beans are $6.28, the spread is –.13 or 13> under ($6.15 – 6.28 = –.13).

Spreading   The purchase of one futures contract and the sale of another in an attempt to profit from the change in price differences between the two contracts. Intermarket, intercommodity, interdelivery, and commodity product are examples of spreads.

Stock index futures   Based on stock market indexes, including Standard and Poor's 500, Value Line, NYSE Composite, Nikkei 225, the Major Market Index, and the Over-the-Counter Index, these instruments are used by investors concerned with price changes in a large number of stocks, or with major long-term trends in the stock market indexes. Stock index futures are settled in cash and are generally quoted in ticks of 0.05. To determine the contract value, the quote is generally multiplied by $500.

Stop order   An order that becomes a market order once a certain price level is reached. These orders are often placed with the purpose of limiting losses. They also are used to initiate positions. Buy stop orders are placed at a price above the current market price. Sell stop orders are placed below the market price; for example, if the market price for December corn is 320>, a buy stop order could be placed at 320> or higher, and a sell stop could be placed at 319> or lower. A buy stop order is activated by a bid or trade at or above the stop price. A sell stop is triggered by a trade or offer at or below the stop price.

Stopped out   When a stop order is activated and a position is offset, the trader has been stopped out.

Storage   The cost to store commodities from one delivery month to another. Storage is one of the carrying charges associated with futures.

Straddle   For futures, the same as *spreading*. In futures options, a straddle is formed by going long a call and a put of the same strike price (long straddle), or going short a call and a put of the same strike price (short straddle).

Strangle spread   Makes maximum use of the premium's time value decay. To utilize a strangle most profitably, choose a market that is trading within a given range (volatility peaking), and sell an out-of-the-money call and an out-of-the-money put.

Strike price   The specified price at which an option contract may be exercised. If the buyer of the option exercises (demands performance), the futures contract positions will be entered at the strike price.

Strong basis   A relatively small difference between cash prices and futures prices. A strong basis also can be called a *narrow basis*, or a *more positive basis*; for example, a strong basis usually occurs in grains in the spring before harvest when supplies are low. Buyers must raise their bids to buy. As the cash prices rise, relative to futures prices, the basis strengthens. A strong basis indicates a good selling market, but a poor buying market.

Supply   The quantity of a good available to meet demand. Supply consists of inventories from previous production, current production, and expected future production. Because resources are scarce, supply creates demand. Only price must be determined.

Support   A horizontal price range in which price hovers due to buying pressure before attempting a downward move.

Surplus fund   A fund established by an exchange for the protection of customers' monies; a portion of all clearing fees are set aside for this fund.

Swap   A contract to buy and sell currencies with spot (cash and carry) or forward contracts. The contract provides for the buying and selling to occur at different times; thus, each party acquires a currency it needs for a predetermined period of time at a predetermined price, and locks in a sales price for the currency as well.

Symbols   Letters used to designate which futures or options price and which contract month is desired. Symbols are used to access quotes from various quote systems.

Synthetic position   A hedging strategy combining futures and futures options for price protection and increased profit potential; for example, by buying a put option and selling (writing) a call option, a trader can construct a position that is similar to a short futures position. This position is known as a synthetic short futures position, and shows a profit if the futures prices decline, and receives margin calls if prices rise. Synthetic positions are a form of arbitrage.

Systematic risk   The risk affecting a market in general; for example, if the government's monetary and fiscal policies create inflation, price levels rise, affecting the entire market in much the same way, thus creating a systematic risk. Stock index futures can be used to substantially reduce systematic risk. Compare with unsystematic risk.

Technical analysis   Technical analysis uses charts to examine changes in price patterns, volume of trading, open interest, and rates of change to predict and profit from trends. Someone who follows technical rules (called a technician) believes that prices will anticipate changes in fundamentals.

Technician   One who uses technical analysis to forecast price movements.

Terms   The components, elements, or parts of an agreement. The terms of a futures contract include: which commodity, its quality, the quantity, the time and place of delivery, and its price. All the terms of futures and futures option contracts are standardized by the exchange, except for price, which is determined through open-outcry in the exchanges' trading pits.

Tick   The minimum allowable price fluctuation (up or down) for a futures contract. Different contracts have different size ticks. Ticks can be stated in terms of price per unit of measure, or in dollars and cents. *See also Point.*

Time value   The premium of an out-of-the-money option reflecting the probability that an option will move in-to-the-money before expiration constitutes the time value of the option. There also may be some time value in the premium of an in-the-money option, which reflects the probability of the option moving further into the money. To determine the time value of an in-the-money option, subtract the amount by which the option is in-the-money (intrinsic value) from the total premium.

Trading range   The prices between the high and the low for a specific time period (day, week, life of the contract).

Trend   A significant price movement in one direction or another. Trends may go either up or down.

Underlying futures contract   The futures contract covered by an option; for example, a 300 Dec. corn call's underlying futures contract is the December corn futures contract.

Unsystematic risk   The risk of price change for an individual stock, commodity, or industry. Anything from an oil discovery to a change in management could affect this sort of risk. Unsystematic risks are reduced or eliminated through diversification of holdings, not by hedging with index futures. Compare with systematic risk.

Uptrend   A channel of upward price movement.

Value   The importance placed on something by an individual. Value is subjective and may change according to the circumstances. Something that may be valued highly at one time may be valued less at another time.

Variable limit   Most exchanges set a limit on the maximum daily price movement of some of the futures contracts traded on their floors. They also retain the right to expand these limits if the price moves up- or down-limit for one, two, or three trading days in a row. If the limits automatically change after repeated limit moves, they are known as variable limits.

Variation margin call   A margin call from the clearinghouse to a clearing member. These margin calls are issued when the clearing member's margin has been reduced substantially by unfavorable price moves. The variation margin call must be met within one hour.

Vertical spreads   Also known as a price spread, this type is constructed with options having the same expiration months. This can be done with either calls or puts. *See Bear call spread, Bull call spread, Bear put spread,* and *Bull put spread.*

Volatile A description of a market that is subject to wide price fluctuations. This volatility is often due to a lack of liquidity.

Volume The number of futures contracts, calls, or puts traded in a day. Volume figures use the number of longs or shorts in a day, not both. Such figures are reported on the following day.

Wash sales An illegal process in which simultaneous purchases and sales are made in the same commodity futures contract, on the same exchange, and in the same month. No actual position is taken, although it appears that trades have been made. It is hoped that the apparent activity will induce legitimate trades, thus increasing trading volume and commissions.

Wasting asset A term often used to describe an option because of its limited life. Shortly before its expiration, an out-of-the-money option has only time value, which declines rapidly. For an in-the-money option, only intrinsic value is left upon expiration. For futures options, this is either automatically exercised or cashed out. At the end of its life, an option that has no intrinsic value becomes worthless (i.e., it wastes away).

Weak basis A relatively large difference between cash prices and futures prices. A weak basis also can be called a *wide basis*, or a *more negative basis*: (e.g., a weak basis usually occurs in grains at harvest time when supplies are abundant). Buyers can lower their bids to buy. As the cash prices decline, relative to futures prices, the basis weakens (gets wider). A weak basis indicates a poor selling market, but a good buying market.

Writer One who sells an option. A writer (or grantor) obligates himself to deliver the underlying futures position to the option purchaser, should he decide to exercise his right to the underlying futures contract position. Option writers are subject to margin calls because they may have to produce the long or short futures position. A call writer must supply a long futures position upon exercise, and thus receive a short futures position. A put writer must supply a short futures position upon exercise, and thus receive a long futures position.

Yield (1) The production of a piece of land (e.g., "His land yielded 100 bushels per acre."); (2) The return provided by an investment; for example, if the return on an investment is 10 percent, the investment yields 10 percent.

Glossary 2

SECURITIES
MARKET TERMINOLOGY*

12b-1 fees   Advertising and promotional costs incurred by a mutual fund and charged against the assets in the fund under a Rule 12b-1 plan filed with the SEC. Funds filing a 12b-1 plan may distribute the shares themselves or distribute them through an underwriter and charge an additional sales load. The maximum 12b-1 fee charge is .75 percent of net assets.

401(k) Plan   A qualified corporate retirement plan in which the employee can take part of his or her compensation in the form of contributions to the plan.

401(b) Plan   A qualified retirement plan, similar to a 401(k) but restricted for use by teachers and employees of certain nonprofit organizations.

Accelerated Cost Recovery System (ACRS)   A statutory schedule of depreciation deductions for assets put into service after 1980 and before 1987. Salvage value is disregarded in computing ACRS allowances. Replaced by Modified Cost Recovery System (MACRS).

Acceptance, Waiver, and Consent Procedure   A disciplinary procedure used when the Department of Enforcement of the NASD believes a violation has occurred and the member or associate does not dispute the violation. With this procedure, the Department of Enforcement prepares and asks the respondent to sign a letter that accepts the charges, waives rights to have a hearing and appeal the decision, and consents to imposition of sanctions.

Account Guarantee Acknowledgment   A written acknowledgment to the firm that it may use the money and securities in the guaranteeing account without restriction to carry the guaranteed account

*Glossary courtesy of The Center for Futures Education, Inc.

and pay any deficit in the guaranteed account. The margin to be maintained is then calculated by combining the two accounts.

Accredited investor   An investor in an offering who meets certain criteria under Regulation D, who does not have to be counted for purposes of limitations on the number of purchasers in an offering. *At least one of the following criteria must be met to be an accredited investor:* (i) a buyer with a net worth individually or with a spouse, of $1,000,000 or more; (ii) institutional investors including banks, insurance companies, registered broker/dealers, and large pension plans; (iii) tax-exempt organizations with total assets in excess of $5,000,000; (iv); private business development companies; (v) directors, officers, or general partners of the issuer; and (vi) entities owned entirely by accredited investors.

Accretion   The process of adjusting the cost of a bond purchased at a discount. Only original-issue discount municipal bonds are accreted.

Accumulation period   For a variable annuity, the time from when the first payment into the annuity is made to when the first annuity payment is made.

Accumulation units   An accounting measurement used to measure an annuitant's ownership of the separate account during the deposit period of a variable annuity contract.

Acid test ratio   *See Quick Ratio.*

ACRS   *See Accelerated Cost Recovery System.*

Actively traded securities   Securities that have a current worldwide average daily trading volume over 60 consecutive calendar days (ADTV) of at least $1 million and an issuer with common equity securities having a public float value of at least $150 million. This condition is used for an exemption from Regulation M, which restricts the trading of an existing security by participants in a public offering of that security.

Additional bond test   An income test, which ascertains that revenues must meet certain levels to allow the sale of additional bonds against the financed facility. A provision in the trust indenture of an open end revenue bond.

Additional takedown   The profit to a syndicate member selling municipal bonds to broker/dealers who are not members of the syndicate.

Adjustment bonds   *See Income bond.*

ADR   *See American Depository Receipt.*

Ad valorem taxes   A tax levied "by value," usually used to describe property taxes.

Advance/Decline ratio   The ratio of the number of stocks increasing in price to the number of stocks decreasing in price. Also called the "breadth of the market."

Advertising Under NASD rules, means promotional items that have uncontrolled distribution. In other words, the firm has no way to know who will see the item. The material is published or designed for use in newspapers, magazines or other periodicals, radio, television, telephone or tape recording, video tape display, signs or billboards, motion pictures, telephone listings (other than white-page listings), or other public media. Does not include communications that are neither advertising nor sales literature.

Adviser's client account An account with a brokerage firm in which an investment adviser pools the funds of all his customers, keeping a record of each customer's percentage of the account. The brokerage firm does not know the identity of the individual customers. The investment adviser pays for securities and meets margin calls. The customers make their checks out to the investment adviser. Also called an omnibus account.

Affiliated persons Persons (individuals, corporations, trusts, etc.) in a position to influence a corporation's decisions. Includes officers, directors, and principal stockholders (those with 10% ownership or more) of the corporation, and their immediate families. Also called insiders or control persons.

Affirmative defense A defense in a legal proceeding that attacks the legal grounds for an accusation rather than the truth of the facts.

Affirmative determination The inquiry a registered representative makes to ensure that a customer who has custody of the securities certificates in a trade can deliver the certificates in good delivery from within three days of the trade date. The registered representative must talk with the customer and make a notation on the order ticket about his conversation with the customer.

Agency sales ticket A memorandum of each brokerage order received or given, whether executed or not.

Agency transactions: Transactions in which a broker acts only as an agent for the customer, putting together a buyer and a seller, and makes a commission on the sale.

Agent One who acts for another. When a firm acts as agent, it is acting as a broker, bringing together a buyer and a seller. As agent it does not buy or sell for its own account.

Aggregate indebtedness A firm's unsecured liabilities, including any customer-related liabilities. Aggregate indebtedness does not include subordinated agreements or loans fully collateralized either by fixed assets such as real estate or by the firm's securities.

Agreement among underwriters The contract that governs the syndicate members in a negotiated offering.

Agreement of limited partnership The contract between the general partners and the limited partners that governs the limited partnership.

Aggregate exercise price   In an options position, the total amount of money involved in the resulting stock trade if the position is exercised. If a customer is long one XYZ July 50 put, the aggregate exercise price is $5000.

Alpha   A statistical measurement used to determine the percentage of the change in a stock's price due to factors internal to the company, rather than to the stock market's fluctuations.

All-or-none (AON)   A limit order for multiple round lots that bars partial execution of the order. The customer waits until the entire order can be filled in a single trade.

All-or-none underwriting   A type of best-efforts underwriting that withdraws the offering if it cannot be sold completely.

Alternative minimum tax   A tax on certain "preference items," most of which are tax deductions allowed under the normal income tax calculation. Taxpayers pay either the regular tax or the alternative minimum tax, whichever is greater.

Alternative orders   An order with two parts. When one part is filled, the other part is automatically canceled. For example, a customer may enter an order to buy at 32 or 38 stop. He is trying to buy the stock for $32.00 or less, but if the price increases to or above $38.00, it becomes a market order.

Alternative Trading System (ATS)   An electronic system that brings together buyers and sellers of securities and completes trades by matching orders according to a predefined logic. Electronic Communication Networks (ECNs) are alternative trading systems that have sufficient volume in non-government securities and commercial paper that they must be registered with the SEC. Unregistered ATSs include the Arizona Stock Exchange, BRASS, and Optimark. The Arizona Stock Exchange is an electronic call market in which buy and sell orders are combined into one large daily trade that takes place at a single price. BRASS is a system management network to rout orders, and Optimark is an electronic trading system that can be purchased by an exchange or broker, but is not an exchange or broker in itself.

American Depository Receipt   A receipt for shares of a foreign corporation on deposit with a foreign branch of an American bank.

American Stock Exchange (AMEX)   The second largest traditional stock exchange, based in New York City.

American-style options   Options that may be exercised at any time before expiration. (*See European-style options.*)

Alternative Minimum Taxable Income (AMTI)   The amount on which the alternative minimum tax liability is calculated.

Amortization   A reduction in a debt or fund by periodic payments covering interest and part of the principal. In municipal bonds, amortization refers to adjusting the cost of a bond for any premium paid.

Annual report   The yearly report of a corporation's financial condition. It includes a balance sheet, income statement, and other descriptive information of interest to investors.

Annuity   Money is paid (usually to an insurance company) to someone who invests the money for a set period of time and then pays money to the annuitant (the one receiving the annuity) when he/she reaches a certain age. Fixed annuities guarantee a fixed payment amount, while variable annuities pay a varying amount depending on the fixed amount of initial investment.

Annuity units   An accounting measurement used to determine the annuitant's ownership in the separate account during the annuity period when payments are being made to the investor on a variable annuity contract.

Anti-dilution clause   A clause in the trust indenture of a bond offering that provides that the conversion price (or conversion ratio) of a convertible bond be adjusted in the case of stock splits or stock dividends paid to common stockholders.

AON   *See All-or-none.*

Arbitrage   Taking advantage of minor aberrations in the market to try to profit as the market returns to normal. Arbitrage might take advantage of imbalances in prices between two markets for the same security (such as a domestic and a foreign market) or between two types of securities whose value depends on the same underlying security (such as a stock and a bond convertible into the stock).

Arbitration   A method of settling disputes. The parties present their arguments to a panel of one or more arbitrators who will render a decision. There are no appeals from arbitration.

Asked price   The lowest price a seller of a security is willing to take for a unit of a security at a particular time. (Note that the OTC market uses the term "asked," while the exchanges use the term "offered" or "offering.")

Asset   Anything of value owned by a company or individual. Assets include cash, investments, and physical property.

Asset allocation   A fundamental concept in portfolio management in which an investment adviser determines the investment profile for a client, including his or her risk tolerance and time horizon, then uses this information to split the client's funds between appropriate classes of investments. As relative movements in the market for the various asset classes change the mix of assets in the portfolio over time, the adviser must rebalance the portfolio.

Asset class   A group of investments with similar risk and return characteristics, such as cash equivalents, government bonds, municipal bonds, corporate bonds, common stock (or industry groupings within the broad category of common stocks), real estate, precious metals, and collectibles.

Assignment For options, the notice from the OCC telling the broker/dealer that an option written by one of its clients has been exercised.

Assistant Representative-Order Processing A Series 11 representative who only accepts unsolicited customer orders for execution. Cannot solicit customers, give investment advise, make recommendations to customers, or effect transactions for the NASD-member's account. Must not be registered in any other capacity for the firm. Compensation cannot be based on the number or size of transactions they handle.

Associated persons Employees of a brokerage firm who are required to be licensed.

ATS *See Alternative Trading System.*

At-the-close order An order to be executed at or near the close of trading. Round-lot orders entered at-the-close are executed in the last 30 seconds of trading.

At-the-money An option contract with a strike price that equals the market price of the underlying stock.

At-the-opening order An order to be filled on the first trade of the day in that stock. If the order cannot be filled on the first trade of the day, it is canceled.

At-risk rule A provision in the tax code stating that a limited partner may only include debt as part of his or her basis in the partnership if he or she is personally liable for the debt (i.e., if it is a recourse loan).

Auction market A market in which the price of a security is determined by supply and demand, through a continuous auction. Exchanges are auction markets.

Auditor's report The public accountant's statement as to the scope of the review of the books and records of the corporation and the accountant's opinion as to the accuracy of the financial statements (i.e., unqualified or to some degree qualified approval).

Automated Confirmation Transaction (ACT) A computer system that matches trade information, determines locked-in trades, and submits them to clearing through the National Securities Clearing Corporation (NSCC)—the primary way that OTC transactions in equity securities are reported. Participation is mandatory for all brokers that are members of a registered clearing agency and for all brokers who have a clearing arrangement with such brokers.

Backing away The illegal practice of publishing a quote that a firm has no intention of honoring.

Balance of payments A summary statement comparing the money coming into a country with the amount of money leaving the country for one period of time. Usually divided into the current account (showing imports and exports of goods and services), the capital account (showing movement of investments), and gold (showing movement of gold). The statement uses double-entry bookkeeping, which ensures that though individual categories may have a deficit or surplus, the overall statement must not.

Balance of trade   The net difference in imports and exports of goods by a country for a period of time. (*Note:* This is not the same as the change in the current account portion of the balance of payments, since the current account also includes imports and exports of services.) More exports than imports produce what is generally considered a favorable balance of trade, while the reverse is generally considered unfavorable.

Balance sheet   A financial report of a corporation, showing the corporation's assets, liabilities, and stockholders' equity at a point in time (usually month-end, quarter-end, or year-end).

BAN   *See Bond Anticipation Note.*

Bankers' acceptances   A short-term instrument used to finance import/export activities. Usually sold at a discount.

Basis   The cost or book value of an investment. The gain or loss on an investment is the sale price less the basis. Basis is often called "cost basis."

Basis book   A series of tables used to determine the dollar price of a serial municipal bond issue (quoted on a yield to maturity basis), or to determine the yield to maturity on a term bond (quoted in the same manner as corporate bonds).

Basis points   A 0.01 percent in yield. Increasing from 5.00 percent to 5.05 percent, the yield increases by five basis points.

Bearer   Certificates (usually bonds) that are not registered in the holder's name, but are payable to the presenting party when due.

Bear market   A situation in a market for investments in which price trends are generally downward.

Bear spreads   An options spread position that is profitable when the stock price decreases. The position is characteristically entered by purchasing a high strike price option and selling a low strike price option.

Best-efforts underwriting   Underwriting without a guarantee to the issuer to sell the securities. The underwriters act as brokers.

Beta   A statistical measurement correlating a stock's price change with the movement of the stock market.

Bid price   The highest price a buyer of a security is willing to pay for a unit of the security at a particular time.

Blanket fidelity bond   A bond that insurance brokerage firms are required to carry to protect customers from the dishonesty or carelessness of brokerage employees and officers. Covers loss of money or securities, forgery, and fraudulent trading. The amount of coverage required is linked to the firm's required net capital under SEC Rule 15c3-1. The minimum bond allowed for all categories is $25,000.

Block trade   A trade of a large number of shares, usually 10,000 shares or more.

Blue Chip Stocks   Stocks of strong, well established corporations with a history of paying dividends in good and bad times.

Blue List   A listing of municipal bonds offered for sale in the secondary market.

Blue List Total   The total par value of the bonds offered for sale on the Blue List. This is a measure of the secondary market for municipal bonds.

Blue Skying   The process of registering a new issue with the states.

Blue Sky Laws   State securities laws. The name is derived from a court decision in which a state judge held that a particular offering had "no more substance than the blue sky above."

Board broker   The employee of the CBOE who maintains the public limit order file, which is similar to a specialist's book, and executes limit orders for customers. Also known as an Order Book Official, or OBO.

Bond   A long-term debt instrument issued by a corporation or government entity. The bondholder loans the issuer money and the issuer promises to pay the bondholder interest at a specified rate on the loan for a specified period of time and then to repay the loan at expiration. The bondholder is a creditor of the issuer rather than a partial owner.

Bond Anticipation Note (BAN)   A short-term municipal note issued in advance of long-term bond financing. The BAN is repaid from the proceeds of the bond issue. BANs are normally general obligations of the issuer.

Bond buyer   A publication that contains news of interest to the municipal bond market; also contains worksheets designed to assist syndicates in preparing their bids for an offering.

Bond index   An index of 20 high-quality, general obligation municipal bonds, also known as the 20 Bond Index.

Bond swap   Selling municipal bonds (usually at a loss) and using the proceeds to buy other municipal bonds, to establish a loss for tax purposes, to diversify a portfolio, to increase cash flow, or increase yield. Also known as tax swaps.

Book entry   A bond registration procedure in which the bondholder does not receive the physical certificates held by a depository. The depository maintains ownership records and forwards interest payments.

Book value   The value of a corporation's assets or liabilities on its balance sheet. Assets are valued at their original purchase price less any depreciation taken for accounting purposes. The book value of common stock is the corporation's assets less its liabilities and the liquidation value of its preferred stock. Book value may have little relationship to market value.

BP option   *BP* is the abbreviation for the British Pound. An option to buy or sell British Pounds.

Branch office   Any location identified to the public as a location where an NASD member conducts investment banking or securities business. However, telephone directories, business cards, etc. may refer to a non-branch, as long as they also give the address and telephone number of the branch office or office of supervisory jurisdiction that supervises the non-branch.

Breadth of the Market   *See Advance/Decline Ratio.*

Breakeven Point   The point beyond which a trade begins to be profitable. Up to this point, it is a losing trade.

Breakpoint   A purchase amount that qualifies for a reduced sales charge for mutual funds.

Breakpoint sale   The prohibited practice of selling mutual fund shares in an amount just under a breakpoint (usually within $1000 of a breakpoint) to earn more commissions.

Broker   *See Agent.*

Broker/Dealer   A brokerage firm.

Broker's broker   A municipal securities firm that acts as broker for other firms. Broker's brokers do not deal with customers and do not trade their own accounts.

Bull market   A situation in a market for investments in which price trends are generally upward.

Bull spread   An options spread position that is profitable if the stock price rises. The position is characterized by a low strike price for the long position and a high strike price for the short position.

Bunching   Combining two or more odd lot orders into one order for a round lot.

Business cycle   A recurring cycle of economic conditions starting with credit expansion, economic activity becoming feverish, then depressed. Recovery occurs when the malinvestments and maladjustments have been corrected.

Buyer's option   A contract giving the buyer the right to specify a later date on which to settle the trade. The specified date must be from six business days to sixty calendar days after the trade date.

Buying power   In a margin account, the dollar amount of securities the customer may purchase without making a cash deposit. The buying power in an account is a function of the SMA (which see).

Buy stop   An order to buy a security if it trades at or above a trigger price. Often used to limit a loss or protect a profit in a short stock position.

Calendar spread   An options spread position with the same strike prices, but different expiration months. Calendar spreads are entered to take advantage of the decay of time premium.

Callable securities   Securities that may be bought back by the issuer before they are due, usually at a premium over the par value. Many bonds and preferred stocks are callable.

Call option An option contract that gives the holder the choice to buy the stock and the writer the obligation to sell the stock at a specified price.

Call rate The rate of interest banks charge broker/dealers on loans collateralized by securities, often called the broker loan rate.

Call spread An options spread position in which the customer is long a call and short a different call on the same underlying security.

Canadian interest cost *See True Interest Cost.*

Cap interval The point at which these special index options are automatically exercised if the underlying index touches or exceeds the cap price on the close.

Capital Asset Pricing Theory (CAPT) A theory of portfolio analysis stating that diversified investments in a portfolio are less risky than the sum of the risks of the individual stocks.

Capitalization The long-term financing of a corporation, including the shareholder's equity section of the balance sheet plus long-term bonds outstanding.

Capital gain A gain recognized when a security is purchased at one price and sold at a higher price. It does not include dividend or interest income.

Cash flow The net profits or losses of a business plus noncash expenses such as depreciation, amortization, and depletion.

Cash settlement A trade that is settled on the same day as the trade date.

Catastrophe call A provision in the trust indenture of a bond issue that allows the issuer to call the bonds if the facility is destroyed by a natural disaster. It is usually called at par.

CBOE *See Chicago Board Options Exchange.*

CD *See Certificate of Deposit.*

Certificate The physical paper that evidences ownership of stock in a corporation.

Certificate of Deposit A document certifying an unsecured time deposit with a bank, usually known as a CD. To be negotiable, it must be for $100,000 or more.

Certificate of Limited Partnership A document summarizing the provisions of a limited partnership. It must be filed with the secretary of state in the state in which the partnership is formed. Filing the certificate creates the limited partnership.

Chicago Board Options Exchange (CBOE) The largest options exchange. Located in Chicago.

CFTC *See Commodity Futures Trading Commission.*

Chinese Wall doctrine Doctrine by which firms must establish barriers restricting information flow between departments to ensure that insider information acquired by one department (legal or investment banking, for example) will not be used in trades of another department or in recommendations to customers.

Churning Excessive trading in a customer's account to give profit to the broker/dealer in disregard of the customer's best interests. Prosecutable under the 1934 Securities Exchange Act.

Circuit breakers Trading halts, curtailment of automated trading systems and/or price movement limits used by the exchanges to attempt to prevent the free-fall of stock or stock index futures markets. Established after Black Monday in 1987 by major stock and commodities exchanges. The breakers are triggered when the market has fallen by a specified amount in a specified period. Amounts that trigger the breakers are changed from time to time.

Class of options Options of the same type (put or call) on the same underlying security.

Closed-end investment company An investment company with a fixed number of shares that trade in the secondary market.

Closing purchase A purchase of an option to eliminate or reduce a short options position.

COD Cash on Delivery. Payment for goods is made upon delivery. *See Delivery versus Payment.*

Code of Arbitration Procedure of the NASD for settling disputes among participants in the securities markets by arbitration. Applies to disputes between and among members, members and their associates, members and public customers, associates of members and public customers, and members and clearing agencies or persons using the facilities of a clearing agency (however, only when the clearing agency has an arbitration agreement with the NASD).

Code of Procedure Procedures of the NASD that detail the form for disciplinary actions against members and their associates for violations of the rules over which the NASD has jurisdiction.

Coincident indicator An economic indicator that reflects changes in the economy. The index of industrial production and retail sales are both coincident indicators.

Collateral Securities or other assets that a borrower pledges to a lender to secure repayment of a loan. If the borrower does not make payments as promised, the lender may legally seize the collateral and use the proceeds from its sale to pay off the loan.

Collateralized Mortgage Obligations (CMOs) Bonds secured with GNMA, FNMA, and FHLMC mortgage-backed securities. Also known as REMICs.

Collateral trust bonds Bonds secured by securities of another corporation.

Combination An options position in which an investor is long both a put and a call option on the same stock or short both a put and a call option on the same stock. The options usually have different strike prices.

Commercial paper   Short-term business notes, drafts, and acceptances maturing in 270 days or less.

Commission   The fee charged by a broker/dealer for acting for others in executing buying or selling orders.

Commodity Futures Trading Commission   U.S. Government Agency that regulates U.S. exchange trading in futures.

Common stock   The most basic type of equity security, representing ownership of the corporation.

Communications that are neither advertising nor sales literature   Items exempt from the NASD's advertising and sales literature rules, including: (1) tombstone advertisements or similar communications; (2) documents intended for the internal use of the firm and not given to the public; (3) communications which only identify the member and/or offer a specific security at a stated price; (4) prospectuses, offering circulars, and so on used in connection with a public offering of a security that has been registered or filed with the SEC or a state (except for the prospectus for investment company shares); and (5) communications merely stating facts, such as the member's new name or address, facts concerning a merger or acquisition, the firm's NASDAQ© symbol, or the NASDAQ© symbol of a security in which the member is a registered market-maker.

Competitive bid underwriting   An offering in which syndicates enter bids for the opportunity to underwrite the issue.

Competitive trader   A person who owns a seat on an exchange and uses it to trade for his own account.

Complaint   Defined by the NASD as a written statement of a grievance by a customer or his agent, involving persons associated with the member concerning the solicitation, execution, or disposition of funds or securities.

Compliance Registered Options Principal (CROP)   A registered options principal who has been designated by the broker/dealer to maintain compliance with industry rules and federal law. He must approve all items of advertising, sales literature, and educational material.

Concession   In a municipal underwriting, the compensation given up to broker/dealers who are not members of the syndicate.

Conduct Rules (formerly known as the Rules of Fair Practice)   Rules maintained and enforced by the NASD that apply to general business activities of members.

Conduit Theory   Theory governing an exemption on paying taxes for Regulated Investment Companies. The theory governing this exemption is that an RIC that distributes most of its income is acting only as a conduit for income on investments.

Confirmation A written report giving details of the trade to the customer or the other broker/dealer involved in the trade. Confirmations must be sent the next business day after the trade.

Consent to service of process Legal document used by the state administrator to simplify filing of complaints under state securities laws. The person or entity signing it (such as the issuer of a security, or a securities registrant with the state) agrees that, for non-criminal complaints, any legal papers regarding the signee that are served on the state administrator in lieu of the signee have the same force and validity as if they were served directly on the signee.

Consolidated Tape System for providing the last sale price and volume of trades in exchange-listed securities. The system has two tapes: Network A and Network B. All trades in NYSE securities, regardless of where they occur, are listed on Network A with an identifier as to where they originated. Transactions in securities listed on AMEX and other regional exchanges are reported on Network B. Participants in addition to the NYSE and AMEX include BSE, CBOE, CSE, CHX, NASD, PSE, and PHLX.

Contemporaneous traders Traders who buy or sell a security at the time of insider trading. Such traders may sue in court for damages.

Continuous issue of redeemable securities Manner in which shares of a mutual fund are issued. The shares purchased are new shares, and when a shareholder wishes to sell shares, he sells them back to the fund itself (redeems them) rather than selling them on the open market. The shares repurchased by the mutual fund are retired: they do not become treasury stock, nor may they be reissued; the shares simply cease to exist.

Continuous net settlement The offsetting of payments and certificates when multiple trades involving a particular security have the same two parties on opposing sides. Used by registered clearing agencies.

Contractual plans A contract committing an investor to invest money over a period of time. The sales charges are deducted over the life of the contract, being higher in the early part of the contract.

Control persons See *Affiliated persons*. Control persons are also called *insiders*.

Control stock Stock owned by control persons.

Conversion price The price of a bond or stock at which it can be converted to common stock.

Conversion ratio The ratio specifying how many shares of a common stock will be received upon converting one bond or share of preferred stock.

Convertible Designation for a bond, debenture, or preferred stock which signifies that it may be exchanged by the owner for common stock or another security, usually one issued by the same corporation. Conversions are subject to terms established in the issue of the original security.

Cooling-off period   The time between the filing of the offering with the SEC and the effective date when it is released by the SEC.

Cost basis   *See Basis.*

Coterminous   Overlapping debt, such as the bonds of a city and a school district in which both debts are being paid by the same tax base (taxpayers).

Coupon bond   A bond in which coupons for interest payment are physically attached to the bond paper. The bondholder must clip the coupons as they come due and present them for payment of interest.

Coupon rate   The nominal yield on a bond or share of preferred stock. For example, a bond with a face value of $1000 that pays $100 per year has a nominal yield or coupon rate of 10 percent.

Covered options   A short options position in which the writer has the means of meeting the obligation (e.g., a person who is short a call option and long the stock).

Credit agreement   An agreement between broker and customer on the conditions of a margin account.

Credit balance   Money on deposit in a customer's account.

Credit spreads   An options spread position in which the premium on the short position is greater than the premium on the long position.

CROP   *See Compliance Registered Options Principal.*

Crossed market   A market in which either a newly entered bid is higher than an existing asked price or a newly entered asked price is less than an existing bid price.

Crossover   The point at which the partnership goes from showing losses for tax purposes to showing income.

Cumulative preferred stock   A preferred stock whose dividends continue to accumulate even though they are not earned or declared.

Currency exchange risk   The risk that the value of an investor's domestic currency may drop against the value of the currency in which an investment is held. Much of this risk can be hedged away through the market for forwards and futures.

Current assets   Assets that are converted to cash within one year.

Current liabilities   Obligations that must be paid within one year.

Current ratio   Current assets divided by current liabilities.

Current yield   The ratio of the current income from an investment to the purchase price or the current price of the investment.

CUSIP number   A number assigned to each issue of securities by the Committee on Uniform Securities Identification Procedures to facilitate tracking lost, stolen, or counterfeit securities.

Custodian   The person appointed by the donor to manage a minor's account. Might be the donor, a guardian, or some other adult or institution such as a bank.

Customer   Any person or entity for whom the broker/dealer holds funds or securities, unless that entity is another broker/dealer. (Though municipal securities dealers may be considered customers on transactions not involving municipal securities.)

Customer agreement   A basic agreement between customer and broker, incorporating the margin agreement, the credit agreement and the loan consent.

Customer book   A listing maintained by the registered representative of every security a customer holds.

Cyclical stocks   Common stocks of companies whose prices vary directly with the business cycle.

Dated date   In a bond issue, the date on which interest begins to accrue.

Day orders   Orders that are canceled if they are not filled on the day they are entered.

Dealer   One who buys or sells stock for his own account, charging a markup when he sells to a customer and a markdown when he buys from the customer.

Debentures   Bonds not secured by any specific property, based on the full faith and credit of the issuer.

Debit balance   Money owed to a broker/dealer by a customer.

Debit spread   An options spread position in which the premium paid on the long position is greater than the premium received on the short position.

Declared date   The date on which a corporation declares a dividend.

Defeasance   Annulment of trust indenture conditions granting new bonds a claim on revenues, and the old bonds a claim on the escrow account containing the proceeds (the money) from the pre-refunding issue.

Defensive issue   Common stock of companies that are relatively unaffected by the business cycle, such as food companies, utilities, and tobacco companies.

Defined benefit plan   A corporate pension plan that guarantees a specific level of benefits for participants, usually based on levels of compensation and years of service (e.g., an annuity purchased by the corporation for the employee).

Defined contribution plan   A corporate pension plan that guarantees the employer will pay a specific amount into the plan each year. Either a money purchase plan, such as a 401(k) or a SEP, or a profit sharing plan, or some combination of the two.

Deflation   A decline in the prices of goods and services.

Delivery versus Payment (DVP) A type of settlement, commonly used by bank trust departments, in which the security is paid for when the broker/dealer has it deliverable in the purchaser's name. Also referred to as DVP or COD.

Demand note A short-term municipal note that permits the issuer to change the interest rate on a weekly or monthly basis, and the holder to sell the note back to the issuer at the same intervals.

De minimus transactions A small amount of transactions allowed in a state for a registered rep who is not registered in that state. Applies when an existing customer of a firm moves to another state or stays in another state for less than 30 days. Subject to restrictions.

Depository Trust Company (DTC) A central depository for the physical certificates evidencing securities held by its members. The members transfer securities among themselves to effect transactions using electronic bookkeeping entries.

Depository trust receipt A written guarantee that can be used for money or stock, and to cover either calls or puts. Unlike escrow receipts or bank guarantee letters, which can only be used once, a depository trust receipt may be used again upon expiration of the option.

Depreciation A noncash expense reflecting wear and tear of property used as part of a trade or business or held for the production of income. Usually, the cost of an asset, less an appropriate salvage value, is "written off" over its useful life by periodically reducing the book value of the asset with an increase to accumulated depreciation and charging an equal and offsetting amount as depreciation expense. Depreciation used for book purposes may be different from the amounts allowed on tax statements.

Derivative security A contract whose value depends on the performance of some other security, index, or other investment. For example, a stock option is a derivative security whose value depends on the value of the underlying stock.

Depression A stage of the business cycle characterized by high unemployment and low levels of business activity.

Designated order In a municipal bond underwriting, an order by the buyer specifying the syndicate member who receives the compensation for the order.

Designated reporting member A broker/dealer who engages in many third market trades, and is designated as such.

Developmental drilling Drilling oil or gas wells in an area of known production.

Diagonal spread An options spread position in which both the strike prices and the expiration months differ.

Dilution Reduction of the percentage ownership of the existing shareholders through the sale of more stock by the corporation.

Direct Participation Program (DPP) An investment program that allows the flow-through of all tax consequences to the investor. The most common form of DPP is a limited partnership.

Discount The difference between some nominal amount for a security and the lower current market price. For example, the discount on a preferred stock or bond is the amount by which it is currently selling below par or face value. For securities sold or loans made "at a discount," the issue or loaned amount is the face amount reduced by the amount of the interest.

Discount rate The rate of interest the Federal Reserve Board charges member banks for reserves borrowed from the Fed.

Discretionary account A customer account in which the firm or its registered representative has the authority to enter orders without the prior approval of the customer.

Discretionary income The amount of income the individual has left after covering his or her essentials such as food, housing, utilities, clothes, and payment of obligations.

Discretionary orders Orders in which the customer allows the registered representative to decide whether to buy or sell, which security; and the number of shares. The order is discretionary even if the customer supplies the other information required to order, such as when to place the order and whether the order is at market price or a limit order at a stated price.

Discretionary power The power of attorney given by a customer to a registered representative or brokerage firm.

Disintermediation The nonuse of financial institutions as intermediaries between savers and the users of funds.

Disproportionate sharing arrangement A sharing arrangement in an oil and gas program granting the general partner a greater share of income than would be merited by his capital contribution. For example, the general partner contributes 10 percent of the total capital but receives 25 percent of the income.

District executive representative Person designated by a member of the NASD to vote on NASD matters related to a particular district for the member. A member may designate one district executive representative for each district in which it has at least one branch office. However, the firm cannot designate a district executive representative in addition to an executive representative in the district that is its principal place of business.

Diversification Reducing risk by spreading investments among several markets and/or industry segments within a market. Diversification reduces the risk that an individual investment will perform worse than other investments in its same class (i.e., non-systematic risk).

Diversified investment management company An investment company with 75 percent of the value of its assets held in cash or cash equivalents, government securities, securities of other investment companies, or securities of other issuers; no more than 5 percent of its total assets in the securities of any one company; and ownership of no more than 10 percent of the outstanding voting stock of any one company.

Dividend   A payment of corporate earnings to shareholders. Dividends are normally paid in cash, but may also be in stock or property.

Dividend Re-Investment Plan (DRIP)   A program offered by some corporations (particularly investment companies) in which shareholders may opt to use their dividends to purchase additional shares in the corporation in lieu of receiving cash payments. Since the shares are purchased directly from the corporation, brokerage fees do not apply. However, the shareholder is still responsible for taxes on the dividends.

Dollar bond   A term municipal bond, quoted in the same manner as corporate bonds.

Dollar-cost averaging   A method of investing in which the investor makes fixed dollar purchases at regular intervals regardless of the price per share. The investor purchases more shares with this method when the share price is low and fewer shares when the share price is high. Thus, the investor benefits from temporary downturns in share price.

Don't know procedures (DK procedures)   Procedures followed by dealers if confirmations between dealers are in disagreement, or if one party fails to confirm a trade prior to the settlement date. Literally means we "don't know" this trade.

DOT System   The Designated Order Turnaround System, which is the automated execution system on the NYSE. It is now called the Super Dot 250 System.

Double-barreled bonds   A municipal bond based on the revenues to be generated by some facility or project, but also backed by the full faith, credit, and taxing power of a government.

Double-exempt bonds   Bonds issued by a territory of the United States that are exempt from both federal and state income taxes in all fifty states. Some states may tax bonds of other states.

Dow Jones Composite Average   An average of 65 stocks, including the 30 stocks in the Dow Jones Industrial Average, plus 20 transportation stocks and 15 utility stocks.

Dow Jones Industrial Average   An average of 30 stocks that are purportedly representative of the entire stock market. This is the average most widely followed by the public.

Due bill   A written admission of a debt. Due bills are given when a stock split or stock dividend is pending and the shares are sold prior to the ex-date, but too late to transfer them to the buyer's name.

Due-bill check A postdated check dated to the payment date of a cash dividend. Due bill checks are used when a cash dividend is pending and the shares are sold prior to the ex-dividend date, but too late to transfer them to the buyer's name.

Due-diligence meeting A meeting held by the issuer and the underwriters shortly before the effective date of an offering. The purpose is to make certain that all disclosures are adequate.

DVP *See Delivery versus Payment.*

Earnings per share The net income of a corporation after taxes and payment of preferred stock dividends, divided by the number of common shares outstanding.

Eastern underwriting agreement A firm commitment underwriting in which syndicate members are liable for their share of any unsold securities, regardless of how much of their allotment they sold. Eastern underwriting agreements have joint and several liability.

Easy money A phenomenon occurring when new money is injected into the economy by the Federal Reserve System. The new money stimulates demand for existing goods, thus making it simple to make more money.

ECN *See Electronic Communication Network.*

Education IRA A tax-advantaged savings vehicle used to pay the qualified higher education expenses of a designated beneficiary.

Effective date In a new issue, the date on which the SEC releases the offering.

Electronic Communication Networks (ECNs) Alternative trading systems that have sufficient volume in nongovernment securities and commercial paper that they must be registered with the SEC. An ECN may register with the SEC as either a broker/dealer or an exchange. ECNs registered as broker/dealers must comply with Regulation ATS, which includes a requirement to link to a registered exchange or the NASD and publicly display their best priced orders for any security in which they have had 5 percent or more of the average daily volume share in the past four out of six calendar months. ECNs registered as exchanges must comply with exchange requirements for self-regulation. ECNs registered as exchanges include Archipelago, Attain, Island, and REDIBook. ECNs registered as broker/dealers include B-Trade, BRUT, Instinet, NexTrade, and Strike. POSIT Crossing Network is registered as a broker, but is not considered an ECN because of its low volume. POSIT is a call market that matches sell and purchase orders six times a day, creating a single trade at the midpoint each time.

Eligible Worker-Owned Cooperative (EWOC) A retirement plan structured as either a cooperative farmers' association or any corporation operating on a cooperative basis except for a tax-exempt organization, a mutual savings bank, an insurance company, or a corporation that furnishes electric energy or telephone service to persons in rural areas. Restrictions apply.

Employee Retirement Income Security Act (ERISA) Act regulating pension plans with regard to eligibility for participation, vesting, funding, fiduciary responsibility, and reporting and disclosure. ERISA also created the Pension Benefit Guaranty Corporation (PBGC), a mandatory pension insurance fund used to guarantee pension benefits.

Employee Stock Ownership Plan (ESOP) A profit sharing plan in which the contribution is made in stock.

Equipment trust certificates A corporate bond offering secured by the equipment of a railroad, airline, or trucking firm, known as rolling stock.

Equity The value of an asset (or part of an asset) that is not indebted.

Equity trader Category of registration both for market makers, agency traders, and proprietary traders in NASDAQ© and other OTC market equity or convertible debt securities and for supervisors of those activities. Does not include traders who primarily execute orders for a registered investment company. Equity traders must pass the test for limited representative-equity trader (Series 55) and, in addition, either Series 7 or Series 62.

Eurodollar bonds Bonds issued outside the United States, but denominated in U.S. dollars.

European-style options Options that may only be exercised on the expiration date. (Most options in the United States are American-style options.)

Excess margin stocks The stocks held in a margin account whose market value causes the equity in the customer's account to be more than 140 percent of the debit balance in the account.

Exchanges Organizations or groups of individuals and/or firms that provide a means of bringing buyers or sellers of securities together. Unless their volume is so small to qualify for an exemption, exchanges must register with the SEC as national exchanges and abide by their rules.

Exchange acquisition A block trade on an exchange initiated by the buyer. The broker/dealer lines up both sides of the trade prior to bringing it to the exchange floor.

Exchange distribution A block trade on an exchange initiated by the seller. The broker/dealer lines up both sides of the trade prior to bringing it to the exchange floor.

Exchange rate The price at which one country's currency can be exchanged for another country's currency.

Ex-dividend date The date on which a stock starts trading without a pending dividend, usually four business days prior to the record date. It is set by either the exchange or the Uniform Practice Committee of the NASD.

Executive representative Individual designated by a member in the NASD to vote for the member in all NASD matters. Must be a registered principal of the member who participates in senior management of the member.

Exercise Demand from the holder of an option that the writer perform according to the terms of the option contract. When a holder exercises a call option, the writer of the option must sell the underlying stock to the holder at a predetermined price. When a holder exercises a put option, the writer of the option must buy the underlying stock from the holder at the predetermined price.

Exercised by exception Automatic exercise of an option that is in-the-money by three-fourths of a point or more on the expiration date, unless the holder gives specific instructions to the contrary.

Exercise limit A maximum number of options of the same class that the OCC allows to be exercised by an investor within five consecutive days.

Exercise price The price at which the trade is executed when the option is exercised. It is also called the *strike price.*

Ex legal Designation at time of trade that is required for municipal securities to be considered good delivery if certificates are delivered without legal opinions or other documents legally required to accompany the certificates.

Expansion The initial stage of the business cycle in which credit is expanded.

Expense guarantee Guarantee by an insurer that expense factors will not change during the payout period on an annuity.

Expense ratio In a mutual fund, the ratio between the operating expenses for the year and the total average net asset value. It usually amounts to less than 1 percent.

Expiration The end of trading for an option. The option may not be exercised after the expiration date.

Exploratory drilling The drilling of oil or gas wells in an area without known production. Exploratory wells are also called "wildcat" wells.

Ex-rights The buyer of a stock sold ex-rights acquires only the stock itself and not any associated right to subscribe to additional stock directly from the company at a discount.

Extension When a customer fails to pay for a purchase of securities by the seventh business day after trade date, the broker/dealer may choose to request an extension, allowing an additional five business days to make payment.

Extraordinary call   A call on a bond issue that is used in unusual circumstances, such as a catastrophe call.

Face-amount certificate   An obligation on the part of its issuer to pay a specific amount or amounts at a specific date or dates at least 24 months in the future. If the purchase is made in periodic payments, the face-amount certificate is an installment type.

Face-amount certificate company   A fairly rare category of investment company that issues face-amount certificates, backed with specific assets, such as real estate or securities. The issuer promises to pay the holder at maturity the face amount of the certificate, which is the return of capital plus accrued interest. Investors may also be able to get a surrender value if the certificate is presented prior to maturity.

Face value   The amount on the face of a bond on which interest payments are calculated. This amount is also the amount due at maturity. May be higher or lower than market value. Also called par value.

Fair market price   The price a willing buyer would pay a willing seller for an asset, in which both are acting rationally with full knowledge.

Feasibility study   A viability study for a municipal revenue bond, to determine its technical and economic profitability.

Federal covered security   A security that is exempt from state registration because either it must be registered with the Federal government under the Securities Act of 1933 or it is exempt from federal registration under the 1933 Act (except that municipal securities may be regulated by the state of which the issuer is a part). Includes securities listed or authorized for listing on the NYSE, AMEX, the National Market System of NASDAQ©, or securities of the same issuer as those above with equal or higher seniority; registered investment company securities; securities offered or sold to qualified purchasers; securities with respect to certain transactions exempt from Federal registration, including some private placements; and securities that are exempt from Federal registration.

Federal funds   Very short-term loans (usually overnight) between banks, without any collateral.

Federal Home Loan Mortgage Corporation (FHLMC or "Freddie Mac")   Purchases conventional mortgages from federally chartered savings and loans.

Federal National Mortgage Association   An independent association that purchases mortgages from banks and other lenders, known as FNMA, or "Fannie Mae."

Federal Reserve Board   Commonly referred to as the Fed or "the Board," it manages the Federal Reserve System.

Fidelity bond   *See Blanket fidelity bond.*

Fiduciary   Someone who manages an account for the beneficiary of the account.

FIFO   First-in, First-out, a method of accounting for which shares or inventory items are being sold from a pool of similar shares or items. Assumes that when a sale is made, the items purchased first are sold first.

Fill-or-Kill   A limit order for multiple round lots that must be executed in its entirety at the stated price, or be canceled.

Financial futures   Contracts to buy or sell specific amounts of a financial instrument at a specific price on some specific date in the future. Underlying securities include Treasuries, CDs, and currencies. Used by banks and other financial institutions to hedge against changing interest rates.

Financial and operations principal   Person in a NASD-member firm who is responsible for the financial reports of the firm, keeping of books and records, supervision of back office operations, and compliance with financial responsibility rules, including compliance with net capital requirements. At least one person in each member firm must be registered with the NASD as such.

Firm commitment underwriting   A promise from the underwriters of an issue to purchase the securities for their own account if they cannot be sold to customers.

Firm quote   A quote committing the firm to buy or sell at least 100 shares of stock or 5 bonds at the stated price. All quotes are assumed to be firm unless otherwise specified.

Five percent policy   NASD policy to limit commissions, markups, and markdowns to five percent. This is a guideline rather than a rule because a number of other factors must also be considered.

Fixed annuity   An annuity policy with fixed monthly payments to the owner. *See annuity.*

Fixed assets   Corporate assets that are used in a trade or business having a useful life of more than one year.

Fixed Income Pricing System (FIPS)   An automated quotation and trade negotiation system for the high-yield bond market that is operated by the NASD.

Fixed-unit investment trust   A trust that buys a fixed portfolio of securities (usually municipal bonds) and sells that portfolio to investors in units. Each unit represents an undivided interest in the portfolio. The holdings of the trust are static. When the holdings mature, the redemptions are passed proportionately to the unit holders. The unit shares do not trade on a secondary market.

Floor brokers   Employees of a broker/dealer who execute the firm's orders on the floor of a futures exchange.

Flower bonds   U.S. government securities that were issued at a discount from par value, but are acceptable at par in payment of estate taxes.

FNMA   *See Federal National Mortgage Association.*

FOCUS report   Financial and Operational Combined Uniform and Single reports that all registered broker/dealers must regularly file with the SEC. Shows the firm's activity volume, cash position, amount of customer exposure, inventory, money and securities owed to or from other broker/dealers, net income, and net capital position. The type and frequency of filing varies by the type of firm.

FOK   *See Fill-or-Kill.*

FOMC   The Federal Open Market Committee, which controls the open market operations of the Federal Reserve Banks.

Forward pricing   In mutual funds, the practice of filling orders based on the next computed net-asset value of the fund.

Fourth market   Trades in which institutions deal directly with each other, without using broker/dealers.

FRB   *See Federal Reserve Board.*

Free credit balances   A credit balance in a customer's account that the customer can withdraw upon request. Not all credits are free credits. For example, the credit balance related to a short sale in a margin account is not a free credit, since the customer cannot withdraw that credit until the short sale is covered. The firm must send customers statements concerning any existing credit balances at least quarterly.

Freeriding   Using the proceeds of a sale to pay for a prior purchase.

Freeriding and withholding   Failure of a member firm to make a bona fide public distribution of a hot issue. Such an issue may not be purchased by any broker/dealer or his employees or families, except under certain conditions.

Frozen account   An account that is not readily usable. The customer must have the money already on deposit to enter a buy order, or the security already on deposit to enter a sell order.

Full authorization or discretion   A power of attorney for an account that gives the person holding it the right to enter orders and also add or withdraw funds.

Fully diluted earnings per share   The earnings per share if all convertible securities were converted into common stock.

Fully paid securities   Securities held in a cash account for which full payment has been made.

Functional allocation   A sharing arrangement in an oil and gas program in which the limited partners contribute all the intangible costs and the general partners contribute all the tangible costs.

Fundamental analysis   The study of certain factors affecting prices such as the management of a corporation, the economy, the industry, supply and demand, and so forth. Compare with technical analysis.

Futures Contracts to buy or sell a specific amount of some product at a specific price on a specific date in the future. The underlying asset might be a financial instrument (financial future), a stock index (stock index future) or an agricultural product, such as wheat, soybeans, or pork bellies. If the underlying asset is a stock index, settlement is made in cash due to the difficulty in delivering a market basket of stocks.

General obligation bonds Municipal bonds that are backed by the full faith, credit, and taxing power of the issuer.

General partner The partner who has the responsibility to manage the business and affairs of a limited partnership, and who has unlimited liability.

General securities firms Brokers or dealers that carry customer or other broker/dealer accounts and receive and hold securities and funds for those accounts. Also called carrying, clearing firms.

Glass-Steagall Act of 1939 The federal law that prohibited banks from acting as dealers or underwriters in any securities other than general obligation municipal bonds.

GNMA *See Government National Mortgage Association.*

Good delivery Acceptable quality for delivery. A security that is in good delivery form must be accepted.

Good-faith deposit In a competitive underwriting, the bidders must make a good faith deposit, to show that they have the capability of handling the offering.

Good faith margin account Type of account allowed under Reg. T for margin transactions in exempt securities, non-equity securities, money market mutual fund shares, or shares in a mutual fund that has at least 95 percent of its assets continuously invested in exempted securities. The initial good faith margin required for purchases is the "amount of margin which a creditor would require in exercising sound credit judgment." For short sales, the initial margin required is the current market value of the security plus the good faith margin.

Good 'Til Cancelled (GTC) order An order to buy or sell at a specific price that stands until the investor cancels it.

Government bond A bond issued by the U.S. government.

Government National Mortgage Association A government owned corporation that is backed by the full faith and credit of the U.S. government, creating pools of mortgages insured by either the Department of Veterans Affairs or the Federal Housing Administration and are sold to investors, commonly referred to as GNMA. Also called Ginnie Mae.

Government securities principal An associated person who supervises government securities activities and is not registered as any other kind of principal. Must be registered, but no qualification exam applies. A principal who also performs tasks of a government securities representative must pass the appropriate exams for that function.

Green shoe offering   A new issue in which the issuer grants the underwriters an option or a warrant to purchase up to 15 percent more shares from the issuer at prices below the public offering price. The additional shares are used to cover certificates borrowed when the manager shorted stock to purchasers. The option is exercisable within thirty days after the effective date of the offering. The additional shares are registered with an amendment to the original registration statement. Profits earned by the manager on covering the short position are distributed to syndicate members pro-rata. So-called because the Green Shoe Company first used this arrangement.

Gross investment income   The total of all interest and dividends received on the securities in a portfolio, such as that held by a mutual fund.

Gross-revenue pledge   In a municipal revenue bond, a trust-indenture provision stipulating that the revenues first go to pay the debt servicing costs. The operating costs may be paid from some other source of revenues.

Group net order   In a municipal bond underwriting, an order in which the compensation is shared proportionately among the syndicate members.

Group sales   Sales in an underwriting made to institutional customers, such as banks and insurance companies, and for which all of the members of the underwriting group share in the commissions proportionate to their takedown in the offering.

GTC Order   A type of order that is good until it is canceled.

Haircut   A haircut is a percent reduction required to certain valuations of assets included in a firm's net capital calculation. Percentages are set by the SEC to allow for three types of potential losses in rapid liquidation: fluctuations in the market value of securities positions, losses in open contractual commitments made in firm commitment underwritings, and losses for aged fail-to-delivers.

Head and shoulders pattern   A technical chart formation that resembles a head and shoulders. It is a reversal pattern, representing the end of an up-trend and the beginning of a down-trend.

Hedge clauses   Cautionary statements or caveats made in a communication, such as an advertisement.

Hedging   An investment strategy by which the investor tries to eliminate all potential future gain or loss on an investment. For example, investors may hedge their investments with stock options, future contracts, or by selling short.

Horizontal spread An options spread position in which the strike prices are the same, but the expiration months are different. Also known as time spreads and calendar spreads.

Hot issues A new issue which, on the first day of trading, trades at a price above the new issue price.

Howey test The test established in the 1946 case of SEC v. W.J. Howey Co. to determine what an investment contract is. According to the Howey test, an instrument is only an investment contract if it involves an investment of money or other tangible or definable consideration in a common enterprise with a reasonable expectation of profits to be derived primarily from the entrepreneurial or managerial efforts of others. The form of the security (whether it is a formal certificate or nominal interests in the physical assets employed by the enterprise) is irrelevant. Thus, notes that a furniture store issues to finance a customer's purchases are not securities, since their primary purpose is to facilitate the purchase. However, notes issued by a corporation for the general use of the company, in which the buyer is primarily interested in the interest to be earned on the notes, would be considered an investment contract.

Hyperinflation A rise in the prices of goods and services at rates of 100 percent or more per year.

Hypothecation A broker/dealer's pledge of a customer stock to a bank as collateral for a bank loan. The proceeds of the bank loan are used to finance the debit balance in the customer's margin account.

Hypothecation agreement Agreement signed by a margin customer that pledges the securities in the account as collateral for the loan and allows the broker/dealer to use the securities as collateral with the bank supplying the loan money. (Also called the margin agreement.) Usually combined with the Loan Consent Form into one document with two signature lines. The combined document is called the Customer Agreement.

Illiquid asset Any asset that cannot be sold or disposed of without any loss in capital value in seven days or less.

Immediate-or-Cancel A limit order for multiple round lots that demands immediate execution at the stated price, and accepts partial execution. Any remaining portion of the order is canceled.

Income bond A bond on which interest is paid "when, as, and if earned." It is normally issued by companies in bankruptcy. Also called "adjustment bond."

Income statement The financial statement showing a corporation's performance over a period of time, such as a month, a quarter, or a year. The income statement shows revenues, cost of sales, and expenses.

Indenture The written agreement that specifies the terms of a bond or preferred stock issue.

Index   A statistical measure of the price activity of some composite group, usually expressed in relation to some previously established base market value. For example, the Consumer Price Index is a measure of the price of a market basket of goods relative to what those goods cost in 1984–1985. The NYSE Composite Index is computed relative to the price at the close of market at year-end 1965.

Indication of interest   A customer statement that he may consider purchasing securities in a new issue. Indications of interest are taken during the cooling-off period, after the customer has received a red herring.

Individual Retirement Account (IRA)   A pension plan allowing individuals to save for retirement while enjoying some of the tax advantages given to corporate pension plans.

Industrial revenue bonds   A municipal bond the proceeds of which are used to assist in the financing of a corporation in that jurisdiction.

Inflation   A rise in the prices of goods and services.

Inflation rate   The rate of increase in the price of goods and services. Commonly used measures of the rate of inflation are the Consumer Price Index, the Producer Price Index, and the GNP deflator.

Initial Public Offering (IPO)   The initial sale of securities to the public.

Inside market   The inside market is the lowest ask (selling) price and the highest bid (buying price) available for a particular security at a point in time.

Insider   Anyone in a position to influence the decisions of a corporation. Insiders include officers, directors, principal stockholders, and their respective immediate families. Insiders of a corporation are also referred to as affiliated persons or control persons.

Instinet   A computer system designed to assist institutions in trading securities among themselves, or fourth-market trading.

Institutional investor   An investor who is a bank, savings and loan association, insurance company, registered investment company, federal- or state-registered investment adviser, or any other person, corporation, partnership, trust, or other entity with total assets of at least $50 million.

Intangible drilling and development costs   The expenses associated with establishing an oil or gas well. These expenses have no salvage value and are immediately tax deductible.

Integration   The practice of including sales before and after an offering with sales during the offering to test whether maximums were violated for Regulation A offerings.

Interbank market   The market for foreign currencies in which the largest participants are the money center banks. The interbank market for currencies exists all over the world.

Interest   Money paid as compensation for the loan of someone else's money.

Intermarket Trading System (ITS)   Electronic system that electronically links seven exchanges (New York, American, Boston, Cincinnati, Midwest, Pacific, and Philadelphia) and, to a limited extent, the NASD (National Association of Securities Dealers). For securities being quoted in more than one market, the system allows orders to execute in whatever market offers the best quotation. The system may be used by brokers affecting trades for public customers and by specialists and market-makers trading for their own accounts.

Interpositioning   A prohibited practice of placing another firm between a broker/dealer and the best available market for a security, denying the customer the best available price.

In-the-money   A call option is in-the-money if the market price of the underlying stock is higher than the strike price of the call. A put option is in-the-money if the market price of the stock is lower than the strike price of the put. An in-the-money option contract is more likely to be exercised than one that is either at-the-money or out-of-the-money.

Intrastate offering   A solicitation to sell stock made only to residents of the state in which it originates. Also known as a Rule 147 offering.

Intrinsic value   The amount an option is in-the-money.

Introducing broker/dealers   Brokers or dealers who use another broker/dealer to carry and clear transactions and accounts for their customers and do not themselves hold customers' fund or securities. The receiving broker/dealer, usually a general securities firm, carries the account with the names and addresses of the customers fully disclosed. Customers write checks directly to the carrying broker/dealer. The introducing broker/dealer can receive securities, but must forward them immediately to the carrying firm. Customers may be public customers or other broker/dealers.

Inventory   The total of a corporation's assets held for sale, including raw materials, work-in-process, supplies used in operations, and finished goods.

Inverted head and shoulders pattern   A technical charting pattern that resembles an upside-down head-and-shoulders. It is a reversal pattern signaling the end of a down-trend and the beginning of an up-trend.

Investment   The use of capital to earn more money, by generating income and/or capital gains.

Investment adviser   In investment companies, the person or firm making the trading decisions. In other uses, a person or firm (i) providing investment advice for a fee; (ii) managing money for investors; or (iii) publishing investment newsletters for paid subscriptions.

Investment Advisers Act of 1940   The federal law regulating investment advisers. Among other things, the law requires investment advisers to register with the SEC.

Investment banker   A firm acting as intermediary either between a corporation issuing new securities and the public or between the holder of large blocks of securities and potential buyers. The investment banker may operate individually or in a syndicate with other investment bankers, and as an underwriter or an agent in the transaction.

Investment company   A company which, instead of manufacturing a product or providing a service, makes investments in securities or issues face amount certificates of the installment type.

Investment Company Act of 1940   The federal law regulating investment companies.

Investment contract   The catchall term for any securities that are not explicitly named but remain within the context of what the SEC was attempting with the 1934 Securities Exchange Act. The 1946 case of SEC v. W.J. Howey Co. established a test to determine what is an investment contract. *See Howey test.*

Investment grade securities   Securities rated by a nationally recognized statistical rating organization in one of its four highest generic rating categories.

Investor brochure   Publication of the MSRB that describes municipal securities trading. Upon receiving a complaint from a customer, the broker-dealer must deliver the brochure to the customer.

In-whole call   The call of an entire issue, as opposed to a partial call.

IOC   *See Immediate-or-Cancel.*

IPO   *See Initial Public Offering.*

Issue   An offering of securities.

Issuer   The corporation offering or proposing to offer securities.

JTWROS (Joint tenancy with rights of survivorship)   a type of ownership right. When one owner dies, his interest passes to his surviving co-tenants.

Keogh (or HR-10) plan   A tax-advantaged investment designed to assist self-employed persons (either full-time or part-time) and employees of unincorporated businesses in saving for retirement.

Layoff stock   Stock that the syndicate acquires and then sells in a rights offering.

Lagging indicator   An economic indicator or signal that reacts slowly to economy changes. Unemployment figures are a lagging indicator.

Leading indicator   An economic indicator or signal that is in the forefront of changes in economic activity. Stock prices are an example of a leading indicator.

LEAPS (Long-Term Equity AnticiPation Securities)   Long-term equity options traded on the CBOE with expirations of up to thirty-nine months distant (although in practice usually no more than 30 months hence). LEAPS are available on a number of blue chip (large capitalization) stocks. Work much the same as other equity options, but are not as time sensitive and tend to have a larger premium (price).

Lease rental bond   A municipal revenue bond that is supported by lease payments on a building, usually a building leased to a government agency.

Legal list   A list of investments compiled by a state government as the only investments acceptable for certain institutions or fiduciaries. States without such lists typically use the Prudent Man Rule.

Legal opinion   A written opinion by a bond counsel stating whether or not a bond issue conforms with all the laws of the issuer, and the state and federal governments. It also addresses the tax status of the bonds.

Letter of intent   In mutual funds, a written statement by a customer promising to purchase a stated number of mutual fund shares. The letter assures the investor a reduced sales charge on the entire purchase, provided it is completed within thirteen months.

Leverage   The use of debt when purchasing investments. Leverage increases the percentage profit, but also the percentage loss.

Leveraged Buy-Out (LBO)   Financial transaction in which a corporation's management repurchases all public shares, usually by incurring substantial debt, and the company goes private. Usually involves fairly stable, mature companies with good cash flows. Equity money for the LBO often comes from the investment banker or LBO specialist that arranges the buyout and underwrites the debt issue.

Liabilities   All claims on the assets of an individual or corporation. Includes accrued payable amounts, long-and short-term debt, debentures, and notes. Does not include the ownership equity.

LIFO Last-in, First-out   A method of accounting for which shares or inventory items are being sold from a pool of similar shares or items. Assumes that when a sale is made, the items purchased last in a group are sold first.

Limited authorization or discretion   A power of attorney that allows the person holding it to enter orders in the account but not to add or withdraw funds.

Limited partner   A partner with limited liability who may not engage in business for the partnership.

Limited partnership   A partnership comprised of one or more general partners with unlimited obligations and liability, and one or more limited partners with limited obligations and liability.

Limited rep-government securities   A registered rep who deals only with government securities (Series 72).

Limit order   An order to buy or sell subject to some limitation as to price.

Liquid assets   Cash or assets easily convertible to cash, such as Treasury bills, money market fund shares, or demand deposits.

Liquidate   Convert into cash, using the cash to satisfy creditors.

Liquidation period   For a variable annuity, the time from the date when the first annuity payment is made to the annuitant to the date when the annuity is fully paid out.

Liquidity   For an investment, portfolio, or account, the ease with which assets may be converted into cash. For a market, the ability of the market to absorb fairly large volumes of sales without drastically affecting the price.

Load fund   A mutual fund that either sells shares through an underwriter or broker/dealer and charges either an up-front or deferred sales charge, or sells the shares directly but charges more than .25 percent in 12b-1 charges per year.

Loan consent form   A customer document that allows the broker/dealer to pledge customer stock to the bank to borrow the money for the margin account. It allows the firm to hypothecate the stock.

Locked market   Market in which the highest bid and the lowest asked prices for a security are equal.

Long   Owning the security or other item with the expectation that its value will increase. When a person is long a stock or an option, he owns the stock or holds the option.

Long straddle   An options position in which the customer is long a call and a put on the same underlying asset. The position is profitable if the price of the underlying asset moves outside the two break-even points. Long straddles are only profitable in volatile markets.

Long-term capital gains   Gains on assets held for more than 12 months. Usually qualify for lower tax rates than short-term gains do.

Long-term Equity Anticipation Securities (LEAPS)   Equity options on the CBOE covering 100 shares of stock with expirations up to 39 months distant.

Lump-sum distribution   A distribution of a participant's entire balance from an annuity or from all of an employer's qualified pension plans in one year.

Maintenance call   In a margin account, the broker/dealer demand for additional funds to restore the equity to the minimum maintenance level.

Maloney Act of 1938   The act that added section 15A to the Securities Exchange Act of 1934, allowing for the establishment of registered securities associations to promote self-regulation of the securities industry, properly supervised by the government.

Management fee   In an underwriting, the special fee paid to the managing underwriter.

Manipulation   The illegal act of creating a false impression of trading volume or price for a security. Includes engaging in wash sales or matching orders, lying, giving or circulating misleading information, or trying to illegally peg, fix or stabilize the price of an issue (i.e., not following the allowable procedure for stabilizing).

Margin   The amount a client pays for a security purchase in a credit (or margin) account with a broker/dealer. Initial margins on purchases are set by the Federal Reserve Board. Minimum margin maintenance amounts are set by the exchanges.

Margin account   An account in which a customer may pay only part of the purchase price of securities.

Margin agreement   The customer consent pledging his securities as collateral for a debit balance.

Margin call   In a margin account, the request for more equity to bring the account up to the minimum margin maintenance level. Margin calls can be met by depositing cash or stock, or by using SMA.

Markdown   A reduction in price below that at which the security is offered. Acting as dealer and buying stock for its own account from a customer, the firm charges a markdown. This is the firm's compensation.

Market-maker   A firm that buys and sells a particular security for its own account.

Market order   An order to buy or sell as soon as possible at the best available price.

Market price   For securities sold on an exchange, the last reported price at which the security sold. For over-the-counter securities, the inside market quote.

Marking-to-market   Adjusting the value of a security or a portfolio to the current market value. Used in margin accounts to make sure the margin amounts comply with maintenance requirements.

Markup   An amount added to the price of a security. Acting as dealer and selling stock to a customer from his own account, the dealer charges a markup. The markup is the firm's compensation in the trade.

Matching orders   A prohibited practice similar to a wash sale but involving two or more firms trading a security back and forth at the same price in an attempt to show more trading volume than is actually occurring.

Maturity class of option   Options of the same type (put or call) on the same underlying asset with the same expiration month. All XYZ January call options belong to one maturity class; all XYZ April call options belong to another.

Maturity date   The date the face value of a bond is paid.

MBIA   The Municipal Bond Insurance Association, which insures entire issues of municipal bonds.

Member order   In a municipal underwriting, an order by a syndicate member for its own account or a related portfolio.

Merger   The process whereby two or more corporations join into a single corporation.

MIG ratings   Moody's Investment Services ratings for short-term municipal obligations. MIG stands for Moody's Investment Grade.

Mil   Equivalent to 0.001 points. A percentage used in tax rates to determine tax liability. Equivalent to .1 percent.

Minimum maintenance   In a margin account, the minimum equity allowed before a maintenance margin call will be issued.

Minimum-maximum underwriting   A type of best efforts underwriting. It is similar to an all-or-none underwriting until the minimum amount is raised, in that the offering is canceled if that amount is not raised. It then becomes a normal best efforts underwriting above that amount. An example is a real estate limited partnership with a $2 million minimum and a $50 million maximum.

Minor   Someone who is under the legal age for his or her state of residence (18 to 21).

Minor Rule Violation Plan Letter   Procedure of the NASD for certain minor violations of rules by members and their associates when the facts are not in dispute. Mechanics are identical to the Acceptance, Waiver, and Consent Procedure, except that sanctions are limited to a fine of $2,500 and/or a censuring letter. The violations that qualify are all related to the keeping, approving, and reporting of data.

Money market account   An account with a bank or broker/dealer in which the funds are invested in short-term interest-bearing securities. Similar to checking accounts, except that they have limits on checks written per month and pay interest. Accounts with banks are insured by the FDIC.

Money market fund   A mutual fund whose assets are low risk, short-term money market instruments such as Treasury bills, commercial CDs, and commercial paper. Usually these funds offer check-writing privileges.

Money purchase plan   Corporate pension plan in which the employer commits to contribute some percentage of each participant's compensation each year, such as with a 401(k) or a SEP plan.

Money purchase plans   Type of corporate retirement plan in which contributions are based on a percent of the participant's compensation without regard to whether or not the business has a profit.

Money spread An options spread position in which the expiration months are the same, but the strike prices are different, also known as a vertical spread.

Moral obligation bond A municipal revenue bond that the state is morally obligated to redeem, should the bonds go into default.

Moral suasion Tactic used by the Federal Reserve Board to pressure banks into doing what it wants. Officials of the Fed might have heart-to-heart talks with the banks' directors, increase the severity of bank inspections, appeal to community spirit, or make vague threats. Since the Fed has the power to close banks, remove officers, and fire directors, the arguments of the Fed are likely to be very persuasive indeed.

Mortality risk The risk that the remaining lifetime for an annuitant will be different than expected by the mortality tables used by the insurance company. If the annuitant chooses to receive payments over his remaining life, the insurance company accepts that risk.

Mortgage-backed security The most common type of pass-through security, secured by homeowners' mortgages and sometimes guaranteed by the Veteran's Administration, the Farmer's Home Administration, or the Federal Housing Administration.

Mortgage bond A bond secured by a lien on real property.

MSRB Municipal Securities Rulemaking Board.

Municipal underwriting An offering undertaken by a syndicate of broker/dealers to sell an issue of municipal securities.

Munifacts A wire service that provides news of interest to municipal bond traders.

Mutual fund An open-end investment company.

Naked option A short option position in which the writer does not have visible means of meeting the exercise requirement.

NASD *See National Association of Securities Dealers, Inc.*

NASDAQ The computer system designed to facilitate trading of over-the-counter securities. NASDAQ© stands for the National Association of Securities Dealers Automated Quotation System.

National Association of Securities Dealers, Inc. (NASD) This is the self-regulatory organization that is responsible for supervising the OTC market.

National exchanges The large exchanges based in New York City are commonly known as the national exchanges: the New York Stock Exchange and the American Stock Exchange.

National Market System (NMS) The most actively traded stocks on the NASDAQ© System.

National Medallion Signature Guarantee A statement (a stamp and signature) given by a participant in the guarantee program to ensure that the sale, transfer, or assignment of a security certificate is not fraudulent. The guarantor could be a commercial bank, credit union, brokerage firm, or other financial institution that is a member of a medallion signature guarantee program approved by the Securities Transfer Association and the SEC. Three such programs exist: Securities Transfer Association Medallion Program (STAMP), the NY Stock Exchange Program (MSP), and the Stock Exchange Medallion Program (SEMP). The medallion program is not a guarantee by a notary public.

National Securities Clearing Corporation (NSCC)   Firm that clears trades for the NYSE, the ASE, and the over-the-counter market.

National securities exchange   The SEC's definition includes three types of entities: national exchanges, regional exchanges and Electronic Communication Networks, or ECNs.

NAV   *See Net Asset Value.*

Negotiable   A term used to describe a security for which title may be transferred by delivery, such as a stock certificate with a properly signed stock power.

Negotiated market   A market in which prices are determined by negotiation between broker/dealers. The OTC market is a negotiated market.

Negotiated underwriting   New offering in which the issuer and the brokerage firm negotiate a contract for the brokerage firm to sell the securities.

Net Asset Value (NAV)   In a mutual fund, the assets of the fund less its liabilities divided by the number of shares outstanding. This is the price a mutual fund shareholder receives when selling shares of the fund.

Net capital   The net worth of the firm less an adjustment for illiquid assets (i.e., the net liquid assets of the firm). The Securities Exchange Act of 1934 establishes uniform and comprehensive net capital standards for all broker/dealers, including members of national securities exchanges and municipal securities broker/dealers.

Net capital ratio   A ratio of the firm's aggregate indebtedness to the firm's net capital. The lower the net capital ratio, the better the financial condition of the firm. For example, a net capital ratio of 6:1 is better than a net capital ratio of 9:1.

Net interest cost   In a syndicate bid on a competitive bid underwriting, the cost of the offering to the issuer. It is adjusted for premium or discount prices, but does not include any net present value computations. (Compare with True interest cost.) The firm offering the issuer the lowest net interest cost wins the bid and underwrites the issue.

Net investment income   For a mutual fund, gross investment income less management fees, Rule 12b-1 fees, and administrative expenses.

Net revenue pledge In a municipal revenue bond, a provision in the trust indenture stating that revenues will first be used to pay the operating and maintenance costs of the facility. The net revenues will then be used to support the debt.

Net proceeds The offering proceeds less all expenses of issuing and costs of distributing securities, including the underwriting compensation.

Net worth Owners' equity of the firm, or all assets less all liabilities. For a corporation, net worth is equal to the total of capital stock, paid-in capital, and retained earnings.

New issue Securities being issued by a corporation for the first time. May be additional shares for a class of securities that are already in existence.

Nine-bond rule Requirement that members of the NYSE first attempt to execute any order for less than ten bonds on the floor of the NYSE before trading in the over-the-counter market. The only exception is when the customer initiates an unsolicited request to trade in the OTC market.

NMS *See National Market System.*

No-load fund A fund that sells shares directly and charges .25 percent or less in 12b-1 charges per year.

Nominal quote A quote that is not a firm quote. A broker/dealer giving a nominal quote is not obligated to trade at that price.

Nominal yield The stated interest rate on a bond issue, often called the coupon rate.

Non-cumulative Term used to describe preferred stocks for which dividends that are not paid are gone forever and do not accrue.

Nonparticipating preferred stock A type of preferred stock that does not pay higher dividends when the corporation has higher earnings.

Nonrecourse loan In a limited partnership, a loan for which the limited partners are not personally liable.

Non-systematic risk Risk that an individual stock or bond will perform badly as compared to the market. Diversification effectively eliminates this risk.

Non-tax-qualified annuity The normal type of annuity. Contributions are not tax deductible; when payments are received, the annuitant is taxed only on the portion representing earnings. The return of capital is not taxed.

Notice of public offering Notice that Rule 135 allows issuers to publish stating that they intend to make a public offering of securities to be registered under the 1933 Act. May be a news release, a written letter to employees or shareholders, or a published statement. Sometimes used to solicit competitive bids for underwriting the offering. Not considered to be an actual offer of the securities.

Notice of sale Same as *Notice of Public Offering.*

NYSE The New York Stock Exchange.

NYSE Composite Index An index of all the common stocks listed on the NYSE.

OBO *See Order Book Official.*

OCC *See Options Clearing Corporation.*

Odd lot Less than the usual trading unit of 100 shares of stock or 5 bonds.

Odd lot theory An investment theory that contends that as a whole the odd lotters are always wrong. Odd lotters' buying is a sell signal. Odd lotters' selling is a buy signal.

OEX The symbol for Standard & Poor's 100 Index options.

Offer The price a seller of a security is willing to take.

Offering A new distribution of shares offered to the public, also known as a public offering.

Offering circular The preliminary version of an offering statement used in a Regulation A offering.

Offering date The later of the effective date of a new issue's registration or the first date the security is actually offered to the public.

Offering price The lowest price a seller of a security is willing to take for a unit of a security at a particular time. (Note that the OTC market uses the term *asked*, while the exchanges use the term *offered* or *offering*.)

Offer of Settlement An offer to settle a dispute made by the respondent in a disciplinary action of the NASD. May be made any time after the respondent is notified of a complaint. All rights of appeal are waived if the settlement offer is accepted.

Offices of Supervisory Jurisdiction (OSJs) A branch office of an NASD member in which registered personnel execute orders; engage in market-making; structure public offerings or private placements; hold customer's funds; hold customer's securities; accept new accounts; review and endorse customers orders; approve advertising or sales literature; and/or supervise associates at one or more of the member's branch offices. The main office would automatically be an OSJ.

Official statement The disclosure document in a municipal bond offering. Issuers of municipal bonds are not required to publish an official statement, but most do anyway.

Oil and gas income program Buying existing oil and gas wells and producing the wells to generate income. The program does not generate intangible drilling and development costs, and does not generate high tax deductions.

Omnibus account A special account a broker/dealer opens with another firm to trade on behalf of a subsidiary or affiliate. Also, an account an investment adviser opens to trade on behalf of his or her clients, in which the brokerage firm does not know the individual identities of the clients.

Open-end investment company *See Mutual Fund.*

Open interest The number of outstanding option contracts.

Open market operations Refers to the Federal Reserve's buying or selling U.S. government securities. The Federal Open Market Committee conducts the policy.

Open order An order that has been entered but not effected.

Option A contract that gives a holder the right to buy (call option) or sell (put option) a fixed amount of a security at a specific price anytime before the stated expiration date (for an American-style option). If the holder does not exercise his option, the option expires and he forfeits the amount he paid for the option (the premium).

Options Clearing Corporation (OCC) The OCC is the actual issuer of option contracts. It acts as a clearing house, or bookkeeper. When an exercise notice is received, it assigns the notice. It is also considered the obligor and guarantor of option contracts, guaranteeing performance.

Options Disclosure Document An OCC prospectus explaining the nature of options, the types of options available, and the basic strategies and risk factors. Must be sent to new options customers when an options account is opened. Updated prospectuses must be sent to existing customers no later than with the confirmation of the customer's next options trade.

Order The specific instructions given for buying or selling a security.

Order Book Official An employee of the CBOE who maintains the public limit order file, which is similar to a specialist's book. Also referred to as an OBO or Board Broker, he executes limit orders for options.

Order period In a municipal underwriting, a short period when all orders are accepted without regard to the priority for orders for the offering.

Ordinary income For tax purposes, income from wages, salaries, and self-employment, demagogically called *earned income.*

OSS System The automated execution system for CBOE options.

OTC Bulletin Board (OTCBB) Quotation system developed for penny stocks and other thinly traded securities. The system lists domestic and foreign equity securities (including registered ADRs) that have at least one market-maker, are not listed on NASDAQ© or a national securities exchange, and are not listed on a regional exchange and eligible for consolidated tape reporting. To be eligible for listing, foreign equity securities must be fully registered with the SEC and domestic securities must be providing current financial information to the SEC.

OTC market *See Over-the-counter market.*

Out-of-the-money Lacking intrinsic value. A call option is out-of-the-money if the market price of the underlying stock is less than the strike price of the call. A put option is out-of-the-money if the market price of the underlying stock is higher than the strike price of the put.

Overlapping debt Multifarious debt that rests on a single debtor. In general, obligation municipal bonds, bonds issued by a city, county, school district, and water district may all look to the same people for taxes to support the debt.

Overriding royalty interest In an oil and gas program, a compensation arrangement giving the general partner a percentage of the gross income, on top of the other royalties.

Over-the-counter market The market for securities that are not listed on an exchange. Various broker/dealers buy and sell these securities for their own accounts.

Parity An option trading for exactly its intrinsic value is said to be trading at parity.

Parity price For convertible securities, the price level at which their exchange value equals that of the common stock.

Participating preferred stock Preferred stock that shares in exceptional earnings of the corporation. Participating preferred stocks may be paid an extra quarterly dividend if the company has a very good year.

Participating (semi-fixed) trusts A unit investment trust that purchases shares of a particular investment company and then sells shares of the portfolio on a contractual basis to investors. Virtually all contractual plans are structured as participating trusts, also referred to as periodic payment plan companies.

Partnership A business entity in which two or more people agree to share equally the risks and profits of the business.

Par value The face value appearing on the certificate. Preferred stocks normally have a par value of $100, bonds, a par value of $1000.

Passive income For tax purposes, income from direct investments in a business venture, such as income from limited partnerships, by an investor who does not actively participate in management.

Pass-through security In a pass-through security, debt obligations are purchased by an intermediary who packages them into new securities backed by the pooled obligations and then sells shares in the pool in the open market. The interest and principal payments made by the debtor flow through the intermediary, who pays them to the investor net of service fees. The most common type of pass-through security is a mortgage-backed security, secured by homeowners' mortgages and sometimes guaranteed by the Veteran's Administration, the Farmer's Home Administration, or the Federal Housing Administration.

Payment date   The date on which a corporation pays a dividend that has been declared.

P/E ratio   *See Price to Earnings ratio.*

Penny stocks   Speculative equity securities (excluding options and investment company shares) with prices under $5 per share. Usually do not meet the listing requirements for NASDAQ© or the exchanges. Their sale through broker/dealers is subject to certain rules as to approval of customers, maintenance of information to support quotations, distribution of account statements, and disclosure of risk, quotations, and compensation.

PHA Bonds   *See Public Housing Authority Bonds.*

Phantom income   In a limited partnership, taxable income that exceeds cash distributions.

Pink sheets   A listing (on pink paper) of OTC securities, their quotes, and the firms that make the market.

Placement Ratio   The ratio of new issue municipal bonds sold during a particular week divided by the dollar amount of new issue municipal bonds available during that week. It is published by the Bond Buyer.

Plan completion life insurance   Insurance with an optional feature stipulating that if the plan holder dies before completing the contract, a life insurance policy will complete the purchase. The insurance proceeds are paid to the custodian bank of the plan, which completes the purchase.

PN   *See Project note.*

Point   A price increment for a security or index. One point is $1.00 for stocks and $10.00 for bonds (1% of $1000 face value). However, a one-point rise in the NYSE Composite Index does not represent $1.

Portfolio income   For tax purposes, an income category that includes capital gains and losses, and interest and dividend income.

Position limits   A limit set by the exchange on which an option trades as to the number of standard options contracts on the same side of the market on the same underlying security that an investor may hold at any given time. Set at 75,000, 60,000, 31,500, 22,500 or 13,500 contracts for each option class. Reviewed semiannually (January 1 and July 1). *See Side of market.*

Positions book   An electronic or paper record maintained by the registered rep that shows which customers have a position in each security.

Pot   In a corporate underwriting, syndicate members estimate their sales to institutional investors. Those shares are set aside (placed in "the pot") and handled by the managing underwriter.

Power of attorney   A written statement executed by a customer to give someone else the right to enter orders in the customer's account. Must be witnessed by a notary public or other public official.

Pre-dispute arbitration clause   An agreement between the firm and either its customer or its employee that states that the parties to the agreement will subject future disagreements to arbitration.

Preemptive right   A corporate shareholder's right to maintain his share of ownership when new shares are sold through a rights offering.

Preferred stock   A type of corporate stock with a stated dividend that must be paid before the common stockholders may receive a dividend. A preferred stock also has priority in liquidation over the common stock.

Preliminary prospectus   A preliminary version of the prospectus that is published as soon as the offering is registered with the SEC. It does not include the final price or spread, and may not be used to solicit orders, but may be used to solicit indications of interest. It is often referred to as a "red herring."

Preliminary study   A short analysis done as part of the negotiation process in an offering to determine if an investment banker wishes to proceed with an underwriting.

Preliminary statement   A preliminary version of the official statement for a municipal bond offering.

Premium   The amount the buyer of an option pays a writer of the option. Also, the amount by which the current market price for a preferred stock or bond is higher than par or face value.

Pre-refunding   Selling a new bond issue to refund (refinance) an old issue prior to the call date of the old bonds. The proceeds of the offering are placed in an escrow account until the call date is reached.

Pre-sale order   An order for a new issue municipal bond taken by a syndicate prior to winning the bid. It is used to help the syndicate gauge the reception the offering is likely to receive.

Price to Earnings (P/E) ratio   The ratio of the price of a common stock to its earnings per share, often referred to as the P/E ratio. It is used to measure how expensive a stock is, relative to its earnings.

Primary distribution   A sale of new stock to the public.

Primary market   The buying and selling of new issues. Resales are handled in the secondary markets.

Prime rate   The interest rate banks charge their best customers.

Principal   (1) In a loan, the amount of the loan, not including interest; (2) in a brokerage firm, a person in an ownership and/or supervisory capacity; and (3) in a trade, a firm acting as dealer.

Principal stockholder   Any person or entity owning ten percent or more of the common stock of the corporation.

Principal transactions   Dealer transactions done directly with customers. The firm must disclose if it is acting as a principal in a transaction.

Private placement   A securities offering under Regulation D that is not registered with the SEC. The offering is generally made to a limited number of persons who meet certain suitability standards.

Private placement memorandum   A disclosure document that must be prepared by the issuer in a Schedule D offering if any offers are made to nonaccredited investors. This document must be given to all offerees, not just the nonaccredited investors.

Private securities transaction   A transaction by a registered representative acting outside the scope of his employment with a broker/dealer. If done without the knowledge and consent of the employer, it is prohibited. This is also known as "selling away."

Proceeds sale   Selling one security, and using the proceeds to buy another.

Production purchase program   *See Oil and gas income program.*

Profile   A summary prospectus for registered mutual funds, permitted by Rule 498 of the 1933 Act. It summarizes key information about the fund and gives investors the option of purchasing the fund's shares based on the information in the profile. An investor who purchases fund shares based on the profile will receive the fund's prospectus with the purchase confirmation. The fund must file a profile with the Commission at least 30 days prior to first use.

Profit-sharing plans   Type of corporate retirement plan in which contributions are made out of net profits, either based on a precise formula or merely made in substantial and systematic way. An employee stock ownership plan (ESOP) is a profit sharing plan in which the contribution is made in stock.

Program trading   Computer-aided trading in which orders are automatically generated at trigger points.

Progressive tax   A tax that rises in rate as the taxpayer's income increases; for example, income tax.

Project note   A short-term municipal note used to finance low income housing projects.

Prospectus   The disclosure document for an offering registered with the SEC. The final prospectus is issued on the effective date, when the offering is released by the SEC.

Prospectus delivery period   The period after a public offering during which dealers must usually give a final prospectus to purchasers who buy the security in the secondary market. Extends to 40 calendar days after the offering date, or for 90 calendar days if it was an initial public offering. Calculated for shelf distributions the same as for other issues, even though the offering may continue for some time beyond that point. The delivery period is dropped to 25 calendar days if the security is listed on an exchange or included in NASDAQ© by the offering date.

Proxy   A written authorization by a stockholder giving his voting rights to someone else. Shareholders who cannot attend the annual meeting usually give their proxies to someone else, often to management.

Prudent Man Rule   A standard by which a fiduciary is required to invest the funds under his care in some states. The standard demands that a fiduciary should act with the care, skill, prudence, and diligence that a prudent man who is familiar with such matters would use if he were acting under conditions in which the circumstances, his capacity, the character of the enterprise, and the goal of the enterprise were similar. This is a general standard adopted by some states. Other states, called legal list states, specify the particular investments a fiduciary may use.

Public float value   The aggregate market value of common equity securities held by persons who are not affiliated with the issuer.

Public Housing Authority Bonds   Municipal bonds that provide long-term financing (mortgages) for low income housing projects, commonly referred to as PHA bonds, and guaranteed by the U.S. government. Sometimes they are called New Housing Authority Bonds, or NHAs.

Public Offering   Securities offerings that are made to the general public.

Public offering price   For a mutual fund, the price at which an investor may buy a share, or the net asset value plus the sales load. If the fund does not charge an up-front sales charge, the public offering price is the net asset value.

Purchaser's representative   In a Rule 506 offering under Regulation D, pertaining to a private placement, investors are encouraged to appoint someone to act as their representative. He is to analyze the offering to ensure that it is a suitable investment.

Put bond   A bond with a put option that allows the owner to sell the bond back to the issuer at certain intervals, usually at par.

Put option   An option that gives the holder the right to sell the underlying asset, and the writer the obligation to buy the asset at a specified price.

Put spread   An option spread position in which the investor is long a put and short a put on the same asset.

Qualified purchasers   Under the Investment Company Act of 1940, individuals with investments of at least $5 million or persons who have discretion over investments of at least $25 million for their own accounts or the accounts of other qualified purchasers. Exemptions from the definition of an investment company are allowed for companies who sell their shares only to qualified purchasers.

Qualified retirement plan   A pension, profit sharing, or stock bonus plan set up by an employer to provide retirement benefits for employees that qualifies for special tax treatment. In general, a plan qualifies if participation in the plan and benefits do not discriminate in favor of the employer's key employees.

Quick assets   Assets that can readily be converted to cash, including marketable securities, accounts receivable, and checking accounts.

Quick ratio   The ratio between quick assets and current liabilities. This is a measure of the liquidity of the company.

Quotation   A bid price or asked price given by a dealer. A two-sided quotation would include both a bid and asked price.

RAN   *See Revenue Anticipation Note.*

Random walk theory   An investment theory holding that all that can be known about a stock is incorporated into its price. It is, therefore, impossible to outperform market averages in the long run. It suggests that stock prices move in a random way that cannot be foreseen.

Real Estate Investment Trust   A closed-end investment company that invests in real estate, either directly or through real estate loans, commonly referred to as a REIT.

Real Estate Mortgage Investment Conduit   Mortgages pooled to sell to investors, commonly called a REMIC.

Reallowance   In a corporate underwriting, the compensation of a firm that is not a member of the syndicate or the selling group for selling shares to the public.

Recession   A mild form of depression, identified by two consecutive calendar quarters of economic decline.

Record date   The date determining shareholders of record (those who own the stock) who are entitled to receive a dividend.

Recourse loan   In a limited partnership, a loan for which the limited partners are personally liable.

Recovery   The phase of the business cycle when economic activity begins to improve from a recession or depression.

Redeemable security   Security that entitles the holder to receive approximately his proportionate share of the issuer's current net assets (or its cash equivalent) upon presentation of the security to the issuer or its designated representative.

Redemption fee   A fee charged some mutual funds upon sale of shares back to the fund, generally not exceeding 1% of the sale proceeds.

Redemption price   Price the issuer must pay if he or she wishes to redeem bonds before maturity or retire preferred stock shares. Also known as call price.

Red herring   *See Preliminary prospectus.*

Reference security   Security X is a reference security for another security, Y, if Y may be converted into, exchanged for, or exercised to purchase or sell X, or if X in whole or part determines the value of Y. For example, if a convertible bond is convertible into common stock, the common stock would be a reference security for the bond, but the bond would not be a reference security for the stock.

Refunding   Selling a new bond issue and using the proceeds to call an outstanding issue (usually done to decrease interest costs or extend maturity). Also called refinancing.

Regional exchanges   The traditional exchanges outside of New York city: the Midwest, Pacific, Philadelphia, Boston, and Cincinnati exchanges.

Registered bond   A bond whose ownership is recorded on the books of the issuing corporation. A registered bond must be endorsed by the registered owner before it is transferable (as opposed to a bearer bond).

Registered Options Principal   A person who is in charge of supervising options trading, commonly referred to as a ROP. Most branch managers perform this function.

Registered Options Trader (ROT)   A person on the floor of an options exchange who buys and sells options for his own account, also known as a Market-Maker. He performs the dealer functions of the specialist on the floor of the NYSE.

Registered representative   An employee of a broker/dealer that is a member of the NASD or a stock exchange who is registered with the SEC and performs the duties of an account executive.

Registrar   The company official who maintains the list of corporate shareholders, and ascertains the correct number of outstanding shares.

Registration   Process by which securities must be filed with the SEC. Registration of new issues is covered under the Securities Act of 1933. Registration of securities admitted to trading on a national securities exchange is covered under the Securities Exchange Act of 1934.

Regressive tax   A tax the rate of which increases as the taxpayer's income decreases.

Regular way settlement   For corporate and municipal securities, settlement three business days after the trade date. For U.S. government securities, the next business day. The word "settlement" applies only to broker/dealers, not customers.

Regulated investment companies   Investment companies that qualify for special tax treatment, avoiding the double income taxation on dividends.

Regulation A offerings   Offerings of $1,500,000 or less that do not have to be fully registered with the SEC.

Regulation D   The federal regulation pertaining to private placements of offerings to a limited number of people meeting certain suitability standards. Private placements need not register with the SEC.

Regulation M   Regulation that restricts the trading of an existing security by participants in a public offering of that security.

Regulation S   Safe harbor that allows both domestic and foreign issuers to distribute and resell securities outside the United States without registering them in the United States.

Regulation T   The federal regulation governing extension of credit by broker/dealers to customers for trading securities. Regulation T mandates payment conditions and governs margin accounts.

Regulation U   The federal regulation of bank loans collateralized by securities, including broker/dealer hypothecation of stock.

REIT   *See Real Estate Investment Trust.*

REMIC   *See Real Estate Mortgage Investment Conduit.*

Re-offering scale   In a municipal bond underwriting, the initial yields at which the bonds are offered to the public.

Representative   Any associate of an NASD member firm who is engaged in the investment banking or securities business for the member but is not a principal. Representatives can include assistant officers, people who supervise or train employees, and people who solicit or conduct business in securities. Member firms must register all representatives with the NASD.

Repurchase agreement   A contract committing a U.S. government securities dealer to sell U.S. government securities to a purchaser (often to a municipality or institutional investor), with a provision that he repurchase the securities at a set price at a specified time, usually the next day. This is a money market instrument.

Reserve requirements   A specified percentage of customers' deposits that a bank must keep on deposit with the Federal Reserve System. The reserve requirements vary according to whether the deposits are time deposits or demand deposits.

Resistance   A charting pattern in which a stock price tops out or levels off. Breaking the resistance level is a buy signal for a technical analyst.

Restricted account   A margin account with a balance below 50 percent equity.

Restricted securities   Securities that have been purchased directly from the issuer or an affiliate of the issuer rather than through a public offering. Affiliated persons might obtain restricted securities by exercising stock options included in the person's compensation plan. Nonaffiliated persons would normally purchase restricted stock through a Regulation D offering or in a transaction subject to Rule 144A, Private Resales of Securities to Institutions. Subject to holding periods before resale.

Retention   (1) When securities are sold in a restricted margin account, at least 50 percent of the sale proceeds must remain in the account and be applied to reduce the debit balance. (2) In an underwriting, the number of shares sold on a retail basis by a syndicate member. This is the syndicate member's allotment, less any shares held in "the pot" for sale to institutional investors, and any shares given up to the selling group.

Revenue Anticipation Note   A short-term municipal note sold when the issuer is expecting to receive a large sum of money, usually from the federal government, commonly referred to as a RAN. When the funds are received, the RAN is repaid.

Revenue bond   A municipal bond that is to be paid from the revenues of a specific project, such as a stadium. If the revenues are insufficient to support the debt, the bond goes into default. The issuer is not required to use other revenues to redeem the bond.

Reverse split   A process by which multiple stock shares are combined into one share such that the stockholder's equity (both in total and for the individual stockholder) remains unchanged, but each stockholder holds fewer shares worth more each. For example, in a one-for-two reverse split, each stockholder receives one share for every two shares held. The new shares are worth twice as much as the old shares, but since the stockholder has half as many shares, his investment remains unchanged.

Reversionary working interest   In oil and gas programs, a sharing arrangement whereby the general partner does not share in revenues until the limited partners have recouped their initial investment.

Rights   Certificates allowing shareholders to purchase enough new shares to maintain their percentage of ownership in the corporation.

Rights of accumulation   In mutual funds, the right to reduce sales charges when a shareholder's total purchases exceed a breakpoint. There is no time limit for rights of accumulation.

Rights offering   A rights offering occurs when a corporation makes new shares (called "rights") available to its existing shareholders, thus allowing them to maintain their existing proportion of ownership in the corporation.

Riskless transaction   A transaction by a broker/dealer who, upon a customer's request, buys a security for its own account first, then sells it to the customer as a dealer, and charges a markup. Riskless transactions are also known as simultaneous transactions.

Rollover   Distribution from an employer's qualified pension plan into an IRA or the direct and immediate transfer of funds from one IRA to another (such as switching between funds). Usually does not generate a penalty or tax on the withdrawal.

Rollup of a DPP   A transaction in which a direct participation program not listed on an exchange or NASDAQ© is "rolled up" into another public DPP, a public trust, or a public corporation. The form of the rollup could be an acquisition, merger, or consolidation.

ROP   *See Registered Options Principal.*

ROT   *See Registered Options Trader.*

Roth IRA   Individual retirement account for which contributions are taxed but qualified distributions are not.

Round lot   The normal trading unit of a security: 100 shares of stock or 5 bonds in the OTC market (1 bond on the NYSE).

Royalty   In oil and gas programs, a percentage of revenues paid to the owner of the mineral rights in return for allowing the partnership to drill on the property.

Rule 134 communication   Tombstone advertisement or other purely factual communication about an offering that is not a solicitation.

Rule 144   The federal law regarding resale of securities without registration if the securities are owned by affiliated persons or the securities are restricted.

Rule 144A   Rule that exempts private placements of some issuers from the SEC registration and disclosure requirements, and allows qualified institutional investors (insurance companies, investment companies, pension plans, investment advisers, etc.) to trade these securities among themselves without some of the restrictions imposed to protect the public. Securities must not be of the same class as securities listed on a registered national securities exchange or quoted on a U.S. automated inter-dealer quotation system (or be convertible or exchangeable into a class thus listed or quoted). Issues of foreign securities are sometimes traded in this fashion.

Rule 147   An exemption from federal registration for securities offered within a single state and thus regulated by that state. The issuer and the purchasers must meet certain requirements. Limitations on resales apply.

Rules of Fair Practice   *See Conduct Rules.*

Sallie Mae   *See Student Loan Marketing Agency*

Sales charges   Any charges or fees paid by the investor and used by the investment company to cover sales or promotional expenses, regardless of whether they are paid up-front, deferred, or assessed against the assets of the fund. Also called sales load.

Sales literature   All promotional items with a controlled distribution, meaning the firm knows in advance who will see the item. Examples include reports given to customers, circulars, market letters, performance reports or summaries, telemarketing scripts, seminar texts, research reports, form letters, or reprints or excerpts of any other advertisement, sales literature, or published article. Does not include communications that are neither advertising or sales literature.

Savings Incentive Matching Plan for Employees (SIMPLE)   Plan created to give small business owners (including self-employed individuals) the ability to offer retirement plans to employees without incurring excessive costs or administrative burdens. To be eligible, companies must have 100 or fewer employees. The plan must normally be the only retirement plan of the employer.

SEC *See Securities and Exchange Commission.*

Secondary distribution   In underwritings, the sale of previously issued shares, such as treasury stock or shares held by insiders. Large block trades may also be called secondary distributions.

Secondary market   The market in which previously issued securities are traded among public investors. Most securities transactions occur in the secondary market.

Securities Act of 1933   The federal law regulating new issues, requiring their registration with the SEC.

Securities and Exchange Commission   The federal agency that regulates the securities markets and administers federal securities laws. Commonly known as the SEC.

Securities differences   Differences in securities positions between what is on the books of the firm and what certificates are actually held by the firm.

Securities Exchange Act of 1934   The federal law regulating the markets for existing securities, and governing public companies, broker/dealers, and exchanges. It allowed for the creation of self-regulatory organizations, such as the NASD.

Securities Information Center   The agency that takes reports on lost, stolen, or counterfeit securities. Commonly known as the SIC.

Securities Investors Protection Corporation (SIPC)   Organization that insures customers of brokerage firms in the event of the bankruptcy of a brokerage firm, much the same way the FDIC insures customers of banks. The SIPC is a nonprofit corporation that is not an agency of the U.S. government. The NASD requires virtually all brokerage firms to be members of the SIPC. The only exception is firms that deal only in mutual funds and variable annuities. The SIPC is funded by assessments on member firms. The SIPC insures customers for up to $500,000 of cash and securities on deposit with a member firm. Of the $500,000, no more than $100,000 may be cash on deposit with the member.

Security   SEC definition includes: investment notes, stocks, treasury stocks, bonds, or debentures; certificates of interest or participation in a profit-sharing agreement or in oil, gas, or other mineral royalty or lease; collateral-trust certificates or voting-trust certificates; investment contracts; certificates of deposit for one of the above; options, rights or warrants on one of the above or on any group or index of the above; or foreign currency options or rights. Includes temporary securities but does not include currency, or any note, draft, bill of exchange, or banker's acceptance with a maturity of less than nine months. Commodity futures contracts or commodity options are not generally considered securities, but fall under the jurisdiction of the Commodities Futures Trading Commission. While whole life, term, and universal life insurance are not considered securities, even though they may include some investment risk, variable life insurance is considered a security.

Self-regulatory organizations (SROs)   Private organizations owned and operated by their members and to whom the SEC delegates much of its authority to oversee both securities markets and participants in those markets. All SRO rules and regulations must be approved by the SEC. An SRO may be either a national exchange, such as the New York Stock Exchange (NYSE), or a national securities association such as the NASD.

Seller's option   The seller chooses the date on which the trade is settled. The date must be no less than six business days, but no more than sixty calendar days after trade date.

Selling away   *See Private Securities Transactions.*

Selling dividends   Inducing a customer to buy mutual fund shares just prior to an ex-dividend date, so that he receives the dividend. Because the price of the shares is likely to drop by the amount of the dividend, the customer is effectively getting his own money back, and is taxed on the dividend, besides.

Selling group   A select group of broker/dealers who assist the syndicate in selling the new issue in a corporate underwriting.

Selling group agreement   Agreement between members of the selling group and the managing underwriter, signed when the offering has been released by the Securities and Exchange Commission.

Selling group concession   In a corporate underwriting, the compensation paid to the selling group members.

Selling short   Selling a security or future that the seller does not own, either to lock in a gain on a long position or to make a gain on an anticipated decline in the market.

Sell stop   An order to sell a stock if the price falls to or below a specified price. It is often called a "stop loss" order.

Semi-fixed unit investment trust   A contractual plan investment company that creates its own portfolio, consisting solely of shares in an underlying mutual fund. The plan sells shares of its portfolio to investors on a contractual basis. *See participating trust.*

Separate account   In a variable annuity, the investment account into which the annuitant's funds are deposited. The account is segregated from the insurance company's other investments, and registered as an investment company under the Investment Company Act of 1940.

Serial bond   An issue with bonds of different maturities.

Series bond   A bond offering that took place over a period of time.

Series of options   Options of the same type (put or call) on the same security, with the same exercise month and strike price.

Service fees   Fees and charges assessed against an investment company's assets that cover ministerial, recordkeeping, or administrative activities.

Settlement   In a trade, the exchange of money and the security. Regular way settlement takes place three business days after trade date.

Shelf distribution   Method of distributing shares in which the seller registers the shares with the SEC, but does not immediately sell them to the public . The shares are "put on the shelf" and held for later sale at any time within two years of the registration that market conditions seem appropriate. Originally designed for use by insiders of the issuer, such as major shareholders who own unregistered shares acquired directly from the issuer, but now expanded to allow issuers to use the process.

Short   In options, the position of the writer of an option. In securities, the position of a seller of stock he does not own, but hopes to buy later.

Short against the box   A position of an investor who is long and short the same security, usually for tax purposes, to lock in a sales price, but defer the gain into the year the short position is covered.

Short interest theory   An investment theory according to which a large volume of short sales constitutes a buy signal.

Short sale   The sale of a borrowed security. If the seller can buy back the security at a lower price, he reaps a profit.

Short straddle   An options position in which the investor sells both a call and a put on the same security. The position is profitable if the stock price remains between the two breakeven points.

Shortswing profit rule   A federal law that forces insiders who sell securities of their company and take a short-term profit to pay that profit to the company.

SIC   *See Securities Information Center.*

Side of market   Description of an options position referring to whether a person would buy or sell the stock upon exercise of an option. Long call positions are added to short put positions to arrive at the buy side of the market. Long put positions are added to short call positions to determine the sell side of the market.

Simplified Arbitration   Arbitration procedure of the NASD that must be used for disputes of less than $25,000, which either involve public customers or are employment disputes that qualify for this type of arbitration. Usually only one public arbitrator handles such disputes.

Simplified Employee Pension (SEP) plan or SEP-IRA   Essentially an IRA with more liberal contribution limits, established and financed by an employer for all its eligible employees. The employer may set up a SEP even if it has already established a qualified pension or profit sharing plan. The company may or may not be incorporated.

Simplified Industry Arbitration Arbitration procedure of the NASD that must be used for disputes of less than $25,000 that do not involve a public customer and are not employment disputes that qualify for Simplified Arbitration. One to three securities industry arbitrators arbitrate the dispute. Unless one of the parties requests a hearing or a majority of the panel call for a hearing, the matter is decided solely on the pleadings and evidence filed.

Simultaneous transaction *See Riskless Transaction.*

Sinking fund A fund established to accumulate resources for the retirement of bonds.

Sinking fund call A repurchase of bonds by the issuer in which the money used to refund the bonds comes from a fund established for that specific purpose.

SIPC *See Securities Investors Protection Corporation.*

SMA Special Memorandum Account. In a margin account, SMA is a line of credit that is granted when the account generates equity in excess of 50 percent.

Sole proprietorship A business entity that is owned and operated by a single individual.

Special assessment bond A municipal bond that is backed by tax assessments levied on the property of residents who benefit from the facility being financed, such as an improved sewer system.

Special bid A bid for a large number of shares. Announcement is made on the consolidated tape that a firm is bidding to purchase a number of shares.

Specialist An exchange member who makes the market in a particular security. He must maintain a "fair and orderly" market.

Specialist's bid A specialist's bid for a block of stock owned by a customer. The purchase is a negotiated transaction.

Specialist's offer A specialist's sale of a block of stock to a customer in a negotiated transaction.

Special offer An offer for a block of stock that is reported on the consolidated tape.

Special Reserve Account for the Exclusive Benefit of Customers (SRA) Account required for all brokerage firms that hold customers' cash and securities for the protection of customers. May be maintained in one or more banks. Must be kept separate from the firm's other bank accounts. Assets in the account may not be used by the bank as collateral and the bank may not attach any claim to the account. The amount of cash or qualified securities the firm must deposit in the SRA is calculated either weekly or monthly based on the excess of customer credits over customer debits (i.e., the net credits).

Special situation   Circumstances that may cause a company to buy or sell its securities other than the fundamental prospects of the corporation. An example is a company that has received a tender offer by someone trying to buy all outstanding shares. The decision to buy or sell stock is made more on the basis of the likely success or failure of the tender offer than on the long-term prospects of the company.

Special tax bond   A municipal bond that is supported only by the revenues from a specific tax. It is considered to be a revenue bond; for example, a state pledging its gasoline taxes to finance construction of roads.

Split   Division of stock shares into multiple shares such that the stockholder's equity (both in total and for the individual stockholder) remains unchanged, but each stockholder holds more shares worth less each. For example, in a two-for-one split each stockholder receives two shares for every share held. The new shares are worth half as much as the old shares, but since the stockholder has twice as many shares, his investment remains unchanged.

Spousal IRA   An individual retirement account that may be established for one of a pair of married persons filing a joint return, even if the individual has either no income or a small amount of income.

Spread   An option position in which the investor is long an option and short another option of the same type. For example, he is long 1 ABC July 50 Call and short 1 ABC July 55 Call. Also the difference in price between what the principal who offers an IPO pays and what the investor pays for the newly offered securities.

Stabilizing bid   In a corporate underwriting, a bid by the managing underwriter to buy outstanding shares of the issuer's stock. This is done to support the stock price so the new issue can be distributed. For example, if a company offers a new issue at $30 per share, and the price of the old shares falls below $30, the managing underwriter may enter a stabilizing bid at $30 or slightly less to support the price.

Standard & Poor's 100 Index   An index of 100 stocks published by Standard & Poor's Corporation; the index on which OEX options are based.

Standard & Poor's 500 Index   An index of 500 stocks published by Standard & Poor's and considered representative of the overall stock market.

Standby underwriting   A corporate underwriting related to a rights offering. The syndicate agrees to underwrite any shares not sold through the rights offering. Standby underwritings apply only to offerings of common stock.

Standardized yield   For a mutual fund, the annualized net investment income for a period as a percent of the net asset value for the fund.

Statutory disqualification Status when a person is restricted by the SEC from being either a member in a self-regulatory organization such as the NYSE or the NASD, or an associate of a member.

Staying power An investor's ability to maintain his or her positions by meeting margin calls and/or holding onto his or her investments through down markets rather than having to liquidate at a disadvantageous time.

Sticky offering Offering in which underwriters have set the price too high, making shares difficult to sell to the public.

Stock dividend A dividend in the form of stock. Shareholders are given additional shares of stock, rather than being paid cash. Stock dividends are stated as a percentage. For example, if a 10 percent stock dividend is paid, the owner of 100 shares receives an additional 10 shares.

Stock exchange An organized marketplace for securities.

Stockholder of record The owner of a company's stock that is recorded on the books of the company.

Stockholders' equity The dollar value of all holdings of preferred and common stock, including any paid-in surplus, plus retained earnings.

Stock Index Futures Futures contracts based on an index of securities prices. Settlement is made in cash.

Stock power Instead of endorsing the back of a stock certificate, a customer may sign a separate form, called a stock power, which then is attached to the certificate to make it negotiable.

Stock split Issuing additional new shares for those now outstanding. For example, a 2-for-1 stock split doubles the number of shares outstanding. The price is likely to fall to one-half the previous price.

Stop limit order An order activated when the stock price trades at or through a trigger price. The order then becomes a limit order.

Stop loss order Another name for a stop order.

Stop order An order that is activated if the stock price trades at or through a trigger price. The order then becomes a market order. *See also Buy Stops and Sell Stops.*

Stopping stock An execution guaranteed by a specialist to a floor broker for customer orders. The specialist guarantees the order will be filled at a specified price or better.

Straddle An options position in which the investor either buys a call and a put on the same security (a long straddle), or sells a call and a put on the same security (a short straddle).

Street name Form of registration for a security in which it is held in the name of the broker/dealer carrying the account rather than in the name of the customer owning the security.

Strike price The price at which the stock trade will take place if an option is exercised. Also known as the exercise price.

Student Loan Marketing Agency ("Sallie Mae")   Agency issuing non-guaranteed securities based on student loans.

Subchapter M   A tax code provision favoring investment companies, avoiding double taxation of income. Investment companies qualifying for this treatment are called "Regulated Investment Companies."

Subject quotes   A quote subject to confirmation by someone else. It is not a firm quote, but a nominal quote.

Subordination agreement   Agreements that the firm makes with a lender in which the lender agrees to subordinate itself to all other creditors of the firm, present or future. In other words, if the firm went out of business, all other creditors would be paid before the lender on the subordination agreement.

Subscription agreement   In a limited partnership, the document a limited partner signs when he joins the partnership. It typically asks many questions regarding the investor's suitability for the program.

Summary complaint procedure   An NASD procedure investigating possible violation of the rules. If the violation is not severe, and the facts are not in dispute, NASD may offer summary complaint procedure. If accepted, the maximum penalty is censure and a fine up to $2500.

Summary prospectus   A document for use by most issuers that are not investment companies that summarizes information in the registration statement and can be used as a prospectus to solicit orders. The summary prospectus must be labeled at the beginning or end with the words "Copies of a more complete prospectus may be obtained from [insert name[s], address[es] and telephone number[s]."

SuperDot   An electronic order-routing and execution-reporting system used by the NYSE.

Support   A charting pattern indicating buying pressure. If the stock price declines below the support level, a technical analyst views the decline as a sell signal.

Syndicate   In an underwriting, a group of firms acting together to market a stock or bond issue. They are required to buy unsold shares for their own accounts if they fail to sell them to their customers.

Syndicate letter   In a competitive bid underwriting, the contract governing the syndicate.

Systematic risk   The portion of an investment's risk that is coincident with the market and thus cannot be eliminated by diversification. Measured by the security's beta coefficient. Also called market risk.

Tail fee   An amount paid to an underwriter when the offering is not completed as agreed and then the issuer subsequently makes a similar distribution.

Takedown   In a municipal underwriting, the profit of a syndicate member selling bonds to a customer.

TAN *See Tax Anticipation Note.*

Tax Anticipation Note A short-term municipal note offered before receiving tax revenues, commonly referred to as a TAN. It may be issued three to six months before property tax bills are sent out. They are general obligation issues, and are repaid from property taxes.

Tax-qualified annuities Plans available only to employees of non-profit organizations, such as schools, churches, and charities, also known as 403(b) plans. When the employee makes the contribution to the annuity, it is tax-deductible. When the contract is annuitized, the entire payment is taxable as ordinary income.

Tax swap *See Bond swap.*

Technical analysis Analysis of investments based on technical factors, primarily on charting. This is the practice of determining investment strategies based on chart patterns.

Tenants-in-common A joint account in which, if one party to the account dies, his or her share goes to his or her estate, not to the surviving tenant(s)-in-common.

Tender offer An offer to buy all or a large block of the securities of a particular company. The offer must be made to all shareholders.

Term bond A corporate or municipal bond issue with all the bonds maturing at the same time. Municipal term bonds are called dollar bonds, and are quoted in the same manner as corporate bonds.

Third market Over-the-counter market trades in securities listed on an exchange.

Tight money A reduced rate of money creation by the Federal Reserve System.

Time spread An options spread position in which the strike prices are the same, but the expiration months are different.

Time value In an option contract, the premium minus the intrinsic value (the in-the-money amount).

Tippee Person who is given material secret information by an insider to a corporation and buys or sells a security while in possession of such information. The possession of such information gives the holder an unfair (and illegal) advantage over the investor on the other side of the trade who does not have the information. Both the tippee and the tipper may be prosecuted.

Tombstone advertisement For a new issue, an advertisement showing the security being sold, the price, and the names of the broker/dealers from whom a prospectus can be obtained.

Total capital Owners' equity, adjusted for unrealized profits and losses, plus subordination agreements.

Total contract price In a bond trade, the price of a bond plus the accrued interest.

Total return On a mutual fund, the increase in value of an investment in the fund over a given period, assuming reinvestment of distributions. Includes capital gains and unrealized appreciation and depreciation in value of the fund's assets in addition to net investment income. The total return is the appreciation in investment value an investor who reinvested all distributions would have achieved over the period described. Does not take into account taxes the investor would have had to pay on dividends and does not consider the sales load for the initial purchase of the fund shares.

Trade date   The date a firm accepts a bid or offer for a security, even if time differences mean that the acceptance may not reach the firm making the bid or offer until the next day. The trade date may be different from the day the order was placed with a firm.

Trader   An individual who either buys and sells from his own account for profit or handles trades for a brokerage firm and its clients.

Trading authorization   A power of authority given to someone outside the firm, such as an investment adviser. The person holding this power is said to have trading authority in the account. The trading authorization will typically be given in the investment adviser contract.

Trading flat   Bonds trading without accrued interest, such as income bonds, bonds in default, and zero coupon bonds.

Transfer agent   The person or firm that cancels the shares in the name of the seller and reissues shares in the name of the buyer.

Treasury bill   A U.S. government security maturing in less than one year. It is issued at a discount, and matures at par.

Treasury bond   A U.S. government security maturing in more than ten years. It is issued with a coupon rate, and is quoted in 32nds.

Treasury note   A U.S. government security maturing in one to ten years. It is issued with a coupon rate, and is quoted in 32nds.

Treasury receipt   A type of zero coupon bond representing only the principal payment on a Treasury bond with twenty years to maturity. Since there are no interest payments, they trade at a steep discount.

Treasury stock   Stock that has been repurchased by the issuing corporation. It has no voting rights, does not receive dividends, and is not used in calculating earnings per share.

Treasury strip   When a Treasury receipt is created by stripping the coupons from a 20-year Treasury bond, the 40 interest coupons for the bond are sold separately as Treasury strips.

Triple-exempt bond   A bond exempt from federal, state, and local taxation.

True interest cost   In a competitive bid municipal bond offering, a method of calculating the interest cost that takes into account the time value of money. The calculation is done in constant dollars, considering not only what payments are made, but also when they are made. The other method of determining the bid is the net interest cost, which does not involve any net present value computation. True interest cost is also referred to as Canadian interest cost.

Trust Indenture Act of 1939   The federal law requiring all bond issuers to create a trust indenture, which is the contract between the issuer and the bondholders. The trust indenture appoints a company (usually a bank) to act as trustee on behalf of the bondholders.

Turnover rate   The number of shares traded in a year as a percentage of the total shares outstanding. May be calculated for a particular security, a portfolio (such as a mutual fund), or a securities exchange.

Two-dollar broker   An independent floor broker on the floor of an exchange who assists other members in executing their orders.

Type of option   There are two types: puts and calls.

UGMA   *See Uniform Gift to Minors Act.*

Uncovered options   A short options position in which the writer has no obvious means of fulfilling the exercise requirement. For example, a person who is short a call option and does not own the stock. They are also called naked options.

Underlying security   For any given option contract, the security that the holder of an option has a right to buy or sell.

Underwriter   A syndicate member in a firm commitment underwriting. The term is usually only given to those who have a financial commitment to buy the stock for their own account.

Underwriter's book   Place in which the syndicate manger in an underwriting records indications of interest in order to determine how well the offering is being received. This information is used to price the issue and determine the share of each member of the syndicate.

Underwriter's concession   In a corporate underwriting, the profit of a syndicate member selling securities to a customer.

Underwriting   The process in which broker/dealers form a syndicate to sell a new issue of securities.

Underwriting spread   The amount the underwriters retain for distributing an offering. Composed of the management fee paid to the syndicate manager for management services and the underwriter's concession paid to each member of the syndicate (including the manager) for the shares they are allotted. The selling group concession paid to the selling group members for their assistance in distributing the securities comes out of the underwriter's concession.

Undesignated order   In a municipal underwriting, an order in which the entire syndicate shares proportionately in the compensation. They are also called group orders or group net orders.

Undivided interest   Form of ownership such as a shareholder has in a mutual fund in which he owns a proportionate share of each of the fund's holdings rather than a particular piece of the fund's holdings.

Uniform Gift to Minors Act　The law governing gifts of money or securities to a minor, commonly referred to as UGMA. The donor must appoint a custodian (frequently the donor) to manage the account.

Uniform Practice Code (UPC)　NASD rules governing members' dealings with each other.

Uniform Securities Act　A model developed by the National Conference of Commissioners on Uniform State Law that serves as a basis for most state securities laws. The model makes it easier for securities professionals to do business across state lines. However, individual states, even those that adopted a version of the Act, might have individual variances.

Unit Investment Trust　An investment company that creates a portfolio of securities, often municipal bonds, and then sells the portfolio to investors.

Unlisted stock　A security that is not listed on a stock exchange.

Unsecured liabilities　Loans or other obligations not collateralized by either fixed assets such as real estate or by the firm's securities. Could be payable to customers, banks or other lenders, suppliers, other broker/dealers, employees or anyone else having a business relationship with the firm.

Uptick　A higher price than the previous trade.

Uptick rule　A federal law requiring that short sales be executed on an uptick or a zero plus tick.

Variable annuity　A type of annuity that assigns the investment risk to the annuitant. If the investments perform well, the monthly payment increases, and vice versa. Variable annuities must be registered as investment companies with the SEC.

Venture capital　Equity investment for a company not large enough to go public that is supplied by partnerships set up to pool funds and invest in untried companies, by wealthy individuals, or by large institutional investors. Venture capitalists take on high risks in hopes of making extraordinary returns on some of their investments.

Vertical spread　An options spread position in which the expiration months are the same, but the strike prices differ. They are also called money spreads.

Warrant　A security that gives the holder the right to buy the common stock of the issuer at a specified price for a period of time, usually years. Warrants resemble rights, except warrants are long-term.

Wash sale　(1) Buying and selling the same security, usually through different brokerage firms, in an attempt to manipulate the price and inflate the trading volume without actually taking a position in the market. (2) In tax law, selling a security at a loss, and repurchasing the same or similar security within thirty days before or after the sale; the loss is not tax deductible.

Western underwriting agreement   In a firm commitment underwriting, an agreement that makes syndicate members liable severally, but not jointly. If one syndicate member cannot sell his or her entire allotment, only he or she must buy the unsold securities. Usually used in corporate underwritings.

When, as, and if issued   Settlement does not take place until the certificates are printed. New issues trade "when, as, and if issued."

White's ratings   A bond rating measuring the marketability of a bond, rather than its credit risk.

With recall   In the municipal bond market, a dealer quote with an option to buy the bond at a guaranteed price for some period of time (often one hour); the dealer retains the right to recall the bonds and cancel the option.

Without recall   In the municipal bond market, a dealer quote with an option to buy the bond at a guaranteed price for some period of time (often one hour). The dealer cannot recall the bond and cancel the option.

Workable indication   In the municipal bond market, a nominal quote of an approximate price. It is usually a one-sided quote; that is, either a bid price or an asked price.

Working capital   A corporation's current assets less its current liabilities.

Workout quote   In the over-the-counter market, a nominal quote. The actual price is subject to negotiation.

Wrap fee   A wrap fee is an amount charged to a client of an investment advisor for several services wrapped together, such as portfolio management, asset allocation, custodial services, execution of transactions, and preparation of quarterly performance reports. The wrap fee is calculated as a percentage of net assets in the clients account rather than on transactions. Traditional wrap programs typically charge wrap fees of 1 to 3 percent.

Wrap fee brochure   A written disclosure statement or brochure that includes at least the information designated in Schedule H to Form ADV for a wrap program, including the fees, services, and policies of the wrap program, and any restrictions on clients. One sponsor of each wrap fee program must prepare the wrap fee brochure. Advisers must deliver the wrap fee brochure to potential wrap fee clients and also offer it annually to any existing wrap fee client in lieu of the standard adviser brochure.

Wrap program (Wrap)   Program offered by an investment adviser that wraps several services together for a fee based on the size of the client's account. Traditional wrap programs are based on the original model developed by E.F. Hutton in 1975, with minimum investments between $100,000 and $200,000, fees between 1 percent and 3 percent of the net assets in the account, and "wrapped" services that include portfolio management, asset allocation, custodial services, execution of transactions, and preparation of quarterly performance reports. In one variation (with smaller minimum investments), the adviser selects a mixture of mutual funds for the client. Wrap programs, unlike registered investment companies, are tailored to the individual investor. Wrap fee programs that offer similar advice to a number of clients must be carefully structured to conform to the safe harbor provisions in Rule 3a-4 of the Investment Company Act of 1940.

Wrap program sponsor   A person or entity is a sponsor of a wrap fee program if he receives compensation for sponsoring, organizing, or administering the wrap fee program, selecting investment advisers in the program, or for giving advice to clients about selecting advisers in the program. The sponsor typically manages the client's account using discretion and previously determined investment objectives.

Yellow sheets   A listing of corporate bonds traded in the OTC market, showing the market-makers and their quotes.

Yield curve   A chart showing yields of bonds with various maturities. Short-term debt normally has a lower yield than long-term debt.

Yield to call   The yield of a bond to its call date. The calculation is similar to a yield to maturity calculation, except the bond is assumed to mature on the call date at the call price.

Yield to maturity   The yield of a bond, taking into account the gain or loss at maturity.

Zero coupon bond   A bond without interest payments. Because they pay no interest, they trade at a steep discount from par.

Zero plus tick   A trade that was preceded by a trade at the same price, but the prior change in price was an uptick.

INDEX